CREATED RICH

**How Spiritual Attitudes
and Material Means Work Together to
Achieve Prosperity**

A Financial Guide For Bahá'ís

Patrick Barker

Naturegraph Publishers

Library of Congress Cataloging-in-Publication Data:

Barker, Patrick, 1950–
    Created rich : how spiritual attitudes and material
means work together to achieve prosperity : a financial
guide for Bahá'ís / by Patrick Barker.
        p.   cm.
        Includes bibliographical references.
        ISBN 0-87961-241-X (alk. paper)
        1. Bahá'ís--Finance, Personal.   2. Finance,
Personal--Religious aspects--Bahá'í Faith.   I. Title.
HG179.B298   1995
332.024'2979--dc20   95-35994
                                                                        CIP

Cover drawing by Shidan Toloui-Wallace

Books for a better world

Naturegraph Publishers, Inc.
3543 Indian Creek Road
Happy Camp, CA 96039
USA

Dedication

To my beloved children, Eric Townshend and Medora Asíyih.
May they inspire me to even greater depths of service.

Acknowledgements

I would like to express my sincere thanks to the following people who were helpful in encouraging me to write this book: Dr. Elaine McCreary, for reviewing my early chapters and providing a much needed spiritual insight for the book's format; Eugene and Myriam Tobin, Mark and Harriet Gilman, Shirley and Pete Ibsen, and Julie Porch, whose comments on the first few chapters provided me with helpful suggestions and needed encouragement; as well as Kiven Shaidu Wirngo, one of my African friends, who immediately saw the potential of this book and encouraged me to pursue it with all my heart.

Thanks to all my Alaskan friends for their encouragement while I was writing the book, especially Dr. Carlos and Cathy Plasencia, Dr. Richard and Dee Newman, Mehran and Kim Manie-Oskoii, and many others too numerous to name. Also, special thanks to my long-time friends, Bobby and Alice Thaggard, for making practical suggestions in some of the chapters. They are both living examples of many of the principles contained in this book.

I extend my deepest appreciation to Hand of the Cause of God, Dr. ʻAlí Muhammad Varqá, Trustee of Huqúqu'lláh, and to Mr. Parvíz Hatamí of the office of Huqúqu'lláh, for reviewing and commenting on Chapter 5, which discusses the law of Huqúqu'lláh and the Baháʼí funds; and to member of the Universal House of Justice, Mr. Ian Semple, for reviewing the first third of the book entitled "Spiritual

Philosophy" and making constructive suggestions which allowed me to fine tune the spiritual subtleties involved in this subject. Many thanks go to Jean Reece, whose informal editorial review of the entire manuscript not only gave me a fresh perspective, but also made the work more readable. Her comments were right on the money, so to speak.

Thanks to my mother-in-law, Jacqueline Bryant, who consistently encouraged my efforts, as well as to my own parents, Raymond and Shirley Barker, for generally supporting my efforts to succeed in life. I am grateful to my dear children, Eric and Medora, whose patience allowed me to complete this work and to whom the book is dedicated. They, like all the rest of the world's children, are the inheritors of our actions. Of course, the one who proved to be the most invaluable to the entire project was my dear wife and financial partner in life, Lauren, whose priceless encouragement provided me with the inspiration to write and publish this book. Her enthusiastic support and first draft editing of the manuscript were essential to its birth and completion. Regardless of how tired she was after a long day of service and many hours of working, she would assume the care of the children in the evening, which allowed me time to write. Were it not for her, this book would still remain one of my unfulfilled dreams.

Finally, though I have never met him, I owe much to Art Williams, whose financial services organization helped me put my own financial house in order. I am one of many millions who have been richly rewarded by his common sense approach to money matters. Many thanks also go to Shidan Toloui-Wallace for designing the book's cover and to Barbara Brown of Naturegraph for enthusiastically supporting the idea of this book and to her son, Keven Brown, for doing a superb editing job. With all of his other commitments, Keven found enough time to complete this project on schedule.

Table of Contents

Part Two: Essential Requirements

Introduction

Throughout the Bahá'í World, there is a growing backlash to the pernicious and rampant surge of materialism now strangling the spirituality of humankind. Nowhere is this more true than in the developed nations of the world. The Bahá'ís living in these countries are struggling to overcome their immersion in this all-consuming sea of materialism. However, as a result of this struggle, the friends are receiving mixed messages concerning the nature of money and wealth. On the one hand, they are told in the Bahá'í writings that the Bahá'í Fund, which is primarily composed of money, is the "lifeblood" of the Cause of God, whose vitality is essential for the continued work of the Faith; while on the other hand, they are receiving negative messages from various elements in society who revile money as the root of all evil and the source for the crass materialism presently afflicting their lives.

Not surprisingly, if Bahá'ís allow themselves to succumb to this negative view, it will encourage a general disdain for money and, in the guise of moral superiority, promote poverty over riches. Fortunately, this view is not supported in the Bahá'í teachings. On the contrary, where poverty is mentioned in a positive sense, it is only used as a metaphor to describe detachment from the material world, not as a favorable human condition in a literal sense. While it is clear from the Bahá'í writings that the extremes of wealth and poverty, as they exist in the world today, will eventually be eliminated, we should not assume the position of passively waiting for this to happen. Bahá'u'lláh exhorts His followers to earn their living by crafts, trades, and professions that will uplift the world of humanity, and He has exalted such work to the rank of worshiping God.[1] Our work performed in a spirit of service to our fellow human beings is one of the most powerful means of carrying forward an ever-advancing civilization.

Wealth is highly praised by the central authorities of the Faith when it is acquired legitimately and used correctly. In fact, the acquisition of wealth by one's own efforts and hard work is viewed by Bahá'u'lláh as a necessity for those who have achieved spiritual maturity.[2] After all, we were created rich and noble, not poor and ignoble. An important ingredient distinguishing the Golden Age of the Faith from today's civilization is that, in the future, humanity's essential material needs will be met universally so that more worthy ideals can be pursued by all with greater leisure. Part of Bahá'u'lláh's purpose is to elevate the condition of people so that they can build a divine civilization and partake of the myriad bounties of the Kingdom of God. Such a purpose does not bespeak of poverty and destitution.

1. *Tablets of Bahá'u'lláh*, p. 26.
2. *Ibid.*, p. 35.

9

Furthermore, the Bahá'í funds and the institution of the Right of God, both of which are used to support the vital worldwide goals of the Bahá'í Faith, cannot but benefit if more Bahá'ís become wealthy and master the basic principles of prosperity. In a letter written in 1923 from Shoghi Effendi to the American friends, he prays "that the bountiful Lord may...prosper them in their material affairs and pursuits, that the Cause which stands today in sore need of material help and assistance may advance, rapidly and unhindered, towards the fulfillment of its destiny." [1] The financial needs of the Faith in the 1990s, when the entire Bahá'í world is passionately undertaking the sacred task of erecting on Mount Carmel the buildings of the World Administrative Center of their Faith and the terraces of the Shrine of the Báb, are just as great as they have ever been.

The writing of *Created Rich* has resulted from conversations with many Bahá'ís who have expressed a desire to put their financial houses in order without having to understand a lot of complicated financial jargon. They were interested in a simple approach to money and investing which did not go against the teachings of the Bahá'í Faith. To my delight, as I undertook research to write this book, I found that the Bahá'í writings contain many positive statements on both the value of wealth and the principles necessary to achieve it. I have endeavored to use these statements whenever possible to support the premise of achieving prosperity. Although this book is primarily geared to those Bahá'ís living in the industrialized nations of the world, the practical and spiritual principles contained herein can also be applied by those living in other parts of the world.

For easy readability, this book is divided into three parts of five chapters each. Under the heading of each chapter a quote from the Old Testament is used to introduce the theme of that chapter. I found this to be particularly useful, since so much wisdom is also found in the scriptures of other religions. Furthermore, there are many people who have become highly successful by following the guidance contained in these ancient aphorisms.

Part One of the book covers the spiritual philosophy supporting the acquisition of wealth. Since the root cause of our financial difficulties is due to not following certain spiritual principles and not from a shortage of money, this section highlights the spiritual components of prosperity, explains the various attitudes associated with poverty and prosperity, shows the difference between material means and materialism, and emphasizes the need to obey the law of Huqúqu'lláh and contribute to the funds of the Faith. Within a spiritual context, this section describes why we should become prosperous.

Part Two highlights the essential requirements for achieving wealth. It shows the value of investing in one's future, the commitment level required for success, and the prerequisites of providing for

---

1. Bahá'í Administration, p. 53.

one's family. It also describes a simple mathematical technique for multiplying money as well as how to set and reach achievable goals. This section supports the necessity for achieving prosperity during our lifetime.

Part Three outlines the specific steps or practical principles needed for acquiring wealth. The mechanical aspects for accumulating wealth can be reduced to three basic components: redirecting income, managing expenses, and investing wisely. If you can master these three components in your lifetime you can easily achieve prosperity. This section also describes the many opportunities now present in the global economic system, as well as an important investment vehicle, for achieving financial independence. In a realistic manner, it describes how to become wealthy.

Never before in human history has it been possible to achieve so much wealth for so many people. The advent of the promised Day of God has ushered in a golden age never before experienced by humanity. How we utilize this new-found prosperity in conjunction with the teachings of Bahá'u'lláh will have a great influence on how rapidly and successfully the New World Order is implemented throughout the planet.

Patrick Barker
Haifa, Israel
Email: pbarker@bwc.org

Part One
Spiritual Philosophy

Chapter 1

Reasons For Prosperity

Where there is no vision, the people perish.—Proverbs 29:18

Like any of the laws of God, the principles governing the acquisition and growth of wealth are simple and straightforward. Money is plentiful for those who understand and implement these principles. If we fail to learn or do not observe these principles, we will rarely acquire more than a bare minimum throughout our working career. It is important for Bahá'ís to learn and practice the principles of prosperity if they desire to acquire more than just a bare existence after a lifetime of hard work and effort. Mastering these basic principles can greatly increase our confidence and provide additional avenues for serving the Faith. This chapter discusses many spiritual and material reasons for achieving prosperity as well as the wisdom of focusing our vision on a wealthy future.

Requirements of Prosperity

Bahá'u'lláh has defined the condition of man at his creation: *"O Son of Spirit! I created thee rich, why dost thou bring thyself down to poverty? Noble I made thee, wherewith dost thou abase thyself?"* [1] Although the meaning of this Hidden Word primarily concerns the spiritual nature of man, it can be applied to his material side as well. God has created man rich and noble, yet man reduces himself to poverty and abasement. As followers of God's new Revela-

---

1. Hidden Words, Arabic, no. 13.

tion, we should strive to set the example, both spiritually and materially, by reflecting the richness and nobility of God's creation in our
personal lives. Eventually, as humanity advances toward the Most
Great Peace, the abasement brought about by the extremes of poverty and wealth will be eliminated. But for now, our obligation is to
do what we can to build the foundation of that future civilization.

Becoming serious about building the structure of the New World
Order is essential. Many Bahá'ís need help and guidance in putting
their financial houses in order. Whatever our past financial endeavors,
they are unimportant, since our future prosperity depends upon the
financial plan of action we carry out now. Although this can be partially accomplished through a maturation of spiritual views and
attitudes, practical methods are also required for achieving success.
The opportunities for building our nest egg are time-limited, for at
some point in our life it will be too late to fully reach our objective.
Therefore, each one of us should take action now for a more prosperous future.

There are two requirements fundamental to achieving financial
success: The first is the need to develop a positive mental attitude
toward money, prosperity, and financial responsibility; the second is
the need to develop a practical and effective strategy to build enough
wealth to become financially independent. These requirements are the
basis of both the why and how of prosperity and financial independence.

Bahá'u'lláh has not only permitted His followers to partake of all
the wondrous bounties in God's creation, He has even encouraged
them to do so. However, misunderstanding Bahá'u'lláh's words and
erroneously defining detachment have caused many to take a negative
view toward money, riches, and prosperity. We do not realize that we
have been created to be rich, both materially and spiritually, and are
endowed with a nobility of the highest order: *"For I have created
thee rich and have bountifully shed My favor upon thee."* [1] We may
even presume that the rewards of our present sacrifice will be de-
ferred until after our death and entrance into the Abhá Kingdom.
This is a misleading assumption. God has created us rich and noble
from conception, but it is up to us to realize this richness and nobility
through our actions and the choices we make now.

The Financial Needs of the Bahá'í Faith

In addition to helping us further our own material well-being,
achieving financial prosperity will strengthen the lifeblood of the
Cause of God, since only Bahá'ís can contribute to the funds of the
Faith and are privileged to observe the law of Huqúqu'lláh (the Right
of God). Although contributing to the Fund is applicable universally

1. *Hidden Words*, Arabic no. 11.

and not restricted to the wealthy, the flow of sufficient money from the non-wealthy is limited by definition—if you have little to give, you cannot give much. This limiting condition also applies to observing the Right of God, for if everything you have is considered necessary, then no surplus is available on which to base the payment of Huqúqu'lláh. When understood in its spiritual context, being prosperous allows us the opportunity to contribute more of our resources to the Cause of God.

It is evident that the Bahá'í Faith, with such far-reaching goals as the establishment of a new world order and the creation of a golden age of peace and unity, cannot hope to accomplish such feats without financial resources. *"God hath made the achievement of everything conditional upon material means."* [1] In order for the teaching work to go forward and the Administrative Order to function properly, funds are needed. The Bahá'í Fund provides the financial support for most of the work of the Faith and is the monetary vehicle by which the Bahá'í community is able to function and grow.

One of these functions, depending on the size of the Bahá'í community, is the establishment of a physical center of operation for holding feasts, firesides, holy day observances, deepenings, children's classes, and meetings of the spiritual assembly and its various committees. This requires money. Purchasing and disseminating Bahá'í literature, advertising and hosting various proclamation and community events, and teaching and enrolling the masses also require money. Eventually, when every local Bahá'í community begins to build its own House of Worship and all the other necessary buildings surrounding this main structure and its gardens, more funds will be needed, not only for construction, but also for maintenance and operation. We may wish to expand our vision of the future to include these realities by planting the necessary seed money now in order to ensure their eventual realization.

During the present Age of Transition, the financial needs of the Faith are growing exponentially as it assumes an ever greater role in laying the foundation for the Kingdom of God. The Faith will require the benefits derived from an increasing level of prosperity by individual Bahá'ís during this expansion period. The degree of financial resources available to each Bahá'í community is dependent upon the prosperity, generosity, and sacrifice of its individual members, while the wise administration of such financial resources by its elected representatives is a major factor in determining the extent of every community's growth. Moreover, a Bahá'í community whose lifeblood is anemic will reflect this material weakness in the paucity of its activities and a lack of depth in its maturity. Ultimately, the growth of the Faith is dependent upon both the spiritual as well as the material wealth of the individual believer.

---

1. Bahá'u'lláh in *Huqúqu'lláh: The Right of God*, no. 33, p. 11.

On Becoming Prosperous

In a letter to the members of the American National Spiritual Assembly (which also included Canada) on November 26, 1923, the beloved Guardian wrote:

> My fervent prayer at the three Holy Shrines is that the bountiful Lord may bless His American friends who constitute the vanguard of His host in the Western world, and prosper them in their material affairs and pursuits, that the Cause which stands today in sore need of material help and assistance may advance, rapidly and unhindered, towards the fulfillment of its destiny.[1]

In view of this statement, not only should the North American Bahá'ís continue to prosper in order to support the Cause of God, but they should also reacquaint themselves with the primary purpose for becoming prosperous in the first place. By understanding that wealth is simply a means to an end, the friends can renew their quest for material prosperity and continue to share their wealth in support of the institutions of the Faith.

In our attempt to be the instruments for fulfilling the Guardian's fervent prayer, we should strive to understand the principles governing money. This is important if Bahá'ís hope to maintain control over their own personal finances and, if elected to an administrative body, those of the Faith. The successful establishment of a financial system founded on spiritual principles requires the practice of personal economy and social generosity in monetary matters. If not confined within the bounds of moderation, one's personal finances can become a source of severe mental stress and spiritual distraction. By learning the rules which govern the acquisition and growth of money, we are able to better master our own personal finances. This will cause new horizons of success and happiness to open before our eyes as we learn to escape the clutches of materialism by mastering the precepts of financial responsibility. Once this occurs, money will become our servant, instead of our master.

Bahá'ís should become comfortable with money. If we are not, we have either overblown its importance or lost sight of its significance, neither of which is healthy for building the foundation of a divine civilization. We must become efficient and accountable in the proper use of money; otherwise, its misuse can impede the rapid establishment of the future Bahá'í Commonwealth, an endeavor requiring substantial financial resources.

To safeguard the dignified promotion of the Faith and in keeping with the wishes of the beloved Guardian's prayer, the health and strength of the Bahá'í Fund should be of paramount importance to every loyal adherent of Bahá'u'lláh. Becoming prosperous is one way

---

1. *Bahá'í Administration*, p. 53.

we can ensure that our Faith's lifeblood remains healthy and strong. In fact, because the extent of the financial resources available to the Faith is limited to the collective wealth of the Bahá'ís worldwide, it is even more vital that every Bahá'í achieve financial success, since no other source of revenue is available to the Faith outside the generous and continuous support of its faithful and conscientious members.

Also, individual Bahá'ís should understand how to invest and know how to manage their money, for how else can they expect to acquire and contribute enough material resources to generously support both the Faith and themselves? If for no other reason than protecting the precious resources of the Faith from potential loss through financial ignorance, Bahá'ís should plan to become knowledgeable and successful with money.

In a letter to all national spiritual assemblies outlining the amount of funds needed for continuing the work on the Arc on Mount Carmel during the Three Year Plan, the Universal House of Justice said: "It is inevitable that in a project of such size, a large portion of the money will have to come from those Bahá'ís who are endowed with wealth, whether this be to a moderate degree or of a considerable magnitude." [1] Although this challenge to the financial resources of the worldwide Bahá'í community should be well within its capacity to meet, this statement from the Universal House of Justice underscores the need for individual Bahá'ís to become prosperous by mastering the principles of personal or family finances.

The Ultimate Purpose of Wealth

In writing about the foundation of justice and the creation of a divine civilization, 'Abdu'l-Bahá describes the blessings that material wealth can bring to society by the efforts of one individual, especially if that individual maintains a proper attitude toward the acquisition and use of wealth. He also states the condition upon which wealth becomes truly praiseworthy:

> Wealth is praiseworthy in the highest degree, if it is acquired by an individual's own efforts and the grace of God, in commerce, agriculture, art and industry, and if it be expended for philanthropic purposes. Above all, if a judicious and resourceful individual should initiate measures which would universally enrich the masses of the people, there could be no undertaking greater than this, and it would rank in the sight of God as the supreme achievement, for such a benefactor would supply the needs and insure the comfort and well-being of a great multitude. Wealth is most commendable, provided the entire population is

1. Letter from the Department of the Secretariat on behalf of the Universal House of Justice, October 31, 1993.

wealthy. If, however, a few have inordinate riches while the rest are impoverished, and no fruit or benefit accrues from that wealth, then it is only a liability to its possessor. If, on the other hand, it is expended for the promotion of knowledge, the founding of elementary and other schools, the encouragement of art and industry, the training of orphans and the poor—in brief, if it is dedicated to the welfare of society—its possessor will stand out before God and man as the most excellent of all who live on earth and will be accounted as one of the people of paradise.[1]

The wisdom of 'Abdu'l-Bahá in this particular passage encourages us to acquire wealth through our own labors and to partake of its fruits by using it to promote an ever-advancing civilization. The entire population must prosper for civilization to flourish and for humankind to be benefited in the highest degree. Like anything else in life used outside of its purpose, if our wealth is not used in the service of humanity and ultimately in the worship of God, it becomes useless and even dangerous to our well-being. The principle of detachment should apply to our goal of financial independence as it should to everything else in life. If we desire riches simply for their own sake, or if no benefit comes to the society around us from our being financially independent, then the acquisition of wealth becomes a material liability and an obstruction to our spiritual progress. If, on the other hand, our motivation for acquiring wealth is, as 'Abdu'l-Bahá indicates, the promotion of an ever-advancing civilization and helping others find the opportunity to better themselves, then nothing can be said against it.

The social function of wealth is to *"universally enrich the masses of the people"*[2] through the promotion of education, agriculture, sciences, arts, and any other agency that will improve the welfare of society. Wealth's ultimate purpose is not in its being concentrated in the hands of a few individuals or groups of individuals, but in its being shared and disseminated within the community for the benefit of all. Private and public wealth should be expended for the betterment of society so that it can do the greatest good for the most people.

Although wealth finds its ultimate purpose in the betterment of mankind, its acquisition should not become an end in itself. For those who have been transformed by the Revelation of Bahá'u'lláh, this entire world, including its riches, is but a temporary way station on the path to a higher destiny. Of such people, Shoghi Effendi writes:

> Though willing to share to the utmost the temporal benefits and the fleeting joys which this earthly life can confer, though eager to participate in whatever activity that conduces to the

---

1. *The Secret of Divine Civilization*, pp. 23-24.
2. Ibid., p. 23.

richness, the happiness and peace of that life, they can, at no time, forget that it constitutes no more than a transient, a very brief stage of their existence, that they who live it are but pilgrims and wayfarers whose goal is the Celestial City, and whose home the Country of never-failing joy and brightness.[1]

Another area where the ultimate purpose of wealth is demonstrated is in its passing from one generation to the next. Although a person is permitted to dispose of his or her wealth in any way desired, Bahá'u'lláh has given specific guidelines in the Kitáb-i-Aqdas concerning the inheritance of wealth for those who die intestate (without leaving a will). These guidelines remind us of the function of wealth and encourage us to avoid its concentration in the hands of one or more individuals. For those who die intestate, the estate of the deceased is divided among seven categories which include children, spouse, father, mother, brothers, sisters, and teachers. In some cases, where there are no surviving members in the above categories, nephews, nieces, aunts, and uncles, as well as the Universal House of Justice, can be inheritors of the estate of the deceased.

Of course, since our spiritual inheritance will far and away outlast every trace of our material legacy, we should be putting our greatest emphasis on the acquisition of spiritual wealth. This is our ultimate goal, though we are free to partake of the temporary bounties of God's physical creation while existing on this plane. Both areas of development are highly commendable.

Whenever we leave money to our children, we may be doing them a disservice if we have not taken the time and effort to educate them in the proper use of money or the value of wealth. The danger inherent in all forms of simply giving away something is that it usually fails to teach the receiver anything of value. Take, for example, the lesson of the fisherman and the hungry man: When the fisherman gave the hungry man a fish, he fed him for a day; but when the fisherman taught the hungry man how to fish, he fed him for a lifetime. The same lesson is true with all manner of charity. By merely giving away money and material goods, we only alleviate a temporary situation of neediness; but when we also teach self-reliance and self-help, we eliminate a permanent condition of poverty. Being in a chronic state of welfare breeds discontent, since it is ultimately degrading to one's station, whereas teaching self-reliance and giving one an opportunity to be self-supporting, engenders gratitude. This latter condition may also cause the recipient to return something of value to the community, whereas the former condition is a constant drain on the resources of society. This is probably one of the reasons Bahá'u'lláh prohibited mendicancy and made earning a livelihood obligatory. 'Abdu'l-Bahá also made the House of Justice and the wealthy responsible to care for those who are unable to earn their own livelihood.[1]

For philanthropy to be most effective, it must be intertwined with education. When 'Abdu'l-Bahá gave examples of the uses of wealth for philanthropic purposes, He said that it should be *"expended for the promotion of knowledge, the founding of elementary and other schools, the encouragement of art and industry, [and] the training of orphans and the poor."*[2] Thus, when philanthropy is used to educate, encourage, and train people to do something useful, it provides them with the means of extracting themselves from the clutches of poverty. Philanthropy leading to self-reliance is one of the most appropriate uses of wealth and is one of the solutions to humanity's various economic and social woes.

Achieving Prosperity

There are many spiritual beacons on the road to prosperity. One of the most important concerns our attitude toward wealth and its acquisition. If we confuse materialism with material means, we cannot adequately understand the significance of our work being elevated to the level of worship; if we denounce prosperity in favor of poverty, we cannot enjoy the bounties provided by a loving Creator and, worse still, we ridicule the sufferings of the Manifestations of God, whose sacrifices have opened the door to man's spiritual as well as physical well-being. By coming face-to-face with our innermost feelings concerning money, we can deduce our true attitude toward wealth and its acquisition. Pursuing financial independence means forsaking all negative attitudes concerning money and developing a purity of motive regarding its acquisition.

Once we realize that it is allowable to partake of all the bounties of our Lord, we can begin developing a strong commitment to establishing a plan for financial independence. Nevertheless, we should realize that however laudable our high aims and pure motives, they will never be sufficient unless they are supported by sound principles and practical methods. Learning these principles and methods is simple, but they are difficult to put into practice, since they require the highest level of self-discipline and determination to succeed.

Understanding why you are acquiring wealth is also important to your prosperity plan, since the results of your current decisions have an impact on your future options. The why is simple: if you do not begin an investment program for a future income, then you are guaranteed not to have an income, or at least not a sufficient income, to support yourself during your non-income producing years. If you live long enough to retire, and many of us will, how do you expect to

---

1. *The Kitáb-i-Aqdas* n56, p. 194.
2. *The Secret of Divine Civilization*, p. 24.

support yourself if you have little or no money set aside for your golden years? If you have not acquired adequate financial reserves, where do you expect the money to come from—charity, social security, other government benefits, rich relatives, or maybe even the Bahá'í Fund itself? In order not to be a financial burden on anyone, we should always practice personal economy, strive to be self-supporting, and consistently invest a portion of whatever we earn toward our future financial well-being.

In the end, your best chance for achieving financial prosperity is to consistently invest a portion of all you earn and let it grow unencumbered. The growth of money needs time and nourishment to produce fruit, so the earlier you start planting your seeds of wealth, the sooner and richer will be your harvest. And since the financial prosperity of the Faith can be no greater than the collective prosperity of each of its individual members, we should begin our prosperity program right away.

Chapter 2

The Treasury of Detachment

Humility and the fear of the Lord bring wealth and honor and life.
—Proverbs 22:4

Detachment from all save God is one of the most indispensable attributes of the human soul. Bahá'u'lláh says that *"no man shall attain the shores of the ocean of true understanding except he be detached from all that is in heaven and on earth."*[1] Detachment is essential to understanding the purpose of existence and a quality unique to the soul of man. Its importance, especially within the context of financial independence, cannot be overestimated. Detachment is to man's spiritual life what flavor is to food. Although flavor is an invisible component of food, it is vital to its taste and distinctive quality. Without flavor, food is unpalatable and simply provides nourishment for the body. In other words, it has no spirit. Likewise, without the quality of detachment human beings are spiritually lifeless creatures.

The Ceaseless Wonders of His Bounty

All of our material wealth is derived from the earth; yet, when measured against the rest of our galaxy, which contains hundreds of billions of suns, the earth is but a very small speck of dust. Although the Milky Way is about 100,000 light years[2] in length and 10,000

---

1. *Kitáb-i-Íqán,* p. 3.
2. Travel in space is measured in light years. Light, the fastest known substance in the universe, travels at a speed of 186,282 miles or 299,792 kilometers per

light years wide at its center, it is only one of many billions of galaxies in the known universe. The significance of what we call the known universe, with its billions upon billions of Milky Way-like galaxies, is trivial and inconsequential when compared with the infinite panorama of creation itself, a process which has neither a beginning nor an end. Given this comparison in size and significance, the earth and all of its riches recede to irrelevance when contrasted with the immensity and magnitude of the entirety of God's creation.

Concerning creation's origin and vastness, Bahá'u'lláh states: *"A sprinkling from the unfathomed deep of His sovereign and all-pervasive Will hath, out of utter nothingness, called into being a creation which is infinite in its range and deathless in its duration."* [1] By meditating upon this verse, we are able to get a glimmering of the true insignificance of earthly wealth and possessions. If creation itself, of which the known universe is but a part, is only a sprinkling from the fathomless ocean of God's Will, what ultimate value can we attach to the earth, much less to our own spectacle of insignificant riches which are extracted from this same earth? Not only is our material wealth confined to this planet, but it is also confined to the limits of our mortal existence. Beyond this contingent world, it has no value; and beyond a certain period of time, it has no form, since all things eventually return to the dust from which they were created.

If this is the state of our comprehension of the inorganic condition of the universe, how insignificant is our knowledge of its more complex life forms, much less our understanding of the spirit animating its very essence? Since we are limited by the nature of our creation, it is important to acknowledge these limitations and confine our preoccupations to those things within the range of our abilities.

Six Ornaments of Detachment

An ornament is something which adds beauty or honor to something else. In describing the beauty of God's creation, Bahá'u'lláh says: *"A drop of the billowing ocean of His endless mercy hath adorned all creation with the ornament of existence."* [2] Existence, then, is the ornament which embellishes creation and makes it more pleasing. Likewise, Bahá'u'lláh has revealed six ornaments which add beauty to the spiritual life of man and help clarify the meaning of detachment. These six ornaments are found in the Tablet of Tarázát and are briefly mentioned here, though further study may be necessary to fully understand their significance.

---

second. A light year, then, is the distance light would travel in one year's time, which is about 5.88 trillion miles or 9.45 trillion kilometers. The nearest star to our sun, traveling at light speed, is two years away.
1. *Gleanings from the Writings of Bahá'u'lláh*, XXVI, p. 61.
2. *Gleanings*, XXVI, p. 61.

The first of these ornaments is that *"man should know his own self and recognize that which leadeth unto loftiness or lowliness, glory or abasement, wealth or poverty."*[1] As long as we are aware of the purpose for existence and follow the path leading to the comprehension of God, we are on the path of gaining a true knowledge of ourselves. Long ago, a wise philosopher expressed this concept as "know thyself." In varying degrees, it has been observed by nearly every generation of humanity. Ultimately, our success in acquiring financial responsibility will be based on the extent we truly know and understand our own selves.

The second ornament of beauty to adorn the station of humanity is *"to consort with the followers of all religions in a spirit of friendliness and fellowship, to proclaim that which the Speaker on Sinai hath set forth and to observe fairness in all matters."*[2] Consorting with all peoples in a spirit of friendship, joy, love, and unity is the hallmark of the Bahá'í Faith, since Bahá'ís believe in the oneness of mankind. The application of this concept will preserve the structure and promote the tranquility of the world of being. Genuine affection for our fellow human beings implies a sense of detachment, since real love for others is impossible without detachment from selfish desires and conceptions. And, in order to observe fairness in all matters, we must be detached lest our attachment to something or someone falsely influence our judgment.

The third ornament that is well-pleasing to God is a good character: *"A good character is, verily, the best mantle for men from God....The glory and the upliftment of the world must needs depend upon it."*[3] A good character is the foundation from which the application of justice and righteousness is practiced. It incorporates all of the best qualities of man and is conducive to a saintly station. Those possessing a good character are less likely to succumb to the deleterious cravings of the material world, since money and wealth are unable to exert any negative influence over such people.

The fourth ornament honoring the station of man is trustworthiness. Bahá'u'lláh describes the importance of adorning oneself with this ornament: *"Trustworthiness is the greatest portal leading unto the tranquility and security of the people. In truth the stability of every affair hath depended and doth depend upon it. All the domains of power, of grandeur and of wealth are illumined by its light."*[4] Bahá'u'lláh also says of trustworthiness: *"He who partaketh thereof hath indeed partaken of the treasures of wealth and prosperity."*[5] A person's value depends on keeping promises and commitments, telling the truth, and honestly dealing with others. In other

1. *Tablets of Bahá'u'lláh*, p. 35.
2. Ibid., pp. 35-36.
3. Ibid., p. 36.
4. Ibid., p. 37.
5. Ibid.

words, a person's value is measured by the level of his or her trust-worthiness. If you cannot be trusted or relied upon, then you have no credibility; and without credibility, there can be no integrity. The crowning point of trustworthiness is to become so honorable that even your enemies will seek your counsel and abide by your recom-mendations, knowing that they can depend on your integrity. This quality is a reflection of detachment from all things but God.

The fifth ornament is the "_protection and preservation of the stations of God's servants_"[1] and it concerns truthfulness, sincerity, fair-mindedness in all matters, not denying anyone's due reward, showing deference to those who manifest the spirit of service in their professions, and not abusing anyone or anything. Through a rectitude of conduct and by refraining from reprehensible deeds and behavior, we are preserving the stations of God's servants.

The sixth ornament which adds beauty to the station of man is knowledge: "_Knowledge is one of the wondrous gifts of God. It is incumbent upon everyone to acquire it._"[2] Man's repertoire of knowledge, especially in the field of the arts, crafts, sciences, and all other sources of material means, is due to the bounty and blessings of God. With the coming of the Revelation of Bahá'u'lláh, human knowledge has increased exponentially to the point where this period of history has been called the Information Age. Because information is so readily available, human beings have the potential to increase their knowledge, hence their prosperity, beyond measure. However, it is our responsibility to acquire such knowledge as will benefit others, as well as ourselves.

Cleansing the Heart

Detachment is required for obtaining the knowledge of God and worshiping Him through our service. This is possible only when we release our grip on materialism and no longer make it a priority in our lives. Those who possess material wealth without also possessing the ornaments of detachment mentioned above will be unable to cleanse their hearts and receive the divine treasures. The heart of man is the recipient of spirituality and the repository containing the gems of divine reality. God has declined to possess all things except the human heart, which He has reserved exclusively for Himself. By cleansing our hearts, we extricate ourselves from worldly desires and distractions and enter into the lofty realms of detachment and near-ness to God.

The writings of Bahá'u'lláh state that the entire creation has been fashioned for the benefit and training of humankind. However, although we have the right to partake of those things permitted by

1. _Tablets of Bahá'u'lláh_, p. 38.
2. Ibid., p. 39.

God, God does not wish for us to be attached to any one of these things. For example, it is permissible for a believer, who is detached from the world, to eat rare and delicate foods with utensils of pure gold, if it is his wish and he can afford to do so. As long as man is not attached to the things of this world and remembers the purpose for his existence, there is no harm partaking of all the bounties and benefits of God's creation. Bahá'u'lláh explains:

> Know ye that by "the world" is meant your unaware-
> ness of Him Who is your Maker, and your absorption in
> aught else but Him....Should a man wish to adorn him-
> self with the ornaments of the earth, to wear its appar-
> els, or partake of the benefits it can bestow, no harm
> can befall him, if he alloweth nothing whatever to inter-
> vene between him and God, for God hath ordained every
> good thing, whether created in the heavens or in the
> earth, for such of His servants as truly believe in Him.
> Eat ye, O people, of the good things which God hath
> allowed you, and deprive not yourselves from His won-
> drous bounties. Render thanks and praise unto Him, and
> be of them that are truly thankful.[1]

Bahá'u'lláh repeatedly admonishes the human race to forsake heedlessness and the cravings of worldly desires. This is to educate the soul and refine its character in order that we may obtain a share of the gems of divine virtue from the treasury of celestial wisdom. However, instead of pursuing heavenly qualities, the hearts of men are usually preoccupied with the acquisition of worldly pleasures and vanities, which are ultimately worthless and even contemptible in the sight of God. Note the semantic difference between Bahá'u'lláh's use of the term "the world," most often used in the Writings to refer to human materialistic doings, and His reference to "the earth," meaning God-created nature.

The following Hidden Words epitomize the importance of cleansing the heart for the descent of the favors and bounties of God:

> O Son of Man! The temple of being is My throne;
> cleanse it of all things, that there I may be established and
> there I may abide.[2]

> O Son of Being! Thy heart is My home; sanctify it for
> My descent. Thy spirit is My place of revelation; cleanse it
> for My manifestation.[3]

> O Son of Earth! Wouldst thou have Me, seek none other
> than Me; and wouldst thou gaze upon My beauty, close
> thine eyes to the world and all that is therein; for My will

1. *Gleanings*, CXXVIII, p. 276.
2. *Hidden Words*, Arabic, no. 58.
3. Ibid., Arabic, no. 59.

and the will of another than Me, even as fire and water, cannot dwell together in one heart.[1]

O My Servant! Free thyself from the fetters of this world, and loose thy soul from the prison of self. Seize thy chance, for it will come to thee no more.[2]

Sanctified from Riches

The path to material prosperity is fraught with danger, because the acquisition of wealth is potentially a powerful barrier to our spiritual progress. This is why Bahá'u'lláh advises: "*Sanctify thyself from riches, that thou mayest obtain a lasting share from the ocean of My eternal wealth.*"[3] But being sanctified from riches does not necessarily mean being without wealth; it simply means that wealth should not become a barrier or distraction which inhibits the progress of the soul. Like everything else in life, wealth has a proper and specific purpose. It becomes harmful to man only when used or viewed outside of the limits for which God created it. In the Tablet of Tarázát, mentioned above, Bahá'u'lláh clarifies that wealth is a necessity for those who have attained spiritual maturity: "*Having attained the stage of fulfillment and reached his maturity, man standeth in need of wealth, and such wealth as he acquireth through crafts or professions is commendable and praiseworthy in the estimation of men of wisdom.*"[4]

Although wealth in immature hands is a mighty barrier between the soul and God, the splendor of a rich person who is detached from his riches is a source of illumination to those who inhabit the heavenly realms. Bahá'u'lláh states:

O Ye that Pride Yourselves on Mortal Riches! Know ye in truth that wealth is a mighty barrier between the seeker and his desire, the lover and his beloved. The rich, but for a few, shall in no wise attain the court of His presence nor enter the city of content and resignation. Well is it then with him, who, being rich, is not hindered by his riches from the eternal kingdom, nor deprived by them of imperishable dominion. By the most great name! The splendor of such a wealthy man shall illuminate the dwellers of heaven even as the sun enlightens the people of the earth![5]

The attainment of such a potent condition is possible only when we are detached from this material world. This is one of our greatest challenges—to become wealthy without becoming attached to our wealth and the power it represents. In the first volume of his monu-

---

1. *Hidden Words*, Persian, no. 31.
2. Ibid., Persian, no. 40.
3. Ibid., Persian, no. 11.
4. *Tablets of Bahá'u'lláh*, p. 35.
5. *Hidden Words*, Persian, no. 53.

mental work, *The Revelation of Bahá'u'lláh*, Adib Taherzadeh describes attachment in these words:

> Attachment to this world can be described as anything which prevents the soul from drawing nearer to God. Bahá'u'lláh has taught that this world and all that is therein is created for the benefit of man. He is entitled to possess all the good things he can earn, and enjoy all the legitimate pleasures that life bestows upon him. But at no time must he become attached to them. Bahá'u'lláh further teaches that man must take a great interest in this life, work for the betterment of this world and assist in the building of a new world order for mankind.[1]

The possession of wealth and the role of detachment is analogous to the flow of water from a lake. Whenever water from a lake is released and flows onward, the lake remains alive and healthy. It is only when a lake retains everything it has that it becomes a lifeless and even lethal body of water. The Dead Sea in the Holy Land is a good example of this condition. The Dead Sea only receives, it does not give; and because it does not give, it is totally without life—a dead salt sea with no animal or plant life living within its waters. However, the Sea of Galilee, the main body of water flowing into the Dead Sea via the Jordan River, is a freshwater lake teaming with fish and aquatic flora and is the source of life to the people and agriculture of Israel's semi-arid lands. The Sea of Galilee gives bountifully of itself and has abundant life, while the Dead Sea gives nothing and is totally destitute of life.

Giving is a natural condition of life and Bahá'u'lláh confirms this by saying: *"To give and to be generous are attributes of Mine; well is it with him that adorneth himself with My virtues."*[2] Shoghi Effendi likens our contributions to the Bahá'í funds to the flow of water in a fountain or spring:

> We must be like the fountain or spring that is continually emptying itself of all that it has and is continually being refilled from an invisible source. To be continually giving out for the good of our fellows undeterred by fear of poverty and reliant on the unfailing bounty of the Source of all wealth and all good—this is the secret of right living.[3]

The beloved Guardian has here given the key for understanding the essence of detachment. Outwardly, there is an underlying fear associated with the constant outflow of our resources, yet inwardly, this is a source for generating true wealth since it gives us a direct experience with detachment. When water continuously flows from a fountainhead, it becomes the source of life and growth to everything

---

1. *The Revelation of Bahá'u'lláh*, vol. 1, p. 75.
2. *Hidden Words*, Persian, no. 49.
3. *Lifeblood of the Cause: Bahá'í Funds and Contributions*, no. 1, p. 1.

it touches. When water ceases to flow, it becomes stagnant and the organic matter it contains begins to decay and die.

Similarly, when money stops flowing, either in an economic system from a shortage of investment capital, or in the Bahá'í Faith from a lack of individual contributions, prosperity and growth cease to occur. When this happens in the Faith, the activity level begins to decline. If this situation is not corrected within a short period of time, it could lead to the atrophy and death of the community. The vitality of every Bahá'í institution, like that of every national economy, depends on the continuous flow of funds—the source of its lifeblood. This vitality is measured by the extent of its members' participation and generosity. Communities with high levels of teaching and consolidation activities are considered prosperous, while those not experiencing this spiritual vibrancy are not yet mature enough to receive the full measure of God's bounty. Notice that the prosperity of a community is not dependent on how much money it has, but in how active its members are in following the guidance and instructions of its institutions.

Chapter 3

Prosperity and Poverty

The wealth of the rich is their fortified city, but poverty is the ruin of the poor.—Proverbs 10:15

People have always striven to be prosperous. In the material world, prosperity is usually identified with wealth, wisdom, strength, and knowledge, while poverty is generally associated with pauperism, ignorance, weakness, and fear. This, of course, does not include the mystical definition of poverty as the state of detachment from all things except God.

Gold as a Symbol of Attachment

When reading the writings of the Manifestations of God, we should not confuse what is symbolic with what is literal. In religious writings, riches in general, and gold in particular, are commonly used as symbols of attachment. Wealth can either be used as a tool to enhance our spiritual life by improving our moral qualities, or it can provide the means for diminishing these qualities.

Man's basic religious attitude toward wealth has usually been accompanied by a perplexing array of contradictions ranging from greed and superstition to enlightenment and practical economy. Whenever the metaphors of the Manifestations of God are interpreted literally, the danger of fanaticism arises. One of the dangers is in confusing wealth with materialism and detachment with piety. One can be wealthy without being materialistic as easily as one can be detached without being pious. Wealth and detachment are not mutually exclusive conditions.

In the holy scriptures of all religions, gold, or the attitude of man toward gold, has always been a symbol of attachment to the material world. This is because gold, and the power it symbolizes, has a tendency to make people forget about the purpose of their material existence—which is to prepare themselves spiritually for the next world and to promote an ever-advancing civilization in this one. Although very few people today actually possess their wealth in gold, the idea of gold representing wealth is generally accepted. We may own land, stocks, bonds, cash, and various other possessions, yet, in today's modern world, gold remains a standard symbol for measuring wealth and riches.

In His writings, Bahá'u'lláh states: *"O Son of Being! Busy not thyself with this world, for with fire We test the gold, and with gold We test Our servants."* [1] In this statement, Bahá'u'lláh indicates that wealth, as represented by gold, can become a barrier to one's spiritual advancement. It is naive to think that the literal possession of gold, which few people actually have in any sizable quantity, is what tests our attachment to the material world. If this were the case, then very few people would be tested, since very few people keep their assets in gold. Therefore, gold should only be considered as a symbol for wealth and a symbol for our attachment to it.

In another place Bahá'u'lláh states: *"O Son of Man! Thou dost wish for gold and I desire thy freedom from it. Thou thinketh thyself rich in its possession, and I recognize thy wealth in thy sanctity therefrom."* [2] Again, gold is used as a symbol for attachment to the material world and should not be interpreted literally. Although wealth can prevent us from relying on God for sustenance and make us forgetful of our spiritual self, it can also be used as a source of good for humanity. The construction of the Arc on Mount Carmel, "an endeavor which is central to the work of the Faith in eradicating the causes of the appalling suffering now afflicting humanity," [3] is one example of using wealth for the good of mankind.

Finally, as a point of comparison, the acquisition of wealth is similar to the acquisition of knowledge. Both are praiseworthy, but both can be dangerous to the progress of the soul if we form an attachment to them. Knowledge is highly praised in this Dispensation, yet it can also be a source of arrogance and pride, and become a barrier between the soul and God. [4] When this occurs, knowledge becomes a chain which binds us to the material world. Therefore, knowledge, like wealth, has a dual influence. It can either be used to

1. *Hidden Words*, Arabic, no. 55.
2. *Ibid.*, Arabic, no. 56.
3. Letter from the Universal House of Justice to all National Spiritual Assemblies, January 4, 1994.
4. *Kitáb-i-Íqán*, p. 69.

find truth or to reflect vain imaginings. Both wealth and knowledge are tools to help us advance on the pathway toward God. How we use these tools is up to us.

Man's True Wealth

The true wealth of humanity is not in material riches or comforts. Our true reality is spiritual, not material, and although the true nature of our existence is reflected within the shell of our physical reality, we were created for a much more noble purpose. 'Abdu'l-Bahá mentions over twenty attributes and virtues which constitute the criteria of man's spiritual wealth in the human world. These include the following:
- the divine appearances and the heavenly bounties,
- the sublime emotions and the love and knowledge of God,
- universal wisdom, intellectual perception, and scientific discoveries,
- justice, equity, truthfulness, and benevolence,
- natural courage and innate fortitude,
- respect for rights and keeping agreements and covenants,
- rectitude in all circumstances and serving the truth under all conditions,
- the sacrifice of one's life for the good of all people,
- kindness and esteem for all nations,
- obedience to the teachings of God and service in the Divine Kingdom,
- the guidance of the people and the education of the nations and races.[1]

Notice that none of the above qualities absolutely requires money for success. However, if used correctly, money can increase the potency of most of these attributes. Additionally, 'Abdu'l-Bahá says that these virtues require assistance from God, or the divine teachings, before they can be manifested in the human reality.

Although our material possessions are not a measure of our true wealth, we can create an abundance of material wealth through the use of these attributes. The point is that the acquisition of material wealth is a means to an end and can be directly linked to one's spiritual attitude. Unfortunately, a disproportionate amount of publicity has been given to those who have gained their riches through unscrupulous or illegal means and who believe their greatness consists solely in the accumulation of worldly goods.

Humanity's true wealth should also be reflected in the leaders of the people. In a divine or ideal civilization, 'Abdu'l-Bahá says that rulers would disregard any thought of amassing enormous riches for themselves and realize that their true wealth is in the enrichment of

---

1. *Some Answered Questions*, chapter 15, pp. 79-80.

their subjects; ministers of state would devote their time to developing methods for insuring the progress of the people; and those of learning and knowledge would devote themselves to scientific research and educating students of capacity. Those possessing these attitudes would be able to discover ways for improving the community and increasing its wealth and comfort.[1]

Requisites for Prosperity

In the same way that evil is the absence of good and darkness is the absence of light, poverty is the absence of wealth. Although poverty is the absence of something else, no one would assert that it is not a fact. It merely has a negative existence. To paraphrase 'Abdu'l-Bahá, when there is no wealth, there is poverty; wealth is an existing thing, but poverty is nonexistent.[2] A rich man can gather together all of his wealth and give it away, but it is impossible for a poor man to accumulate his poverty. It is wealth which has substance, not poverty. Wealth is what truly exists, while poverty is merely a lack thereof. Although wealth reflects the fabric of reality, most people deprive themselves of it during their lifetime. A lack of wealth can be attributed to the absence of one or more of the following nine characteristics:

Positive Mental Attitude: If we view money and wealth in a negative light, it is nearly impossible for us to become financially prosperous. Ironically, the Manifestations of God have suffered abasement and afflictions in order that humankind may achieve prosperity and abundance: "*We have accepted to be abased, O believers in the Unity of God, that ye may be exalted, and have suffered manifold afflictions, that ye might prosper and flourish.*"[3] Once our attitude toward wealth, and all of the other blessings of God, becomes positive, we will be able to prosper and flourish as is our God-given right. Similar to the effect of prayer upon the soul, our mental attitude requires a constant flow of positive thinking in order to maintain its progress on this plane of existence.

Desire for Wealth: Many people don't feel it is important to become wealthy, so they never give it a second thought; or they drift along in life naively wishing for something to make them a millionaire overnight. Wishing for wealth is a far cry from having a desire to be prosperous. Achieving financial freedom requires effort and persistence. Changing from a poverty mentality to a prosperity consciousness usually requires a transformation spanning many years. If we wish to create a strong desire for financial independence, we must reprioritize our thinking by accepting wealth as an important endeavor and prosperity as a normal way of life.

---

1. *The Secret of Divine Civilization*, pp. 20-22.
2. *Some Answered Questions*, chapter 74, p. 264.
3. Bahá'u'lláh in *Bahá'í World Faith*, p. 33.

Practical Plan of Action: By not having an effective strategy for becoming financially independent, most people can only complain about the impossibility of ever achieving wealth. Financial independence requires a specific plan of action, and although there are many books outlining the practical steps for acquiring wealth, most people fail to formulate, much less follow, any plan which incorporates these principles. The chapters in Part Three of this book delineate one way most people can achieve wealth through a practical plan of action.

Consistency: Regardless of how practical our plan for achieving wealth, if we don't follow it, it will never work. We must develop consistency when it comes to achieving goals, especially those involving financial independence. Think of your plan as a road map to financial success. If you fail to follow the planned route, it is unlikely that you will reach your destination. But through consistent effort, your goals are guaranteed to be successful. Consistency is also very important for achieving spiritual goals. For instance, if we do not pray, study the Writings, and contribute to the Fund regularly, or do not live the life and teach the Faith, it is unlikely that we will develop spiritually. Consistency is critical to both our spiritual and material life.

Persistence: Achieving success in any endeavor requires a certain amount of so-called failures in order to guide our efforts in the right direction. Anytime we are tested on the road to prosperity, it is simply to sharpen our abilities to do better. Failure should never be viewed as a reason for quitting, since this will never allow us to reach our goals. Persistence is a guaranteed way of winning. No failure is ever permanent, unless we make it so by quitting.

Trusting Your Intuition: A person's intuition or common sense concerning money matters is not always acknowledged, much less adhered to, on the road to prosperity. Although we should be open to new ideas, we should weigh such ideas with a strong dose of common sense in order to get an intuitive feel for their value. Too often we rely on the advice of "experts" for basic financial decisions we should be making for ourselves. Always remember that when it comes to your money, rarely does anyone else have your best interest at heart. The more knowledge we have about money matters, the better prepared we will be to handle financial decisions. In the same way that all people should have an elementary knowledge of health, basic financial knowledge is also necessary when making financial decisions.

Humility: If we become smug or complacent about our financial situation, it is a sure sign of impending catastrophe. Wealth is a bounty from God which should be acknowledged and appreciated. Although it is natural for man to be prosperous, it is also wise for him to remain thankful and humble while going through the various stages of prosperity. What can be bestowed upon us can also be taken away.

Pure Motive: Any desire for prosperity should be accompanied by a worthwhile purpose, if it is to achieve any lasting significance. A pure motive is the focal point for achieving any worthwhile purpose. Purity of motive is one of the building blocks of spiritual growth. Whenever we are faced with difficulties in our quest for wealth, we should review the pure motive that formed the basis of our goal in the first place. This procedure will help generate enough strength to overcome most difficulties and provide the necessary impetus for continuing our efforts to reach our objective.

Detachment: As explained in the previous chapter, detachment is critical for achieving our ultimate purpose on this plane of existence. It should also form the fabric of our prosperity consciousness. The person who is materially wealthy and also completely detached from worldly things is truly blessed in the sight of God.

The Characteristics of a Poverty Mentality

A poverty mentality is one of the most insidious obstacles preventing prosperity. It impedes both our material and spiritual progress, since it adversely affects the way we think and look at the world around us. A poverty mentality negates our efforts to manifest noble qualities. Negativity is at the heart of a poverty mentality. Negative emotions have no real power of their own; they simply mirror the potency we give them. Although we should acknowledge these emotions, we should not dwell on them or allow them to control our life. After acknowledging them, the next step is to eliminate these self-destructive tendencies if we intend to become prosperous. The emotions manifested by a poverty mentality include the following:

Apathy: When people have no curiosity about the world around them, they are apathetic toward life. Apathy retards any desire to grow and prosper, and promotes a dangerous disinclination to carry forward an ever-advancing civilization. A blasé or uninvolved attitude can lead to heedlessness and an uncaring outlook on life. Apathy kills the human spirit.

Guilt: People who feel excessive guilt manifest the symptoms of a poverty mentality, because they are unable to look at their situation in a positive light. Inappropriate or overabundant guilt can cause the death of a productive and prosperous lifestyle. Appropriate feelings of guilt are a self-defense mechanism for keeping us on the right path. Guilt should only be used as a self-induced motivator for maintaining the integrity of our principles, not as the dominating theme of our existence.

Indecisiveness: Indecisive people are unsure of what they want in life, usually have no solid goals, and constantly vacillate in their decision-making process. If you are unable to make a definitive statement about any issue, or stand by your moral principles, or are confused about why you exist, then you may fall prey to unscrupulous manipulators. There is an old adage which says that if you don't stand for something, you'll fall for anything.

Indifference: People who are indifferent have lost their passion for life, are often inconsiderate of others, are normally incapable of sincere love, and lack vitality. An indifferent person is one who views all things as equally trivial. This condition can infect a person's attitude to the point where a lack of excellence and mediocrity are acceptable behavioral tendencies. People who are indifferent have usually been beaten down by life and are tired of its many disappointments. They are afraid of failing, so they refuse to take another chance at success.

Irresponsibility: People who cannot accept responsibility for their failures, or deny responsibility for their actions, have developed a poverty mentality. Many people are irresponsible when it comes to using credit cards and investing money for their future; others blame someone else or circumstances for their own shortcomings. The former is a temporary misdirection, while the latter is a more serious disorder, needing eradication before one's fortune can change.

Lack of Appreciation: People who never praise others are ungrateful and hinder the advancement of prosperity. Everyone needs and deserves praise of some kind, even if they do average work. Praise encourages people to do better. 'Abdu'l-Bahá always encouraged the friends to look for the good in everyone and everything, since appreciation and positive thinking provide the right conditions for producing positive results.

Low Self-Worth: Feeling that you don't deserve to be prosperous or happy is destructive to one's spirit and opposed to the purpose of existence. An inferiority complex has nothing to do with humility, since humility is an attitude based on spiritual strength and peace of mind. All of us have been created in the image and likeness of God, so our demeanor should manifest self-worth and gratitude, not worthlessness and despair.

Procrastination: The procrastinator is one who delays, who rarely completes any project once it is started, and who believes that all things are subject to postponement. This type of do-nothing attitude is detrimental to success and prosperity. Procrastination has been accurately described as failure in the installment plan, since nothing ever gets started if it is always being delayed; or if started, it is never completed.

Selfishness: Selfishness is an inability to share with others. People who are selfish not only abhor sharing, but also try to prevent the flow of generosity from others. Generosity, on the other hand, is a desire to give or share with other people. Generosity is a quality of God in which all should participate.

Unhappiness: Unhappy people allow negativity to dominate their thinking. A happy person is generally a prosperous person. 'Abdu'l-Bahá always encouraged the Bahá'ís to be happy, as this attitude indicates true wealth and understanding. It is possible for a happy person to be negative every once in a while, but it is impossible for an unhappy person to remain positive for any length of time.

By ridding ourselves of the above negative characteristics, we are able to focus our thoughts on prosperity and its positive influence. All of us periodically manifest some of these negative tendencies. This is only natural. What is not natural is to be constantly negative. This type of thinking can lead to negative behavior and a cynical personality. Negativity makes spiritual development difficult and can cause permanent emotional damage. A positive attitude, brought about by positive thinking, is the best medicine for extracting ourselves from the clutches of a poverty mentality.

The Characteristics of a Prosperity Attitude

Money is not a problem for those with a prosperity attitude; it is only a problem for those with a poverty mentality. There is no shame in being poor. Shame occurs when we constantly worry about money or waste our time and energy on accumulating things which only bring momentary pleasure. Constantly worrying about money and material things can decrease our ability to succeed. Worrying has a tendency to keep us preoccupied with the mundane things of life. For those developing a prosperity consciousness, money is not the most important thing in life. The reason for developing a prosperity attitude is to allow us to function in the material world in a positive way, whether or not we have money. A prosperity attitude makes it easier to master the precepts of prosperity, enjoy greater self-esteem, and develop confidence in our abilities. Once we are committed to doing something worthwhile in life, all these things will follow.

A prosperity attitude contains two very important traits. The first is believing that you deserve to be prosperous; the second is that it is okay to get paid for enjoying yourself. We were created to feel joy and satisfaction in our work and to receive adequate compensation for our labors. When we experience abundance and happiness, we are realizing our true spiritual nature; and the more we experience this nature, the stronger we develop spiritually. A prosperity attitude is our connection with God, since it allows us to create beauty and abundance and is a vehicle for expressing ourselves in the material world. Bahá'u'lláh has even elevated work performed in a spirit of service to the level of worship. So, unless we deliberately manifest a negative attitude, Bahá'u'lláh has made it nearly impossible for us to have anything other than a prosperity attitude in life.

The following characteristics are associated with a prosperity attitude. They include a positive personality, showing enthusiasm, radiating confidence and self-esteem, giving praise to others, keeping an open mind, and praying for guidance and gratitude. If we can master these characteristics and incorporate them into our lives, our quest for prosperity will be successful.

A Positive Personality: Always be positive! No matter what you do for a living, no matter what your relationship is with other people, and no matter how difficult life seems to be at the moment, always be positive. A positive attitude is an essential part of a pleasing personality and one of the most important character traits a person can possess. If we do not have such a positive outlook, our chances of success are small indeed. Life's attitude toward us is a reflection of our attitude toward it. Whether we are positive or negative about life, we will attract the qualities we manifest. If we think negative thoughts, we will become negative; if we think positive thoughts, we are a joy to be around. It is easy to be negative, but it takes effort, patience, love, and understanding to be positive. Nourishing the mind with positive thoughts and exercising the personality with positive actions strengthens the potency of our endeavors and increases the quality of life.

Showing Enthusiasm: Enthusiasm is a powerful way of expressing positive thinking. Without enthusiasm, our projects, goals, and aspirations are devoid of spirit. Enthusiasm has many levels of intensity. When we become interested in something, we have a certain degree of enthusiasm for it; when this interest is maintained or supported by knowledge, our enthusiasm becomes greater still, until finally, we reach the highest degree of enthusiasm for what we are doing when we develop an unshakeable commitment supported by sound principles. It is the intensity of enthusiasm that burns away the obstacles blocking our successes. The Dawn-Breakers had such intensity of enthusiasm as they spread the Faith far-and-wide across Persia.

Radiating Confidence and Self-Esteem: When you develop a prosperity attitude and expend your energy on worthwhile projects, you exude a sense of confidence which attracts good things. Your self-esteem is built on the amount of confidence you can develop and maintain in your daily life. If we lack enthusiasm for what we are doing, we soon lose our ability to maintain this confidence. When we start thinking and acting like the person we want to be, our self-worth increases. This is why we have role models—to provide examples for incorporating ideal qualities and outwardly reflecting them. Having a positive role model to identify with is important for developing confidence and self-esteem.

Giving Praise to Others: Everyone deserves to be praised for the good things they do in life. Taking other people for granted is one of the best ways to end a friendship or love relationship. It does not matter if the other person is your spouse, a devoted employee, or one of your children, everyone wants to feel appreciated. Not taking the time to compliment and show love to people is a sign of negative thinking and, sooner or later, it will come back to haunt you in unimaginable ways. Most people take their job very seriously, so why not praise and acknowledge the work they do? The development of a prosperity attitude requires us to give praise to other people.

Keeping an Open Mind: An open mind is an important element of a prosperity attitude. Nearly all wealth has been generated by new ideas which found a receptive response in an open-minded individual. Human beings were created to carry forward an ever-advancing civilization, but it is impossible to do this with a closed mind. The mind must be open to new ideas, new innovations, new thoughts, and new ways of doing things, if we expect to continue progressing and advancing. If man were not meant to progress on this plane of existence, only one Manifestation of God would be necessary and there would be no need for the concept of Progressive Revelation.

Praying for Guidance and Gratitude: The final characteristic of a prosperity attitude, praying for guidance and gratitude, is by no means the least important. Praying for continued success is just as important as prayers of gratitude for past achievements. It has been said that we should pray as if everything depends upon God and act as if everything depends upon us. By following this line of thinking, our prosperity is assured.

Chapter 4

Material Means Versus Materialism

The labor of the righteous tendeth to life, the fruit of the wicked to sin.—Proverbs 10:16

Society, without the help of divine guidance, is incapable of establishing harmony in its material endeavors or resolving its economic and social dilemmas. Money alone is not the answer. Only the genuine application of the spiritual principles, as revealed by Bahá'u'lláh, can heal the ills of the world. To this end, Bahá'u'lláh has redirected our efforts away from materialism and toward the attainment of spirituality as the basis of all our activities. Knowing the distinction between material means and materialism is essential for understanding the dynamic relationship linking human spirituality and physical well-being. Materialism implies attachment *to* the material world, whereas material means signifies the best method for becoming detached *from* the material world. Materialism divorces human endeavors from God and prevents the attainment of spiritual attributes, while material means elevates our work to the level of worship and is the key for participating in all the bounties of the Lord.

Work Elevated to the Level of Worship

Bahá'u'lláh has made it incumbent upon everyone to engage in some sort of occupation and has elevated this work to the level of worship: *"It is enjoined upon every one of you to engage in some form of occupation, such as crafts, trades and the like. We have graciously exalted your engagement in such work to the rank of worship unto God, the True One."* [1] And since our occupations are *"identical with the worship of God,"* [2] it is important for us to approach our work with a sense of devotion and joy.

There are practical as well as spiritual reasons for working. On the practical side, work supplies the means of our livelihood and helps us to understand the value of service. On the spiritual side, work helps us come nearer to God by fulfilling one of the reasons for our existence, which is to carry forward an ever-advancing civilization. In a letter written on his behalf, Shoghi Effendi says that work "has not only a utilitarian purpose, but has a value in itself, because it draws us nearer to God, and enables us to better grasp His purpose for us in this world." [3] In another letter written on his behalf, Shoghi Effendi says that Bahá'u'lláh considers work to be "the highest form of detachment in this day." [4] Work enables us to fulfill the law of Huqúqu'lláh and provides the means for supporting the growth of the Cause.

One of the spiritual teachings common in religious history is the dire consequences resulting from those who refuse to engage in work: *"Trees that yield no fruit have been and will ever be for the fire."* [5] Everyone, no matter how poor or handicapped, is obligated to work. Conversely, even the rich must work, since "the inheritance of wealth cannot make anyone immune from daily work." [6] With this in mind, we may wish to pursue a career that is both enjoyable and allows us to utilize our God-given talents. From early childhood, parents should cultivate the unique abilities and interests of their children in order to encourage a sense of joyful service during their working years. If we were not fortunate enough to have such parents, we may still have unfulfilled longings. However, this should not be an excuse to keep us from accomplishing our life's purpose.

Bahá'u'lláh has placed very few employment restrictions on His followers. We are free to engage in any of the arts, sciences, crafts, or trades available, provided they remain within the bounds of Bahá'í Law. In a letter written on his behalf, Shoghi Effendi says that "there is no general rule, or any particular standard, requiring a believer to serve in one field to the exclusion of others. Every believer is to choose for himself any avenue of work in which he conscientiously feels he can render the greatest amount of service to the Cause." [7]

Furthermore, our work does not have to be compensated by monetary means in order to be considered worship. Homemaking and child-rearing are essential and extremely worthwhile occupations,

---

1. *Tablets of Bahá'u'lláh*, p. 26.
2. *Lights of Guidance: A Bahá'í Reference File*, no. 2105, p. 623.
3. Ibid., no. 2106, p. 623.
4. Ibid., no. 2109, p. 624.
5. *Hidden Words*, Persian, no. 80.
6. *Lights of Guidance*, no. 2106, p. 623.
7. Ibid., no. 408, p. 119.

though most parents receive no monetary compensation for such service. In a letter written on behalf of the Universal House of Justice on this subject, it stated that "homemaking is a highly honorable and responsible work of fundamental importance for mankind."[1] Homemakers not only do most of the shopping, cooking, cleaning, laundering, and other work around the house, but also are intended to rear the children to reflect the qualities and attributes of God. Although the Writings indicate that the primary responsibility for financial support rests with the husband, whereas the wife is generally considered the primary educator of the children, the Universal House of Justice affirms that "this by no means implies that these functions are inflexibly fixed and cannot be changed and adjusted to suit particular family situations, nor does it mean that the place of the woman is confined to the home."[2] Bahá'u'lláh has made it quite clear that the family, not the individual, is the basic unit of society; so if the family is better served by a reversal of traditional roles on the part of the husband and wife, then this condition should be accepted and encouraged by the members of the community.

The Value of Material Means

Although Bahá'u'lláh has elevated our work to the level of worship, the value of our material means includes much more. Our work, besides providing us with the basic necessities of life, such as food, shelter, clothing, education, and transportation, is also the source from which our profits and future prosperity is made. Strictly speaking, our material means is the basis for every undertaking and an instrument for worshiping God. By earning our livelihood through our work, we are profiting both spiritually and materially.

Furthermore, we are encouraged to become wealthy from the efforts of our learning and labors: *"Thus it is incumbent on every one to engage in crafts and professions, for therein lies the secret of wealth, O men of understanding!"*[3] Our prosperity should result from acquiring specific knowledge, skills, and education which will elevate humanity. However, though many of us will earn, cumulatively speaking, a fortune during our lifetime, most of us will retain very little of this wealth. The opportunity we have for becoming wealthy through our labor is tremendous. Our work is the best source of revenue for building a financially secure future, but only if we conscientiously save and invest a certain portion of our wages. It is the harvest from our investments that can provide the means for enjoying the good things later in life. Without money, which first comes from our labor and later from our investments, we can enjoy very little of the material creation. 'Abdu'l-Bahá assures us: *"All material things*

---

1. *Women in the Bahá'í Faith*, p. 30.
2. Ibid.
3. *Hidden Words*, Persian, no. 80.

are for us, so that through our gratitude we may learn to under-stand life as a divine benefit." [1]

Our material means can provide an avenue of service to others, service which is not only worship, but an instrument for developing our spiritual potential. Commenting on the occupations of people, 'Abdu'l-Bahá says: *"Commerce, agriculture and industry should not, in truth, be a bar to service of the One True God. Indeed, such occupations are most potent instruments and clear proofs for the manifestation of the evidences of one's piety, of one's trustworthiness and of the virtues of the All-Merciful Lord."* [2] Our work is the testing ground for learning and practicing the spiritual qualities taught by the Manifestation of God.

Theoretically, poverty should not prevent people from working. It should actually be a motivator for engaging in some form of occu-pation, since it helps eliminate neediness and the stigma of not being self-supporting. 'Abdu'l-Bahá says that *"we must never live on oth-ers like a parasitic plant. Every person must have a profession, whether it be literary or manual, and must live a clean, manly, honest life, an example of purity to be imitated by others."* [3] However, as a corollary to this injunction, those in authority must provide "every individual the opportunity of acquiring the necessary talent in some kind of profession, and also the means of utilizing such a talent, both for its own sake and for the sake of earning the means of his livelihood." [4] Indeed, future human society will operate in such a way as to provide the skills, education, and opportunities required for a happy and robust lifestyle. Until then, we should do the best we can to seek an occupation which benefits mankind, supports our fi-nancial needs, and provides personal satisfaction, so we can make the most of our life on this planet.

The implications of carrying forward an ever-advancing civiliza-tion provide abundant opportunities for creating unique channels of service. Our livelihood need not be limited to traditional careers. The future will create job opportunities that are totally unheard-of today, just as many of today's jobs were unknown only a few decades ago. Change and progress are propelling us forward. Being on the cutting-edge of change is not as uncommon as it used to be.

What Money Symbolizes

In the modern world, where money is used as the primary source for measuring the value of exchange between people, it is absurd to think that money is unimportant. *Money is very import-ant!* Every nation in the world has replaced the barter system with a

1. *Bahá'u'lláh and the New Era*, p. 103.
2. *Trustworthiness*, no. 52, p. 15.
3. *Bahá'u'lláh and the New Era*, p. 102.
4. *Lights of Guidance*, no. 2106, p. 623.

system of currency as the primary medium of exchange between peoples. This is money's most important feature, without which the modern industrial world could not function or exist.

Price is another determinate of money's value. The amount of money you pay for goods and services measures their value. Everything has a price, though not everything has the same value to every person. This is where the economic law of supply and demand is relevant, since the price of goods and services are determined by the demand made for them and the ability to supply them. Goods which are plentiful normally have a low price, while those which are rare usually command a high price.

Money can also be used as a measure of wealth. As long as money is an acceptable medium of exchange, it can be stored or accumulated. The storing of people's money is one of the primary functions of banks. Our material wealth includes both what we physically own, such as our home and other material objects, and the amount of money we have accumulated in various financial institutions, such as banks, credit unions, mutual funds, and other instruments of the financial services industry.

Money is a universal symbol of power, prestige, and well-being. How we use money is a vivid reflection of our priorities in life. If we waste our resources on excessive materialism or inordinate material gratification, this usually reflects a paucity of spirituality and a profusion of worldliness. On the other hand, if we use our money for the enrichment of mankind, then we are pursuing a praiseworthy and worthwhile course of action. Though it may be true that money cannot make people happy, neither will its absence.

Money is an emotional and sensitive subject to many people. For many couples, "financial difficulties and disagreements are a major cause of divorce." [1] This is partially due to the inability of each individual to handle his or her own personal finances in a responsible way (a skill that can be learned), though it also concerns the spending patterns (too much or too little) of each partner and the emotional disposition about money that each brings to the marriage.

Another aspect of money is that with it good people become better and bad people become worse. If you love humanity, money can help you to establish a foundation of goodwill for unifying people, but if you harbor prejudices or hatred against people, money can aid you to become more destructive and inconsiderate of others, since money increases the potency of one's actions. The person with a high sense of virtue and spiritual rectitude can accomplish a great deal of good with money, but one not so morally endowed can cause dreadful suffering and mischief.

1. Khalil and Sue Khavari, *Together Forever: A Handbook for Creating a Successful Marriage*, p. 61.

In the modern world, the transfer of funds between financial institutions and people is primarily done by check or credit card. A vast computer network is responsible for maintaining the flow of wealth. Even the concept of money is changing as humanity moves closer to a unified society and a one world system of government. Money is more likely to take the form of electronically computerized digits than of paper currency. Except for petty cash or pocket money, few people see or physically touch the vast majority of the money they earn. People normally receive their wages by paycheck, which is then deposited into their bank account, which is then used to write checks to pay for goods and services received. For the most part, checks and credit cards have replaced cash as the primary method of payment for goods and services. As society becomes even more electronically integrated, paper money could lose its appeal as a convenient medium of exchange entirely. In the near future, paper money may be replaced by a computerized system of credit and debit cards, a potentially hazardous situation for those not in complete control of their finances. However, such a system would make it easier to institute a universal currency to replace the present arcane structure and complex transactions between national paper currencies.

Money symbolizes material power and it provides the Bahá'í Faith with the means to grow and develop throughout the world. Money is needed for completing the terraces of the Shrine of the Báb and the remaining buildings of the World Administrative Center on Mount Carmel, for constructing magnificent Houses of Worship throughout the world, and for promoting the worldwide expansion of the Faith. All of these things can be easily accomplished within a short period of time, if the money is available to do them.

Man's Materialistic Tendencies

By itself, however, money cannot solve humanity's economic plight. Man's economic troubles have resulted from a lack of spirituality, not from a lack of funding. The permanent solution to our monetary problems lies in our ability to incorporate the teachings of Bahá'u'lláh into the very fiber of our being and apply them in our daily life. When the human race begins to practice these spiritual principles, it will find solutions to its most dire material afflictions.

Of the many prevalent behaviors of human society in general, and Western civilization in particular, demonstrating the pernicious nature of materialism, at least three exemplify our tendency to emphasize materialism over spirituality. 'Abdu'l-Bahá describes them as *"the attainment of material livelihood, physical comforts and worldly enjoyments."*[1] Although 'Abdu'l-Bahá recognizes the need for moderation in these endeavors, He seems to be speaking of their extremes,

---

1. *The Promulgation of Universal Peace,* p. 335.

which empty the soul of all desire to serve others and worship God. Though beneficial in moderation, they are detrimental to our spiritual development when carried to excess, since they tend to focus our thoughts on the purely material aspects of life. These extremes are intolerable when their destructive potential is understood. It is with regard to this that Bahá'u'lláh warns: *"If carried to excess, civilization will prove as prolific a source of evil as it had been of goodness when kept within the restraints of moderation....The day is approaching when its flame will devour the cities."* [1]

The excessive attainment of material livelihood, the first of man's materialistic tendencies, has to do with pursuing riches at the expense of all other things. It is sometimes known as chasing the almighty dollar.[2] People who are in this category are never satisfied with their standard of living and always think the grass is greener on the other side of the fence. They are continually being distracted by status, money, or prestige. By feeling dissatisfied in their work, which is identical to worshiping God, they are unable to concentrate on its spiritual implications. Modern society places too much emphasis on this mortal and fleeting existence and not enough on the acquisition of spiritual values.

The inordinate desire for physical comforts, the second of man's materialistic tendencies, has to do with all manner of wasteful and excessive consumption. Modern man, especially in the more affluent technologically advanced societies, is consumer oriented. People consume food excessively not for nourishment but for mere pleasure, tend to buy more things than they can reasonably use, and thoughtlessly waste precious natural resources to satisfy their bodily whims. The physical weakening of the human body through inadequate exercise and improper nutrition, the emotional destruction caused by a lack of healthy interaction with other people, and the loss of tranquility through an overabundance of artificial stimulation and noise has contributed to people losing sight of the true function of the material world, which is to act as a classroom for the acquisition and maintenance of spiritual qualities. If our quest for physical comfort leads to laziness or lethargy, it is almost impossible to progress spiritually.

An overindulgence in worldly enjoyments, the third of man's materialistic tendencies, has to do with the never-ending quest for pleasure and entertainment to the distraction of gaining spiritual attributes. The excessive use of television, video games, and the automobile are just a few examples of this craving to be entertained. Nearly everything in our materialistic society has an entertainment value attached to it—from nightly news programs to religious services to raising chil-

---

1. *Gleanings*, CLXIII, pp. 342-343.
2. The term "dollar" is used to denote money or a monetary unit of currency. The 1992 *World Book Encyclopedia* lists 17 countries which use the term "dollar" for their currency, and it is the world's most popular name for currency.

dren. People want to be stimulated and they want to be stimulated excessively. The modern age offers a dazzling array of electronic gadgets and other luxury items to entertain the individual. People are preoccupied with their own indulgences and personal pursuits, and tend to become forgetful of the real needs of the world around them and their own spiritual reality. The material world exists to improve our spirituality, not to diminish it.

The Curse of Materialism

Materialism signifies total reliance on the material world with little or no concern for spirituality. It acts as a barrier between the individual and God and undermines the mental and moral fiber of mankind. It divorces religion from our daily life by laying "excessive and ever-increasing emphasis on material well-being [while] forgetful of those things of the spirit on which alone a sure and stable foundation can be laid for human society."[1] Although materialism has plagued human society for millennia, its power is much stronger today than in past ages.

> Mankind is submerged in the sea of materialism and occupied with the affairs of this world. They have no thought beyond earthly possessions and manifest no desire save the passions of this fleeting, mortal existence....Although it is necessary for man to strive for material needs and comforts, his real need is the acquisition of the bounties of God.[2]

The desire and preference for materialism over spirituality is a malediction of the soul. Materialism has spread to such an extent that most of the people of the world are completely immersed in it. In a letter written on his behalf to an individual believer, Shoghi Effendi describes the deleterious effects of this curse to the world:

> Indeed, the chief reason for the evils now rampant in society is the lack of spirituality. The materialistic civilization of our age has so much absorbed the energy and interest of mankind that people in general no longer feel the necessity of raising themselves above the forces and conditions of their daily material existence. There is not sufficient demand for things that we should call spiritual to differentiate them from the needs and requirements of our physical existence. The universal crisis affecting mankind is, therefore, essentially spiritual in its causes. The spirit of the age, taken on the whole, is irreligious. Man's outlook on life is too crude and materialistic to enable him to elevate himself into the higher realms of the spirit. It is this

1. Shoghi Effendi, *Citadel of Faith: Messages to America, 1947–1957*, p. 125.
2. 'Abdu'l-Bahá, *Promulgation of Universal Peace*, p. 335.

condition, so sadly morbid, into which society has fallen, that religion seeks to improve and transform.[1]

The curse of materialism has also created an obvious threat to the immediate survival of humankind. Called "an evil" by Shoghi Effendi, this "cancerous materialism" is rapidly spreading and contaminating the peoples and regions of the world. According to the Guardian, Bahá'u'lláh has denounced this evil in "unequivocal and emphatic language...comparing it to a devouring flame and regarding it as the chief factor in precipitating the dire ordeals and world-shaking crises that must necessarily involve the burning of cities and the spread of terror and consternation in the hearts of men."[2] Humanity has experienced untold suffering and destruction during this century, due in part to the bane of materialism.

Materialism was a large contributing factor to the outbreak of both World Wars, which resulted in the destruction of Europe and many cities and villages in Asia, North Africa, and the Pacific. Materialism may also prove to be the underlying cause of yet another and possibly final global confrontation before humanity is cleansed of this spiritual disease. In a letter to the American Bahá'í community in July 1954, the Guardian spoke of the planet's future in dire terms if the fire of this cancerous materialism continues to run its course unabated:

> Indeed a foretaste of the devastation which this consuming fire will wreak upon the world, and with which it will lay waste the cities of the nations participating in this tragic world-engulfing contest, has been afforded by the last World War, marking the second stage in the global havoc which humanity, forgetful of its God and heedless of the clear warnings uttered by His appointed Messenger for this day, must, alas, inevitably experience.[3]

Even before the beginning of World War I, the first stage of this global havoc, 'Abdu'l-Bahá, in His travels to both Europe and America, warned against this "all-pervasive, pernicious materialism." The peoples of Europe, and later America, "found themselves suddenly swept into the vortex of a tempest which in its range and severity was unsurpassed in the world's history."[4] It was this first global conflict which totally destroyed the absolute power of Europe's monarchs, the first group of people to be infected by the excesses of crass materialism.

To the degree that modern man has succeeded in separating his political and economic systems from a spiritual framework, and adopted instead various materialistic philosophies, he has created dev-

1. *Lights of Guidance*, no. 449, pp. 134-135.
2. *Citadel of Faith*, pp. 124-125.
3. Ibid., p. 125.
4. Ibid.

astating social, economic, and environmental problems, including the existence of extreme poverty alongside abundant wealth, the destruction of the planet's environment, the depletion and mismanagement of the earth's natural resources, the disruptive divisions between management and labor, the bleeding of national treasuries and manpower through the excessive build-up of armaments and waging ruinous wars, the disastrous erection of trade barriers based on nationalistic priorities, and widespread crime and immorality. Viewed in its entirety, the world "offers us the sad and pitiful spectacle of a vast, an enfeebled, and moribund organism, which is being torn politically and strangulated economically by forces it has ceased to either control or comprehend." [1]

In spite of these problems, and because of them, humanity is gradually acquiring a strong sense of globalism and oneness. Ironically, the crises themselves are the surest sign that humanity is at long last nearing the stage of planetary civilization and universal peace. But the leaders and peoples of the world must overcome their paralysis of will to act, cease their self-indulgent preoccupations, and concentrate their efforts in constructing a global community bound by universally recognized and inviolable principles. *"The purging of such deeply-rooted and overwhelming corruptions,"* advises Bahá'u'lláh, *"cannot be effected unless the peoples of the world unite in pursuit of one common aim and embrace one universal faith."* [2]

1. Shoghi Effendi, *The World Order of Bahá'u'lláh*, p. 188.
2. *Tablets of Bahá'u'lláh*, p. 69.

Chapter 5

Huqúqu'lláh and the Bahá'í Funds

Will a man rob God? Yet ye have robbed me. But ye say, Wherein have we robbed thee? In tithes and offerings.—Malachi 3:8

From the dawn of religious history, it has been an obligation for the followers of religion to give a portion of their wealth to God. The Revelation for this age is no exception, and this obligation is fulfilled in our obedience to the law of Huqúqu'lláh and generosity in contributing to the various funds of the Faith. Such actions correspond with the proper use of wealth. Our spiritual and material blessings depend, in part, on the extent of our willingness to comply with the Writings in this matter.

The Genius of Huqúqu'lláh

Huqúqu'lláh, or the Right of God,[1] is a sacred law and a divine institution. It provides the central authority of the Faith, today the Universal House of Justice, with the means for assuring its financial independence and unfettered operation through the establishment of an obligatory source of revenue from the believers. Although the law of the Right of God can be considered a financial aspect of the Cov-

---

1. In a letter dated September 30, 1993, Hand of the Cause of God and Trustee of the Huqúqu'lláh, Dr. A. M. Varqá, in following the wishes of the Universal House of Justice, asked that the representatives and deputies of the Huqúqu'lláh encourage the use of the vernacular term "Right of God" instead of the more formal Huqúqu'lláh, since such terminology has a more immediate impact on the believers.

enant, in reality, it is *"the source of blessings, and the mainspring of God's loving-kindness and tender love vouchsafed unto men."* [1] It is a means of spiritual progress and "a way of strengthening the link of love and dedication between man and God." [2]

Bahá'u'lláh has repeatedly stated that *"the progress and promotion of the Cause of God depend on material means."* [3] The Right of God embodies, to a large extent, the financial ingenuity of the Faith and is "an important instrument for building and strengthening the structure of the edifice of the World Order of Bahá'u'lláh." [4] When this institution becomes fully functional in all lands there should be an overflowing source of revenue to meet the growing needs of the Faith, since *"the purpose underlying this law is to ensure that the General Treasury is strengthened in the future."* [5] Viewed in this light, the Right of God will surely become an important mechanism for redistributing the wealth of humankind and eliminating the extremes of wealth and poverty in the future.

The law of Huqúqu'lláh ranks in importance only after the two great obligations of recognizing God and obedience to His laws and ordinances. However, the implementation of this law is characterized by "kindness, forgiveness, tolerance and magnanimity," [6] and not by pressure from any source. In fact, to demand the payment of the Right of God is, according to Bahá'u'lláh, *"in no wise permissible."* [7] The attitude of the believer in complying with this law should be one of *"utmost joy and radiance and in a spirit of perfect humility and lowliness."* [8] In other words, abiding by this law requires the utmost maturity on the part of the individual believer.

In the past, material wealth has tended to corrupt and degrade religion. The law of Huqúqu'lláh preserves against such corruption by eliminating the influence of vested interests in its procurement and distribution. Bahá'u'lláh says that *"today is the Day of God when the preservation of the dignity of His Cause must be given precedence over all other things."* [9] Those receiving the payment of Huqúqu'lláh are exhorted to maintain the dignity of the Cause. Likewise, when paying the Right of God, it is important for the believers to compute the amount correctly so that they can faithfully fulfill their sacred obligation. As will be seen below, the genius of Huqúqu'lláh finds its deepest expression in removing every trace of corruption which can taint this source of revenue.

---

1. *Huqúqu'lláh: The Right of God*, no. 29, p. 9.
2. *Huqúqu'lláh: A Study Guide*, p. 14.
3. *Huqúqu'lláh: The Right of God*, no. 1, p. 1.
4. *Huqúqu'lláh: A Study Guide*, p. 14.
5. *Huqúqu'lláh: The Right of God*, no. 19, p. 5.
6. *Huqúqu'lláh: A Study Guide*, p. 7.
7. *Huqúqu'lláh: The Right of God*, no. 9, p. 3.
8. Ibid., no. 2, p.1.
9. Ibid., no. 3, p. 1.

Distinctive Characteristics of the Right of God

The Right of God is not merely another system for raising money in order to further the interests of the Cause, but a point where both the "spiritual and material dimensions" of the Bahá'í Faith "meet and are united."[1] There are five characteristics which distinguish the law of Huqúqu'lláh, not only from the concept of tithing in past Dispensations, but also from the obligation to give to the Bahá'í funds.

The first distinctive characteristic of the Right of God is that it is really a financial obligation to God, since, according to the Kitáb-i-Aqdas, a part of an individual's possessions and income rightfully belongs to God: *"Should anyone acquire one hundred mithqáls of gold, nineteen mithqáls thereof are God's and to be rendered unto Him, the Fashioner of earth and heaven."*[2] The mysteries and benefits associated with obeying this command-ment are *"beyond the comprehension of anyone save God, the All-Knowing, the All-Informed."*[3] However, what we can compre-hend from observing this obligation is succinctly explained by Hand of the Cause of God Dr. 'Alí Muhammad Varqa, the Trustee of Huqúqu'lláh:

> What we can conceive by our human understanding is that the payment of Huqúqu'lláh is the sign of our love and obedi-ence, a proof of our firmness and steadfastness and a symbol of our trustworthiness in the Covenant of Bahá'u'lláh. It cre-ates and develops our spiritual quality which leads us towards perfection; it harmonizes and balances our material endeavor, protects us from excessive desire which is born in our human nature, and when unleashed turns into a protective element for our spiritual growth. When man realizes that a part of his in-come will be honored by the acceptance of the Lord, the pres-ence of God is felt in all his endeavors, and undoubtedly he will strive to live his life in a just and legitimate manner in order that his offering may deserve to be accepted and spent in the path of God.[4]

In past Dispensations, it was praiseworthy for a believer to vol-untarily bestow his wealth for the sake of God. Of course, God has always been and will always be independent of any material need. The blessings derived from the act of giving and the advantages gained from such deeds will always revert to the individuals them-selves. If, according to Bahá'u'lláh, *"the whole world"*, when divorced from its spiritual purpose, *"is worth as much as the black in the eye of a dead ant,"*[5] then how significant can the mere material

---

1. *Huqúqu'lláh:* See the general comments in the Introduction.
2. *Kitáb-i-Aqdas,* K97, p. 55.
3. *Huqúqu'lláh: The Right of God,* no. 10, p. 3.
4. *Huqúqu'lláh: A Study Guide,* pp. 14-15.
5. *Epistle to the Son of the Wolf,* p. 124.

value of our contributions be to God? Furthermore, Bahá'u'lláh says that *"all the world hath belonged and will always belong to God."* [1] What is well pleasing to God is not the amount of our payment (regardless of how large we may feel it to be), but the purity of its offering: *"the acceptance of the offerings dependeth on the spirit of joy, fellowship and contentment that the righteous souls who fulfill this injunction will manifest."* [2] This spirit of pureheartedness should characterize the believer's attitude when offering the payment of Huqúqu'lláh.

The second distinctive characteristic is that the payment of the Right of God has priority over all contributions to any of the other Bahá'í funds, since this money belongs to God and we have no right to it. Although it may come through us, it does not belong to us. What we contribute to the Bahá'í funds is independent of our obligation to pay the Huqúqu'lláh and must not come from what belongs to God. Incredibly, the act of giving back to God what specifically belongs to Him has the added benefit of purifying our wealth. And when our wealth is purified, all who set foot in our home are also honored to enter a material environment which has been blessed by Bahá'u'lláh.

The third distinctive characteristic of the Right of God is that it is an obligation subject to specific laws and guidelines given in the Kitáb-i-Aqdas, whereas our other contributions are not. Contributing to the Bahá'í funds is an act of sacrifice, generosity, and detachment, not an obligation which has dire consequences to the soul if not obeyed: *"He who dealeth faithlessly with God will in justice meet with faithlessness himself."* [3] Although the payment of the Right of God attracts "divine bounty and blessings, its negligence or failure causes deprivation and is interpreted as tantamount to treachery to a Fund rightfully belonging to God." [4] The payment of Huqúqu'lláh is really the fulfillment of our material indebtedness to God, since we are ultimately beholden to God for all of our blessings and material bounties.

The fourth distinctive characteristic of the Right of God is that the amount due to be paid is determined, not on one's income, but on the size of one's accumulated savings and possessions after all necessary living expenses have been paid and losses have been recouped. [5] Although reference is made to computing one's Huqúqu'lláh when one's annual income and expenses are known, indicating that a yearly payment would be the norm, the frequency of payment is not, in fact, laid down and is left to the judgement of the individual. The

---

1. *Huqúqu'lláh: The Right of God*, no. 27, p. 9.
2. Ibid., no. 4, p. 2.
3. *Kitáb-i-Aqdas*, p. 55.
4. *Huqúqu'lláh: A Study Guide*, p. 13.
5. This fact distinguishes the law of Huqúq from that of Zakát. See below under "On Tithing and Sacrifice."

determination of what are "necessary" expenses is likewise left to "the spiritual maturity of every believer and his innermost conscience." [1] Providing stability to the computations, the Law of God gives gold as the standard against which the value of all currencies and other possessions is measured. One reason for leaving the calculation of the Right of God to the individual's own conscience is not to give one a licence to evade payment, but to permit one to grow spiritually through an honest and trustworthy relationship with God and the central authority of the Faith. It is "not a law which is enforced with pressure, but rather a spiritual obligation based on the love of the believer who is eager to obey the will of his Beloved." [2] And this obedience is "a reflection of the highest degree of love and ardent desire" [3] that we can exhibit toward our Lord.

The fifth distinctive characteristic is that the distribution of the Huqúqu'lláh is solely determined by the Head of the Cause of God and not subject to the wishes of the donor. With other Bahá'í funds, we are free to earmark our contributions for any purpose we wish— not so with payment of the Right of God. "Whatever portion of one's wealth is due to the Huqúqu'lláh," explains the House of Justice, "belongs to the World Centre of the Cause of God, not to the individuals concerned." [4] Since this money rightfully belongs to God and not to the person who is obligated to pay it, the payer has absolutely no say in how it is to be spent. In other words, we have no rights over the Right of God. This is the sole prerogative of the Universal House of Justice.

Throughout His writings, Bahá'u'lláh mentions the benefits that will accrue to those who observe the payment of Huqúqu'lláh. In every case, the greatest benefits return to the donors themselves. The following are a few examples of what Bahá'u'lláh has said concerning the payment of the Right of God:[5]

> *It hath been and will always be conducive to divine increase, prosperity, dignity and honor.*

> *Whatsoever proceedeth from Him produceth a fruit the benefits of which revert to the individuals themselves.*

> *The benefits accruing from benevolent works shall fall to the individuals concerned.*

> *It is indubitably clear and evident that whatsoever hath been sent down from the heaven of divine commandment...is intended to confer benefits upon His servants.*

1. *Huqúqu'lláh: A Study Guide*, p. 12.
2. Ibid., p. 11.
3. Ibid.
4. *Huqúqu'lláh: The Right of God*, no. 100, p. 32.
5. All of the following quotations are from *Huqúqu'lláh: The Right of God*.

> There can be no doubt that whatsoever hath been re-
> vealed from the All-Glorious Pen, be it ordinances or pro-
> hibitions, conferreth benefits upon the believers themselves.
> Were the people...to discover the benefits arising there-
> from, they would certainly, one and all, carry them out
> with the utmost joy and eagerness.

In addition to the individual benefits associated with the obser-
vance of the Right of God, Bahá'u'lláh has extended this prosperity
and wealth to the entire community:[1]

> Most of the wealth of men is not pure. Should they fol-
> low what is revealed by God, they would assuredly not be
> deprived of His grace and they would, in all circumstances,
> be protected under His bounty and blessed by His mercy.

> For had everyone perceived the advantage of such a
> deed and desisted from withholding the right of God, the
> friends in that region would not have experienced any
> hardship.

> Had the friends there observed the payment of
> Huqúqu'lláh, the people of that region would have enjoyed
> ease and comfort.

> It is clear and evident that the payment of the Right of
> God is conducive to prosperity, to blessing, and to honor
> and divine protection.

> It is a bounty which shall remain with every soul in
> every world of the worlds of God.

Another benefit of obeying the law of Huqúqu'lláh is that it requires us to maintain accurate financial records to keep track of the
surplus which is subject to payment. This responsibility should encourage us to maintain control over our money and be more accountable in our finances. Observing the Right of God elevates our
financial situation to a level of spiritual significance, since it allows us
to view our income as more than just the source of our material
sustenance. For information on developing a cash flow management
system (or budget), see Chapter 12, "Controlling Your Expenditures."

The Lifeblood of the Cause of God

In a letter from the Guardian at the very beginning of his ministry, he said: "And as the progress and execution of spiritual activities
is dependent and conditioned upon material means, it is of absolute
necessity that immediately after the establishment of local as well as
national Spiritual Assemblies, a Bahá'í Fund be established."[2] The
Bahá'í Fund is not only an institution of the Faith, but it is its very

1. Ibid., from the same source.
2. Bahá'í Administration, p. 41.

lifeblood by which the steady and progressive expansion of the Cause of God is maintained. The importance of the believer's role in supporting the Bahá'í Fund cannot be overestimated.

This section refers to the Bahá'í Fund as one indivisible entity, although there are many distinct Bahá'í funds at the local, national, continental, and international levels. Although we are encouraged to contribute to each of these funds, it is "left entirely to the discretion of every conscientious believer to decide upon the nature, the amount, and purpose of his or her contribution." [1]

In a letter written on January 3, 1985, the Universal House of Justice stated that "to support the Bahá'í funds is an integral part of the Bahá'í way of life." [2] As with all other aspects of being a Bahá'í, contributing to the Fund is both a privilege and a responsibility: "Every Bahá'í...should have confidence that his spiritual progress will largely depend upon the measure by which he proves, in his deeds, his readiness to support materially the Divine institutions of his Faith." [3] Furthermore, these contributions are "a practical and effective way whereby every believer can test the measure and character of his faith, and prove in deeds the intensity of his devotion and attachment to the Cause." [4]

The material needs of the Bahá'í Faith are great and "to offer contributions towards this end is one of the pressing requirements of the Cause of God, is deemed highly essential, and is of fundamental importance. Next to the payment of the Huqúq, it is the obligation of every Bahá'í." [5] "Contributing to the Bahá'í Fund," states the House of Justice, "is a service that every believer can render, be he poor or wealthy." [6] In order for the Faith to seize the emerging and unprecedented opportunities now present on the global scene, it must be given the financial power to capitalize on the opportune moments and favorable circumstances posed by these golden yet fleeting opportunities. Capital reserves are needed. Everyone should do his or her part to insure that adequate financial resources are forthcoming and maintained for the promotion and expansion of the Cause of God.

Although we are obligated to contribute to the Bahá'í Fund, our contributions are to be "purely and strictly voluntary in character" and only appeals "of a general character, carefully-worded and moving and dignified in tone" [7] should be used to inspire and encourage the friends to sacrifice for the Fund. No form of pressure,

1. *Bahá'í Administration*, p. 101.
2. *A Wider Horizon: Selected Messages of the Universal House of Justice, 1983-1992*, p. 164.
3. From a letter written on behalf of Shoghi Effendi, *Lifeblood of the Cause: Bahá'í Funds and Contributions*, Introduction, p. v.
4. Ibid., no. 18, p. 8.
5. From a letter of Shoghi Effendi, *Lifeblood of the Cause*, no. 45, p. 17.
6. *Wellspring of Guidance*, p. 19.
7. Shoghi Effendi, *Bahá'í Administration*, p. 101.

however innocent, should be used as this "strikes at the very root of
the principle underlying the formation of the Fund." [1] Furthermore,
the Guardian says in another communiqué that "in matters of contribution we should not use any compulsion whatsoever....We should
appeal to but not coerce the friends." [2] Regardless of the financial
needs of the Faith, the dignity of the Cause of God must not be
compromised, but should be upheld at all times and under all conditions.

A Matter of Perception

What may hinder us from fulfilling our responsibility to contribute
to the Bahá'í Fund may have nothing to do with this obligation per
se, but with our perception of ourselves or of its application and ultimate benefit to the community. Thinking that you don't have enough
money to contribute to the Fund, for example, can be resolved by
redirecting your cash flow. It is the level of sacrifice, not the amount
of money, which is the most important element in contributing to the
Fund. By reprioritizing your expenses, you can fulfill your spiritual
obligation to contribute. For example, after paying or putting aside
money for your essential monthly living expenses, make your next
payment a contribution to the Fund before making any additional expenditures. No contribution is too small for acceptance at the Threshold of Bahá'u'lláh. No matter how poor we are, we can still
contribute to the lifeblood of the Cause of God and participate in the
progress and advancement of the Faith. The important thing is to
make a start with some amount, then continue by making regular
contributions thereafter.

If the members of the spiritual assembly appear not to be managing the local fund to your satisfaction, you may offer suggestions at
the Nineteen Day Feast, or consult in private with the assembly.
Many times assembly members are not financially astute or aware of
their obligation to administer the funds of the Faith in a mature and
knowledgeable fashion. Educating the members of the assembly on
basic financial principles may be enough to improve the situation.
Ultimately, it is the duty of the community to elect mature assembly
members in accordance with the Guardian's instructions.

Sometimes we may earmark our contributions so that the assembly is unable to spend our contributions for any purpose other than
what we want. Although we are free to earmark our contributions for
whatever purpose we desire, the Guardian expressed his wish that
the friends place enough trust in the members of their assembly to
allow them to exercise "full discretion [to] expend it for whatever they
deem urgent and necessary." [3] By following the Guardian's advice, we

1. Shoghi Effendi, *Bahá'í Administration,*
2. *Lifeblood of the Cause,* no. 10, p. 4.
3. *Bahá'í Administration,* p. 54.

not only demonstrate detachment, but we show faith in the organic development of the Administrative Order. By trusting the assembly with our contributions, we allow it to grow.

God alone is able to judge the level of our offering and its ultimate benefit. When fulfilling our spiritual obligations, we should do so for the love and sake of God, not for some other purpose. Our giving should be an unconditional expression of our love for Bahá'u'lláh, not a measure of what we expect the Faith to do for us.

Finally, whatever our views toward contributing, they can be improved through studying the Writings and forming the habit of a positive mental attitude. A negative attitude is the most perilous obstacle to a healthy relationship with the Fund, since it poisons our heart. Without a positive attitude, we will severely cripple our potential for making money and contributing a portion of it to the Cause.

On Tithing and Sacrifice

Tithing, or contributing a certain portion of one's wealth to a temple, church, or ecclesiastical representative, is an ancient form of religious obligation. Since a person's wealth was thought to derive from the blessings of God, it was considered a spiritual duty to repay God for this generosity in the form of tithes. In the past, a tithe was a tax levied on the believer's profits from his livelihood or on the value of his land. In the Old Testament, one's tithe, or one-tenth of one's produce, went to the priesthood or to the public granary for later use. In fact, a Jew's oblation required him to give the best portion of his crops or flocks to the religious authorities. The early Christians initiated no formal tithing until the sixth century, when it was imposed as a civil tax by the Christian State. Today, most tithing is done as a voluntary act supporting a particular church or ministry. Islam's tithing consists mostly of obligatory alms payments (*zakát*) to the general Treasury, while Sh**í'**ah Muslims also add a payment of *khums* (one-fifth) which goes to the Imámate. The root meaning of *zakát* is "to purify." As in the Bahá'í Faith, Muslims believe that their private property becomes purified and legitimatized by paying a portion of their income to God for the common good.

In the Bahá'í Faith, tithing (*Zakát*) is not entirely identical with the law of Huqúqu'lláh. While Huqúqu'lláh purifies one's surplus after all one's living expenses have been met, Zakát is intended to purify one's *"means of sustenance and other such things."* [1] Bahá'u'lláh states that the Bahá'í law of Zakát follows *"what hath been revealed in the Qur'án."* [2] Note 161 in the *Kitáb-i-Aqdas* on the payment of Zakát explains: "Since such issues as the limits for exemption, the categories of income concerned, the frequency of payments, and the

1. *Kitáb-i-Aqdas*, K146, p. 72.
2. Ibid., Q107, p. 140.

scale of rates for the various categories of Zakát are not mentioned in the Qur'án, these matters will have to be set forth in the future by the Universal House of Justice. Shoghi Effendi has indicated that pending such legislation the believers should, according to their means and possibilities, make regular contributions to the Bahá'í Fund." [1]

Unlike the payment of Huqúqu'lláh and Zakát, however, our offerings to the Bahá'í funds are considered to be special acts of sacrifice, since they entail giving a certain portion of our material means not considered the property of God. Contributing to the Fund is an act of love, which is measured by the sacrifice it entails in giving to God those things which belong to us. The Guardian explains that "it is not so much the quantity of one's offerings that matters, but rather the measure of deprivation that such offerings entail." [2] In 1975, the Universal House of Justice reiterated this point, saying: "it is not the amount of the contribution which is important, but the degree of self-sacrifice that it entails—for it is this that attracts the confirmations of God." [3]

Determining the appropriate level of sacrifice is sometimes difficult to gauge. At some point, we may fall victim to the principle of diminishing returns [4] if we do not practice moderation in all things. Even in the realm of sacrifice, we may do more harm than good if we do not keep our actions within the bounds of moderation, since *"whatsoever passeth beyond the limits of moderation will cease to exert a beneficial influence."* [5] For example, all of us should be self-supporting, but if we give everything we have to the Fund and become wards of the state or the Bahá'í community, this sacrifice, though seemingly magnanimous, is really beyond the bounds of moderation, since it results in our becoming indigent and unable to support ourselves. If our sacrifice involves the suffering or subsidy of others, it is usually not considered true personal sacrifice. Sacrifice entails exchanging something of lesser value for something of greater value. In the case of contributing to the Bahá'í Fund, a portion of our private income is exchanged for the prosperity of the whole Bahá'í community.

When giving to the Bahá'í funds, you may at first wish to employ a set formula for contributing a certain percentage of your income, then progress from that point onward. If, before becoming a Bahá'í, you were already contributing 10% of your income as a tithe to your church, mosque, or temple, there is no harm in continuing this practice when giving to the Fund. However, if you had no such

1. *Kitáb-i-Aqdas*, n161, p. 235.
2. *Lights of Guidance*, no. 838, p. 249.
3. Ibid., no. 841, p. 250.
4. The principle of diminishing returns is an economic theorem which states that when expenditures for a product rise above a certain level, they do not cause a proportional increase relative to the cost.
5. Bahá'u'lláh, *Gleanings*, CX, p. 216.

discipline, then beginning with a different amount may be the correct starting point. Whether we get paid weekly, bi-weekly, or monthly, we will be fulfilling one of our spiritual obligations by regularly sacrificing a portion of our income for the work of the Cause. Also, we must never think that establishing regularity in our contributions (regularity as defined by the individual) is somehow separate from the concept of sacrifice. Those who regularly contribute a portion of their material resources to the Faith are unequivocally sacrificing, though the level of sacrifice may be negligible or substantial (again, according to one's own definition).

The Power of Universal Participation

In explaining the power of universal participation, the House of Justice has likened the body of the Bahá'í community to the human body. In the human body, every cell and organ has its part to play in the healthy functioning of the whole. Likewise, "in this organic, divinely guided, blessed, and illumined body the participation of every believer is of the utmost importance," for the body of the Faith, like a living organism, is "united in its aspirations, unified in its methods, seeking assistance and confirmation from the same Source, and illumined with the conscious knowledge of its unity."[1] This is the essential meaning of universal participation.

Since the work of the Faith cannot go forward without the lifeblood of the Fund, and the strength of this lifeblood is measured by the universal participation of its members, all must share in maintaining the Fund's vigor and health, if it is to remain financially sound and secure. "It is only evident," the Guardian explains, "that unless the flow of donations is regularly maintained by means of generous and continual support by all the believers, individually and collectively, the National Fund will never be able to meet the needs and requirements of the Cause."[2] Furthermore, Shoghi Effendi says that "the institution of the national Fund, the bedrock on which all other institutions must necessarily rest and be established...should be increasingly supported by the entire body of the believers, both in their individual capacities, and through their collective efforts."[3] The healthy state of the Bahá'í Fund is an example of Bahá'í unity to the world at large.

The consequences for the Faith if the Fund is not assured of "the whole-hearted, the ever-increasing and universal support of the mass of believers"[4] is that "the progress of the Faith...will not only be considerably retarded, but will inevitably come to a standstill."[5] There-

1. *Wellspring of Guidance*, p. 38.
2. *Lifeblood of the Cause*, no. 24, p. 10.
3. Ibid., no. 20, p. 9.
4. Ibid., no. 39, p. 14.
5. From a letter written on behalf of Shoghi Effendi, *Dawn of a New Day*, p. 68.

fore, it is extremely important for all believers to participate in contributing to the Fund, regardless of how modest or extensive their financial means:

> There should be a continual flow of funds to the National treasury of the N.S.A., if that body wishes to properly administer the manifold and ever-increasing activities of the Faith. Every Bahá'í no matter how poor, must realize what a grave responsibility he has to shoulder in this connection, and should have confidence that his spiritual progress as a believer in the World Order of Bahá'u'lláh will largely depend upon the measure in which he proves, in deeds, his readiness to support materially the divine institutions of His Faith.[1]

Like the analogy with the human body, universal participation has the benefit of not overtaxing any one system or group of individuals. Every burden is made lighter when everyone participates in carrying its weight. This solidarity of purpose is one of the secrets to overcoming difficulties and winning victories.

---

1. From a letter written on behalf of Shoghi Effendi, *Dawn of a New Day*, p. 68.

Part Two
Essential Requirements

Chapter 6

If Only I Had Invested

Poverty and shame shall be to him that refuseth instruction.
—Proverbs 13:18

If we are not financially independent by age 65, we will be dependent financially. This poignant observation should quicken our resolve to learn how to achieve financial independence long before the time of our retirement. Unfortunately, statistics show that many people will remain in the same financial condition after they reach retirement age as they are before it—financially dependent on someone else for their livelihood. If we do not have our own independent source of income, we are, by definition, dependent on someone else for our livelihood, be it the government, a job, or charity. As this chapter will show, we should have a plan for achieving financial independence and not leave our future welfare to either circumstance or happenstance.

Building Wealth Takes Time

Compared with the rest of the world, nearly everyone in Western society earns a fortune during their lifetime, yet very few have a sizable amount of wealth to support themselves without government assistance when they retire. Striving to become financially independent can be one of life's most challenging and exciting activities. By focusing part of our energy on acquiring money for a worthy purpose, we will find that accumulating wealth is really a lot of fun and not much of a monetary sacrifice. And once we achieve financial independence, we will have more liberty to pursue many other meritorious things in life.

The sad fact is that too many people wait until it is too late to begin planning for their retirement. Retirement planning should begin from the first day of our first job. It is never too early to plan for a financially independent retirement. Those who delay in planning or fail to achieve their goal of financial freedom before retirement are in grave economic jeopardy. Since building wealth takes time, our retirement income must be financed over a long period of time. It is not something which occurs overnight.

Being retired does not necessarily mean that you have to give up working, it simply means giving up *having* to work in order to survive financially. If you are not chained to your paycheck, you can plan your life to be more rewarding and much happier than if you are financially dependent on your current job for support. Your goal should be to acquire enough money to be able to retire at a date of your own choosing, not when you are forced to retire by someone else or by circumstances beyond your control.

In order to clarify this point about the time it takes to build a retirement income, think of financial independence in these terms: If you did not age and could maintain your health indefinitely, how many years would it take you to save enough money to retire with sufficient cash to be considered financially free? If your answer is "I don't know," then you should seriously contemplate where the source of your retirement income will come from, since you do not have an indefinite amount of time to acquire ample retirement monies.

Now is the time for you to be planning for a rewarding future. Like any other growth process, building wealth takes time and nurturing in order to reach fruition. In addition to time, wealth acquisition also requires a specific plan of action for it to be fruitful. If we fail to plan our future, then we are saying that any future will do. If we are not happy with whatever future we happen to drift into, then we have no one but ourselves to blame, since we have taken no action in making our plans. So get started now in developing and implementing your own plan for financial independence. The end result far outweighs any effort it takes to formulate and achieve such a goal.

Famous Last Words

In the following fictive scenario, two Bahá'ís, whom we will call John and George, go through life with two different conceptual and commitment levels concerning their retirement. Both make approximately the same income, have generally the same career opportunities, come from similar backgrounds, and contribute a portion of their income to the Bahá'í funds. The only major distinction is that John has no specific plans for acquiring sufficient funds for a comfortable retirement, whereas George plans to set aside $100 per month toward his retirement. As we will see through the various stages of their lives, this distinction is far more than a simple measure of the vast difference in the amount of wealth available to each one at retirement—it is also a measure of their tranquility and positive outlook on life. As illustrated by this scenario, achieving financial independence can do wonders for improving one's state of mind. The following portrait is as much a commentary on acquiring a positive attitude as it is on acquiring money.

John's commitment level is low, his working knowledge concerning investments is vague, and he has no long range vision regarding his future. He occasionally puts some money aside, but because he lacks a definite plan and the necessary self-discipline for maintaining his investment portfolio, he invariably spends it whenever he comes across anything he likes or feels he needs. He justifies this action as a way of helping his mental condition or because he feels that he deserves such material gratification after some particularly stressful occurrence in his life. He spends nearly every dollar he earns on the things he wants today. He lives the good life now and figures the future will take care of itself. He doesn't have much money, since he feels somewhat guilty about accumulating it. His childhood memories associate money with corruption and a lack of spirituality. Since John does not understand the underlying spiritual purpose of money, he has become a squanderer of his limited financial resources. Another barrier to his financial success is a deep-rooted subconscious reluctance to surpass his father, who never acquired much money after a lifetime of hard work and steady employment. Overall, John is careless and negligent when it comes to financial responsibility and seems destined to suffer the consequences of his shortsightedness.

George, on the other hand, although coming from a background similar to John's, has worked through the many problems which threaten to keep him in a state of financial uncertainty. He realizes that a lot of what he has been told about money and its relationship to spirituality is not true. Intellectually, he understands that money is neither good nor evil, that it is simply a means to measure the exchange of value between people, but emotionally he has not yet developed a full realization of money's significance. In time, George will gain this knowledge as the results of his actions improve his financial and spiritual situation. Although he is aware that money may not bring him happiness, he knows that poverty will not either. His will power and commitment level are high, since he understands that he can fulfill his dream of financial freedom if he puts his mind to work on its realization with a definite plan of action. He has a vision for a better future and keenly desires to partake of the rewards that wise planning will eventually accomplish for him. He begins learning about the principles governing the building of wealth in order to preserve a portion of his income to achieve financial freedom. The desire George has for a better future, his commitment to his wealth acquisition plan, and his positive mental attitude toward money and financial independence give him the necessary tools for successfully overcoming financial uncertainty and potential poverty.

In terms of investment planning and achievement, John and George represent two different viewpoints. Although the precise characteristics and financial conditions of these two individuals may not completely apply to your particular situation, they illustrate the importance of being committed to a prosperous future. The wise administration of your investment program will help avoid needless suffering later in life. This is a key factor in acquiring financial responsibility.

Although John lives life without seriously thinking about the importance of planning and taking action for something as critical as his future retirement, George read somewhere that mutual funds were pretty good investment vehicles, so he establishes an Individual Retirement Account (IRA) in order to invest $100 per month in a growth mutual fund.

The following dialogue illustrates the attitudes and actions of John and George as they go through different stages in their lives and careers. What will be emphasized here are their particular viewpoints and actions concerning financial matters. The results show dramatically the cumulative monetary effects of their efforts at saving and investing (all amounts have been rounded for convenience).

Age 18 to 25: College and Having a Good Time!

These are the very early years of your career development, where going to college and getting a good education is critical to your future success. If you are not college bound or not a college graduate, the same circumstances apply to your life during this period, since you still have to prepare yourself for a career. Being so young, retirement may seem like a long way off, but it's really just around the corner.

JOHN: "Me invest? Are you kidding? I'm just getting started with my education. You can't expect me to be able to invest now, can you? It's hard making ends meet, especially since going to college is very expensive. Besides, I'm young and I want to have a good time before settling down. After all, I'll be in college for four years or so. When I get out and on my own, I'll start investing then, but not now. Right now I want to enjoy my freedom and do the things I've always wanted to do. I also need a car and a new stereo system. Both of these things cost a lot, so I can't afford to set any money aside for retirement right now. Besides, what if the whole financial system collapses, won't all of my saving and investing be a waste of time, not to mention a waste of my money, if it's all lost?"

RESULT: John's preoccupation with living for today and not planning for the future has left him with nothing during his college years. He's also beginning to formulate a doomsday mentality which paralyzes him into inaction concerning any type of future investing.

GEORGE: "Investing for the future sounds like a great idea, but money is hard to come by when you're in college and trying to get an education. I know planning for the future is important and the right thing to do, so I'll make an extra effort to come up with the cash to invest for my future. Since I'm committed to becoming financially independent, I'll sacrifice now by working part-time at a fast food restaurant in order to set aside $100 a month for my retirement. I know it won't be easy, but I believe it'll be worth it in the long run."

RESULT: By sacrificing now for his future welfare, George is able to accumulate $12,000 [1] in his IRA mutual fund by the time he reaches his 25th birthday—just seven years after beginning his investment program. Although he has outstanding college-loan debts, he feels good about graduating from college with a substantial amount of money in his long-range investment portfolio.

Age 25 to 35: Just Getting Married!

You are now out of school and in the early stages of your working career. You are either just getting married or have been married for a few years and are now thinking about raising a family. Being out on your own and making plans for supporting a family has brought you face-to-face with the hard reality of financial responsibility.

JOHN: "You don't expect me to invest for my retirement now, do you? Remember, I've only been working for a few years. Things will be looking up soon and then I'll be able to invest. Right now, I have college loans to repay and I need to dress well in order to make a good impression at work. My wife and I are making adjustments and plan on having children soon. Although we've saved some money, we'll need it for the down payment on the house we're going to buy. We also need to buy a lot of new things for our new home, though we've nearly reached the limit on our credit cards. I'll have to wait until I'm a little older before I can start investing for retirement. There's time enough to begin thinking about the future a little later down the road."

RESULT: John's wait-and-see attitude has left him with nothing but a lot of debt during his early marriage and career years. Although he has many material things, his expenses are out-of-control and constantly match, and sometimes exceed, his income. He's also beginning to feel financially strapped to his job because of being so far in debt—a burden which is digging his financial grave.

---

1. For the purpose of this illustration, George's investment averages 10% return per year for the duration of his working life. Although some financial professionals would consider a 10% lifetime average return in a growth mutual fund to be conservative, especially since the U.S. stock market has had an average annual return of more than 10% over the last 60 years, we will use this figure to emphasize how simple it is to acquire wealth by using the principle of consistency.

GEORGE: "Boy, it sure feels good investing for my future. I've got a good job and I'm making a steady income now. It's much easier to set aside $100 a month when you've already disciplined yourself to do so. Although there's always a temptation to spend my retirement money on things I want now, I refuse to do so. I don't like the idea of starting over from scratch. Although my wife and I desire many things for our new home, we'll just have to wait until we can budget the cash for them. I refuse to finance our desires by going into debt, especially since learning about the awful misery of the credit trap."

RESULT: George's continual sacrifice has enabled him to accumulate $27,600 at age 30, and over $53,200 by his 35th birthday. For the most part, he's subdued the temptation to use his accumulated retirement money on anything but its intended purpose. A beneficial side effect to his accumulated wealth has been an improvement in his attitude and an elevation in his confidence at work, especially since he has vastly increased his net worth.

Age 35 to 45: Children Are Young!

You now have young children to raise which means your expenses have really shot up. You are also struggling for promotion in your climb up the career ladder and feel the pressure to spend a lot of money on clothes and entertainment and all those things which reflect a higher social and economic status. You are also approaching a period in your career where you are susceptible to experiencing a mid-life crisis.

JOHN: "How can I invest now? I'm married and have children to care for. The boss expects me to entertain and look good in order to get ahead in my career. There are also a lot of things I need to buy. Why, I've never had so many expenses in my life. I'm trying to save money, but with all of our bills it's hard to put anything aside. Besides, whenever I begin putting a little money away for a rainy day, something always seems to happen where I feel obligated to spend it on something else. There's always a good reason why I can't seem to save any money. At least my company has established a pension plan for me, so as long as I don't get fired, I guess I'll be okay. Anyway, when the children are a little older, then I can start thinking about investing. There's still enough time."

RESULT: John's negligent attitude and lack of self-discipline have left him with virtually nothing to show for all of his efforts and hard work nearly half-way through his professional career. He's also under the false impression that his company will take care of him in his old age.

GEORGE: "It feels great putting aside money for the future. I don't miss it like I used to. Of course, I still think about spending my savings on the things I'd like to have now, like a new car or an exotic vacation or the latest in electronic equipment, but these desires are under control. Thank God I have enough discipline to protect what I have nurtured all these years. It's scary to think that I could retire with very little money if I weren't investing for myself. It feels so good fulfilling my dream of financial independence. I'll continue to make do with what I have and won't squander my resources. I have better plans for my money."

RESULT: George's 20-year habit of investing has enabled him to accumulate $95,300 at age 40, and over $164,500 by his 45th birthday. If he remains committed to his plan for financial independence, he will easily make it by the time he retires in another 20 years.

Age 45 to 55: Kids in College!

You are now passing through the peak promotion and earning stages of your career, your children are demanding more of your economic resources, and you are starting to realize the nearness of retirement as you settle into mid-life patterns.

JOHN: "I wish I could invest now, but I just can't seem to do it. Whenever I get started saving money, something always comes along which obliges me to spend it. Now I have two kids in college and it's taking every cent and more to keep them there. I've even had to borrow money these last few years just to meet the college bills. But that won't last forever, and then I can start investing. I know it's important, but there never seems to be any money left at the end of the month to invest. No matter how much I make, I just can't seem to get ahead. I sure wish I could do something about it, but I don't know what. If I just didn't have so many debts, then maybe I could save a little. It seems as if I'm in a never-ending cycle of spending everything I earn. Well, maybe something will turn up. There's still enough time left."

RESULT: John's lifetime habits of wishful thinking and indebtedness have left him with nothing but bills and financial stress during his peak earning years. His financial situation is precarious and similar to a house of cards in which any major emergency could be the cause of it crashing down. When he should be approaching the summer harvest of his lifelong labors, he has yet to plant his seeds of wealth.

GEORGE: "It's a struggle getting the kids through college, but I'm determined not to touch my retirement money to do it, even though I could easily pay all their expenses with this money. At least I've made sure they understand the value of saving and investing for their own future, regardless of how tough it may seem. Seeing how much my investments have grown over the years, I only wish I had put more than $100 a month into my retirement fund. Had I done so, I probably could be retired by now and traveling to some interesting parts of the world. Now that I can see the light at the end of the tunnel, all the hard work and sacrifice my family and I have endured have been well worth it. I love the achievements my wife and I have accomplished since beginning our journey of wealth building. All of my other friends are just now starting to think about their retirement. They can't believe I've accumulated so much money by simply investing $100 a month. I find it pretty amazing myself, but I've learned to respect the magic of compound interest."

RESULT: George's lifetime habit of investing has enabled him to accumulate $278,500 at age 50, and nearly $466,000 by his 55th birthday. In terms of money, George is almost at the half-way point of becoming a cash millionaire. Thanks to the effects of compound interest, he is just eight years away from crossing the million-dollar line at age 63.

Age 55 to 65: Career Winding Down!

You are now in the autumn of your career, the kids are gone and starting their own occupations, and you are pretty much settled in your ways. Your own retirement is just around the corner as the sun of your long and productive career begins approaching its nadir. You begin tasting some of the fruits of your labor. It is during this time in your career that your past achievements and the wise management of your finances should provide an aura of respectability to the younger work force. Your position warrants people listening to what you have to say.

JOHN: "I know I should be investing now, but money is real tight. It's not so easy for a man of my age to change his habits. About all I can do is hang on. Why didn't I start investing thirty or forty years ago? The thought of having so little money to retire on when I'm so close to it really scares me, but what else can I do? Without having enough money, my retirement options are severely limited. I don't know what will happen to me when I do retire. My company pension doesn't seem to be enough and the small amount I'll get from Social Security isn't anything to brag about."

RESULT: A lifetime of doing very little about his future retirement has left John with almost nothing to show for a lifetime of hard work, promotion, and a steadily increasing income. After forty years of working for a good company, he has very little money accumulated for the time he will be forced to retire. John's only prospect is his company's pension plan and Social Security benefits which only amount to about 50% of his current salary. Since he is struggling to live on his full salary now, how can he possibly live on only half his income when he retires in a few years? Because of his shortsightedness and lack of planning, he is in dire financial trouble and frightened by the prospects which await him after he retires. His options in life are becoming less with each passing year.

GEORGE: "I feel great about myself and the million dollars I've acquired over the last 45 years of investing. Now I have the option of designing my retirement however I wish. I can even make concrete plans for travel teaching, since I'll be self-supporting and not dependent on others for my livelihood. All of the sacrifices during my early years and a lifetime of self-discipline have borne fruit and are well worth it. My goal of financial independence has finally been reached. In fact, my retirement income will be more than double my current salary. Isn't that unbelievable? I'll be getting more than 200% of my current income when I retire. Is there any doubt why I feel so wonderful? Financial freedom has given me financial security and peace of mind. It has also provided me with a vast array of options never before available. Because I am financially independent, I can travel whenever and wherever I wish, provide assistance to many struggling Bahá'í communities throughout the world, and support a number of traveling teachers and Bahá'í youth on various teaching projects. My wife and I have become a source of stability and strength in our community. I thank God for giving me the necessary persistence and commitment for achieving my plan of financial independence. Without such self-discipline, I would never have been able to achieve so lofty a goal."

RESULT: George's plan for financial independence has enabled him to accumulate $774,000 at age 60, $1,000,000 just prior to his 63rd birthday, and over $1,280,000 by his 65th birthday—his last day at work. By investing $100 a month for the last 45 years and getting an average annual return of 10%, George has become a cash millionaire and will have no money worries during retirement.

Age Over 65: Too Late or Golden Years!

This is the time that we may either dread or look forward to. We must now reap what we have sown during the course of our lives. In terms of building monetary wealth, the ball game is over.

JOHN: "Yes, it's too late for me now. My wife and I are living in a small apartment since we had to sell our home in order to have enough money to live on. It isn't so nice, but what else can we do? I have Social Security and my company pension, but who can really live on that? Thank goodness our children send us money periodically. If only I had invested when I had the money. You can't invest when there's no income; and when there's no income, it's difficult to make ends meet. I'm in a state of semi-poverty. And you know the irony of it all, I can't remember what was so important during all these years that I couldn't spare at least $100 a month toward my retirement. I can't go back to work for my former company because I'm past the mandatory retirement age, so I'll have to work part-time at a fast food restaurant just to make enough money to pay the bills. I feel terrible about having to work after the conclusion of my career, especially for not much more than minimum wage. It's embarrassing and humiliating to spend my golden years trying to make ends meet, especially after letting so much money slip through my fingers. The sadness I see in my wife's face is heartbreaking."

RESULT: John's procrastination, negligence, and overall casual attitude toward investing has left him virtually penniless and somewhat depressed. He's a financial drain on his children, which creates stress for them; he can't enjoy the fruits of his labor because there is no fruit and no rich harvest. His state of near-poverty after working hard all his life has dimmed his vitality and energy. For him, there are no golden years; he simply lives out the remainder of his days regretting his financially misspent life and inability to do much to help himself or help the Faith expand and grow. By depending on his children for part of his support, he is also robbing them of crucial financial resources for investing in their own future. His financial dependency and bad example may possibly extend this problem for at least another generation. Unless his children learn the prosperity lessons he failed to master, a cycle of financial mismanagement leading to semi-poverty at retirement will be perpetuated. Although John has led a full and productive life, he now realizes that his casual attitude toward investing and lack of monetary goals have caused him to become a financial casualty at retirement.

GEORGE: "Life is wonderful! I feel great about my retirement. Although I've worked hard and sacrificed to get where I am, the money I've set aside hasn't diminished my standard of living one bit. In fact, knowing that my pot-of-gold was growing month-by-month gave me additional self-confidence in my work and in my interactions with other people. I continue to have deep personal relationships with many people. Being a millionaire has changed me for the better. I can now devote much more of myself to helping my fellow man. I can also relax and enjoy more of the things that interest me. I can travel and visit the grandchildren without being a burden on my children. And since I'm financially independent, I don't have to worry about the cost of things. If I continue to earn ten percent on the $1.2 million I've accumulated, it will give me a pre-tax income of $128,000 a year, or $10,600 a month, or nearly $2,500 a week to live on. Receiving all of this money from interest without ever having to touch the principal is really terrific. And with my company pension and social security benefits added to this amount, I have more money now in retirement than I ever did while working. Life's been very good to me. My wife is happy and my children are able to see the tremendous benefits of investing for their own future. We even laugh about the times they tried to persuade me to spend my retirement money when they were young. They're so glad that I never listened to them. They understand how foolish it would have been to chop down my money tree before giving it a chance to bear fruit. They also realize the absolute commitment needed for becoming financially free. Retirement is the best thing that could have happened to me."

RESULT: George has fulfilled his dream of financial independence on only $100 a month. His only regret is in not fully funding his retirement account by contributing just $67 more per month when he first started working at age 18. Had he done this, he could have retired with a million dollars halfway through his 57th year. It's interesting to note that had George contributed this additional amount from age 18 until reaching age 65, his retirement fund would have a value of $2.1 million. This means that he could have almost doubled the large amount he already receives from the interest on his $1.2 million. It pays to start your investment plan early, to invest as much money as possible during your earning years, and to receive the best return you can. George is very happy that his sacrifice has paid-off so well. His self-imposed discipline has made him a better person. He is eager to expand his skills and humanitarian endeavors. His life is full and meaningful. He can devote himself to cultural pursuits, travel, education, and much more service to humanity.

Reviewing Your Life's Work

The above story illustrates the need for taking well-planned action in order to become successful and prosperous during your lifetime. Otherwise, you will always be financially dependent on something or someone else for your livelihood, be it your job, your government, or your relatives. Unless you use part of your current income to seed, nourish, and harvest a future state of financial independence, you will always be financially dependent on others for your sustenance and shelter. Unless money becomes your servant by working for you, you will remain its servant by laboring for it.

George always had faith that his lifetime commitment to a richly rewarding future would be realized during retirement. His burning desire for a better tomorrow gave him the strength to follow a plan of action which would assure him a prosperous future. He learned the lessons of wisdom in regard to money and investments. When his primary source of income was cut off, the investments that he had nourished and worked hard to maintain for so many years began bearing fruit and proved to be more than enough to sustain him for the rest of his life.

John, on the other hand, did not follow wise principles in handling money and investing for his future. His descent into semi-poverty after a lifetime of financial negligence, lack of self-discipline, and a casual attitude toward sacrifice was his penalty for not observing the principles of prosperity. His actions and attitudes finally resulted in an emptiness that came from realizing that he had squandered his limited time and precious resources.

Although no one plans to fail financially, most people fail to plan for their future financial well-being. The time to start planning for your future retirement is now, before it's too late. Acquiring sufficient money for your retirement is an endurance race, not a get-rich-quick sprint. You must determine your present financial status, then immediately make a commitment to become financially independent by putting aside at least 10% of everything you earn (from your gross income) for your future retirement. The millionaires of tomorrow are just getting started today. You could be one of them.

The Top Five Percent Theory

Many years ago, Earl Nightingale, the famous motivator of men and women in all walks of life, developed what he called the "top five percent theory" for measuring the desire of people to achieve financial freedom in the United States, arguably the richest country in the world. What he found was shocking.

The results of his investigation concluded that if you randomly selected a population of 100 Americans and followed them for 40 years of their working life, from age 25 to 65, statistically, the financial outcome of these 100 people would likely be as follows: one would be rich (and this from having abundant opportunity for becoming wealthy in one of the richest countries in the world); four would be financially independent (they would be able to maintain the same standard of living throughout retirement as they had during their working years); 30 would be dead (a statistical result of mortality); and 65 would be dependent on others (either the government, employment, charity, or family members) for their financial support. In other words, 95 out of 100 people would either be dead or dead broke at retirement. Only 5% would be able to maintain a comfortable and care-free existence at retirement.[1]

The results of this investigation clearly demonstrate the critical need for people to take control of their financial resources and begin planning for their retirement early in life. As shown in the above illustration with John and George, if you have enough time, you can build a financially secure future with relatively little money. As will be seen in the next chapter, you can completely avoid being one of the casualties of these statistical averages if you are determined and committed to attaining your goal of financial independence.

Toward a Better Future

An anonymous philosopher once said: "Make no small plans for they have no magic to stir the hearts of men."[2] The message in this statement should also apply to our own dreams and plans for a better future. To be effective, our plans must stir our hearts. God did not create such a luxuriant world just to see us ineptly partake of its bounties. We were created rich in order to abundantly partake of all of God's gifts. Our vision of an ever-advancing civilization should encompass the prospect of a wealthy future for all humankind, and it should begin with each of us.

Although the vehicles for investing have become more complex today than during the time of our grandparents, they have also become more numerous. Our grandparents had limited options for cre-

---

1. Kimbro and Hill, *Think and Grow Rich: A Black Choice*, p. 103.
2. Quoted from a talk given by H. N. Humphrey in Philadelphia, Pennsylvania, in 1989.

ating wealth. During their time, the average person basically had two ways to save money: in low-yielding, fixed-income vehicles (like banks, savings and loan institutions, and life insurance companies), or under the mattress (if they didn't trust these financial institutions). Some also ventured to establish their own business or invest in the stock market. Today, there are many ways of acquiring wealth, including one of the most powerful ever created in the financial and economic system— mutual funds. (See Chapter 14, "The Power of Mutual Funds," for an overview of this investment vehicle.) However, it should be noted that our grandparents had one distinct investment advantage over us—they tended to have long-term vision. In contrast, we live in a short-sighted, live-for-today, instant-gratification society, where it is mentally more difficult to set aside any portion of our income for the future.

Another obstacle to investing is that we are bombarded with so many material distractions and superficial desires that it can be extremely difficult to focus on our goal of financial independence. The Guardian has stated that the people of North America are "immersed in a sea of materialism," "an excessive and binding materialism," [1] which is harmful to their spiritual progress. Being immersed in this omnipresent materialism can make it an arduous task to set aside and save a portion of our income when everywhere in society we are being urged to spend all of our money on material gratifications, creature comforts, and self-indulgent pursuits. It takes a supreme effort of mental determination to overcome these material distractions and pursue a worthwhile goal, such as investing for the future.

---

1. *The Advent of Divine Justice*, p. 19.

Chapter 7

Commitment To Financial Independence

An inheritance quickly gained at the beginning will not be blessed at the end.—Proverbs 20:21

Without a total commitment to becoming financially independent and a plan of action for achieving prosperity, your chances of becoming wealthy are slim to non-existent. Your desire to succeed is the measure of your commitment level. Anything short of such an unshakable commitment will defeat the attainment of your desired objective. This chapter offers six suggestions for acquiring the essential seed money to insure a rich harvest; but first, it outlines the components necessary for beginning your journey toward financial independence.

The Commitment Concept

The most basic component for achieving financial freedom is our absolute commitment to it. If we falter here or make any exception in setting aside a certain portion of our income each month for our future well-being, we will likely not be able to achieve our dream of becoming financially independent. This emphasis on being totally committed to financial independence cannot be overestimated. It is by far the most important part of any wealth acquisition plan. Many different investment vehicles can get us to our goal, but if we fail to invest every month, or if we spend what we have already acquired before it matures, then no investment vehicle, however suitable, will be able to help us reach our goal of financial independence. Our total commitment to our wealth acquisition plan is the driving force which guarantees our success in reaching our goal.

In acquiring wealth, our first duty, notwithstanding that there are many noble and meritorious reasons for wealth acquisition, is to determine our own specific and worthwhile purpose for becoming wealthy, since this will provide us with the necessary motivation for achieving financial freedom. For example, your purpose for wealth acquisition might be to provide you and your spouse with the means for a comfortable and independent retirement, to have enough money to educate your children appropriately, to establish your own business, to have the financial means to travel teach around the world or sponsor other traveling teachers, or to support any number of other global and humanitarian projects that you feel are necessary and worthwhile. Determining your dreams in advance will give you the necessary energy and will-power to fuel your desire for success. You should also define what you mean by financial independence, specifically, how much money does this mean to you? Defining a specific dollar amount is important for establishing a goal to work toward. After this is completed, it will be up to you to faithfully follow your plan of action in order to reach your predetermined state of financial freedom.

A Two-Fold Process

Your total commitment to financial freedom may be considered as a two-fold process. The first is consistency in setting aside a certain portion of your income, while the second is vowing never to touch any portion of your investment money until it reaches maturity. The two are part and parcel of the commitment process. Every time you get paid, you should take a certain portion of your paycheck and apply it to your long-term investment fund. Then you should remain inflexibly convinced not to touch any portion of this money for any purpose other than that for which it was originally intended. Our steadfast adherence to this principle is extremely important. We should never be persuaded to spend or lend our investment money, no matter how convincing the plea or compelling the circumstance. Poor planning on the part of a friend or relative does not necessarily constitute an emergency on our part. And since the prodigal son's appetite for money is insatiable, we should beware of short-term solutions to long-term problems. No amount of so-called dire need should convince us to part with our retirement money; for once we make an exception and spend all or part of our investment money, it is much too easy to make another exception, and another, until finally we have nothing left. In order to overcome this temptation, we must believe that all the dire circumstances which may tempt us to spend our accumulated retirement money to cover any so-called severe but temporary situation, will pass or can be settled without the use of our investment money.

We should consider our financial freedom fund in the same light that Shoghi Effendi considered the status of a newly formed National fund. Whenever a National fund was established, it not only took "absolute precedence over individual and private needs," which were "obviously transient when compared to the lasting interests of the Cause," but also the fund was not "to be jeopardized by individual considerations" [1] which might usurp the purpose of that fund. Likewise, we should consider our financial freedom fund—the source from which our future livelihood depends—as taking precedence over any transitory needs of any particular person or circumstance. Even any sacrifices to the Bahá'í Fund, or contributions to other worthwhile causes, should come from the remaining 90% of our income, not from the 10% which is working to build our fortune.

Choosing the Right Vehicle

Of secondary importance, though still significant to our goal of financial independence, is the investment vehicle we choose for building our fortune. Within reason, almost any investment vehicle will get us to our goal. It is simply a matter of available time and money. The amount of time we have to reach our goal will determine how much money we must contribute, and the rate of return we should have, in order to successfully reach our destination.

For example, if we begin at age 25 and set aside $85 every month for 40 years and get a 12% return (a 12% return is used for calculating all figures), we will have $1,000,000 by age 65 (this includes reinvesting all of the dividends and capital gains). However, if we only have 30 years to reach the million dollar mark, we will need to set aside $286 per month; with only 20 years to reach it, we must invest $1,010 per month; and if we want to have a million dollars in 10 years, we must set aside $4,347 per month to achieve our goal. As we can see from these figures, the earlier we start investing, the smaller the contribution needed each month to reach our goal of a million dollars.

If the rate of return is different, our monthly contribution will also be different. For instance, if we only receive an average of 10% return, we would have to set aside $158 per month for 40 years (again by reinvesting all of the dividends and capital gains); $442 per month for 30 years; $1,317 per month for 20 years; and $4,882 per month to reach one million dollars in 10 years. However, if we receive a 15% return on our money, the monthly contribution figures for reaching one million dollars (by reinvesting all of the dividends and capital gains) would be $32 for 40 years; $144 for 30 years; $668

---

1. *Lifeblood of the Cause*, no. 42, p. 15.

for 20 years; and $3,633 per month for 10 years. These figures assume a goal of one million dollars, though our personal retirement needs may be more or less than this figure.

As can be seen in the above examples, it is important to receive a good rate of return in order to reach your goal more quickly. Keeping your money in low-yielding financial vehicles that pay between 1% to 5% interest (like bank savings accounts, certificates of deposit, and whole life insurance cash value policies) can greatly prolong the time or substantially increase the amount of money needed to reach financial independence. For example, in order to reach $1,000,000 in 40 years at 5% interest, you would have to set aside $655 per month, which is over four times the contribution amount at twice the interest rate (10%) and over 20 times the contribution amount at three times the interest rate (15%). If you could only afford to set aside $100 dollars per month in a bank account paying 5% interest, it would take over 75 years for it to reach the million dollar mark, which is far too long for it to be of any practical use to most people during their lifetimes.

Progressive Responsibility

One of the dangers associated with the desire to acquire wealth is the lure of gaining riches quickly through little or no effort. Gambling, which Bahá'u'lláh has forbidden, is one example of trying to get something for nothing. Having a goal for financial independence is not about getting rich quickly. Pursuing a plan to acquire wealth entails earning money through many years of self-discipline and hard work. It requires saving at least 10% of your total income and investing it in a proven investment vehicle. It is a type of endeavor known as "progressive responsibility."

Progressive responsibility, as it relates to prosperity, demands total self-discipline in directing your energies toward productive and legitimate methods for building wealth. It is a gradual process which calls for maturity and trustworthiness in handling money and mastering monetary concepts.

If we were to go from a small net worth to becoming a millionaire overnight, not enough time would have elapsed for us to master the necessary emotional and mental faculties for handling our newfound wealth. If, on the other hand, it took us 30 to 40 years to progressively build, block by block, our millionaire status, we would know the value of what we had earned and be able to handle the many responsibilities associated with it. The primary difference between quick riches and gradual wealth is accomplishment. We would be less likely to misuse or squander a fortune which took many years of painstaking effort to acquire than one gained instantly with no appreciable effort on our part.

The process of building wealth after prolonged effort and sacrifice is really a form of protection for us. Most things worthwhile in life have not resulted from easy acquisition, but have been acquired after painful effort. The plant that is pruned is the one which bears the best and sweetest fruit.

Six Money Sources for Investing

The concern of many people who become aware of their lack of retirement savings, especially later in life, is where they can get the necessary money to invest for their retirement. Whatever your personal predicament, you can still improve your financial situation, but only if you have sufficient time before retirement and the will power to overcome your present financial obstacles. Your commitment level is measured by the strength of two things: The first is your determination to implement as many of the six sources of income listed below as possible; and the second is the amount of money you are willing to invest now. Most people can accommodate additional expenditures for retirement investing if their priorities are revised.

#1 Paying Yourself First

Although this subject is covered in detail in Chapter 11, it is necessary to introduce the most salient points of this concept now, since it is the first and most important of the six suggestions for acquiring extra income for investing. What is described here is the cornerstone for achieving financial success. By paying yourself first, you put you and your family ahead of any other demands on your money. This kind of thinking is absolutely essential if you hope to acquire enough money for your future needs. This point cannot be overemphasized.

You must never fail to pay yourself first, even if it means paying the minimum amount on your credit card balance every month. Your creditors can easily live with minimum payments, since interest continues to accrue on the unpaid balance. You, however, must be your own advocate and demand from your source of income an agreed upon portion of money (at least 10% of your gross income) for investing in your financial freedom fund. You should not be satisfied with anything below this amount, regardless of how difficult it may seem or how many temptations you encounter to spend this money. You should always, without fail, pay yourself first each payday the full amount due you and never use it until it has fulfilled its intended purpose. Your commitment to always paying yourself first is crucial to your financial freedom plan.

Most financially successful people recommend saving at least 10% of one's gross income, while others recommend saving substantially more. This 10% figure seems to be the absolute minimum for achieving a state of financial independence and is sometimes referred to as "the 10% Solution."[1] However, if you wish to reach your goal sooner (i.e., become financially independent earlier), or increase the amount of cash available to you at retirement, then you must either set aside a greater portion of your income or get a higher return on your investments.

#2 Avoiding the Credit Trap

The credit trap is purchasing anything on a charge account which causes you to lose valuable time and money by paying off debt which has little or no appreciable value. It is a financial liability rather than an asset. One financial writer, Dr. David J. Schwartz, in his book *The Magic of Thinking Success*, has described consumer debt as "dumb debt." Most consumer debt is incurred initially through the use, and ultimately by the abuse, of credit cards. For the purpose of finding extra dollars to invest, we will focus on the accumulation of debt through the use of credit cards, although all forms of consumer debt are anathema to gaining financial independence.

Credit cards are neither good nor bad. They are simply financial tools for making certain aspects of our lives more convenient. How we use these financial tools will determine whether or not we are waylaid in reaching our goals. However, credit cards are inherently dangerous to our financial well-being, since they give us a false sense of prosperity just before ensnaring us in the trap of long-term debt.

Regardless of whatever society leads you to believe, whenever you use a credit card and cannot pay off the debt the following month, you are abusing the use of credit and are considered a dumb debtor; whenever you make monthly payments to finance your indulgences, you are a dumb debtor; and whenever your net worth consists mostly of material things which depreciate or lose value over time, you are a dumb debtor. Any use of a credit card which robs you of the potential for acquiring wealth is an abuse of your financial resources and ensnares you in the credit trap.

Generally speaking, in order to avoid the credit trap, we should avoid using "plastic money" or credit cards to pay for things, but buy only what we can afford and pay for in cash. If we do not have the cash to pay for something, then we simply cannot afford it. Do not let the easy availability and convenience of credit cards deceive you into purchasing things for which you cannot readily pay. Unless you are very self-disciplined in the use of money, credit cards are a time-bomb waiting to go off in your purse or wallet.

Credit cards should only be used for convenience or for an emergency. Convenience includes such things as renting a car or paying for anything that is considered a business expense and requires a receipt (e.g., receipts necessary to verify expenses for tax purposes). In this case, at the end of the month, after paying your credit card

---

1. See Charles J. Givens' popular book *More Wealth Without Risk*, pp. 407-417.

balance in full, you will have an itemized receipt for tax purposes. This is an example of using credit cards for convenience.

Using credit cards for emergencies would include any situation for which you do not have ready cash in hand (though you do have it in your savings or emergency fund account) or where a personal check is not accepted. Of course, you would still pay the bill in full when it comes due at the end of the month, since an emergency expense should not be considered a long-term debt obligation. In situations like this, a credit card is used in lieu of cash until the emergency is over or until we can get the cash from our emergency account to pay for the expense.

We should never be careless when using credit. Misusing credit can be the cause of our financial extinction. Treat it like poison and always be careful not to mishandle it. Poison has its uses, but only rarely and in controlled amounts. Bahá'u'lláh says: *"Consider the effect of poison. Deadly though it is, it possesseth the power of exerting, under certain conditions, a beneficial influence."* [1] This same warning should also be applied to using credit cards.

If we accept the modern-day thinking of "buy now, pay later," then we will probably be doomed to a life of never-ending stress and negative net worth. When we become enmeshed in the credit trap, our major reason for existence starts being defined in terms of working at a job in order to pay off our debts and keep our credit rating from going bad. This is a far cry from considering the purpose of work as identical to worshiping God. Whenever we abuse the use of credit, we should determine why this situation occurred, then avoid doing those things which caused it to happen in the first place. Do everything possible to get out from under consumer debt. Your financial survival depends on it.

Finally, although borrowing money from a bank to purchase a house or a piece of income-producing property is considered debt, it is not usually considered dumb debt because property tends to appreciate in value. Buying a home or an income-producing property is considered smart debt because you are using other people's money to purchase an asset. And with rental property, you are not only using other people's money to finance the asset, but you are also using other people's money to pay for your asset through its lease. This use of credit is called leverage. Assets are the building blocks of wealth and leverage allows you to control an asset with very little of your own money. Within reason, leverage is considered smart debt and should be used whenever circumstances are favorable. The subject of property ownership will be briefly covered in Chapter 13, "Maximizing Your Investments."

---

1. *Gleanings*, XCIII, p. 189.

#3 Needs versus Wants

Most of us want a certain degree of material comfort and security. We want to be able to do the many things we consider enjoyable and worthwhile without worrying about how much it costs. We want freedom from the drudgery of having to go to work everyday just to pay our bills and get by, especially if our job is not fulfilling our unique talents, dreams, and aspirations. Although Bahá'u'lláh has made work *"a duty"* which *"hath been prescribed unto every one,"*[1] few people have the financial resources to do the kind of work they desire most—whatever it may be.

The same restriction applies to our material wants and desires, since we usually do not have enough money to buy whatever we desire in life. Because we do not possess unlimited financial resources, it is unrealistic to think that we can acquire all the material things we desire in this world. We may want a luxury yacht or a new sports car or an expensive first-class vacation to an exotic destination, but unless we have the financial resources to pay for them, they are out of our reach. In fact, whatever our material yearnings, if we do not possess sufficient money for their purchase, then we cannot legitimately obtain them and must learn to live without them. Most people are unable to fulfill most, much less all, of their material cravings. However, by prioritizing our desires and disciplining ourselves to go after only those things we truly want, we will be able to satisfy our most urgent cravings.

After identifying our most cherished desires, our next step is to restrict and regulate our cash flow in order to prevent a financial hemorrhage from bleeding dry our primary source of income. If we fail to stem the outflow of our money on indiscriminate cravings for material things, it is unlikely that we will achieve our goals. For example, if our greatest desire is to live well when we retire, then we will find ways to discipline ourself to save and invest the necessary money to accomplish this goal. However, if we have no desire other than to spend every dollar we earn on self-gratification, our energy will be so dissipated that it is unlikely we will be able to derive any lasting satisfaction from these material indulgences. Our consumer-driven and consumption-oriented society is ideal for breeding self-indulgent attitudes.

Furthermore, it seems that most people rarely think about what they want most in life, much less have specific plans for attaining it. They just accept anything that comes along and looks interesting at the moment. Spontaneity in fulfilling our material wants can be the cause of stress and misery. Our material desires should be selective and disciplined if we hope to survive financially in this materialistic society. Living beyond our means is tantamount to financial death; so unless we prioritize our desires to reflect the level of our potential

1. *Gleanings*, C, p. 202.

cash flow, it is doubtful that we will ever find contentment in the material world.

#4 Buy the Right Life Insurance

Buying the right life insurance may seem unimportant in being committed to a wealth acquisition plan, but billions of dollars have been squandered by an ignorant and misinformed public in the purchase of life insurance in the United States alone.[1] The insurance industry is one of the richest and most powerful industries on the planet. Collectively, they have grown to become one of the world's largest and wealthiest financial institutions primarily from selling mostly overpriced and overrated products—whole and universal life insurance policies.

Life insurance is crucial to a family needing financial protection in the event of the breadwinner's death; it is indispensable to the surviving spouse who has small children to raise, a mortgage to pay, other debts to satisfy, and no source of income to replace that of the breadwinner. These facts are not in question. What is in question is the *type* of life insurance a family needs to purchase. Although this subject will be covered in greater detail in the next chapter, for now it is important to get an overview of the purpose and cost-reduction possibilities of life insurance coverage as another source for freeing up extra money to invest.

The major purpose of life insurance is to create a death estate. Your death estate is simply the amount of money needed to support your family for a certain period of time after your death. Life insurance can also preserve your financial assets by preventing their use and depletion to support your family's living standards following your death. Although life insurance essentially replaces the breadwinner's income for a certain number of years, it should not be used as a substitute for prosperity or the acquisition of wealth.

When you purchase a life insurance policy, you are buying the right of your beneficiary to receive a certain amount of cash, called the "face amount," from the insurance company upon your death. And since you are buying a product, it makes sense that your cost for this product (called the premium) should be the lowest one possible. In the purchase of life insurance, getting the highest face amount for the lowest price comes only from "term" insurance; and with term insurance, you pay for only the insurance coverage, nothing else—no "cash value," no "dividends," nothing but a cash settlement upon the death of the person covered. By purchasing any other kind of life insurance product, such as whole or universal life, you pay much more money for the same coverage. Term insurance can provide the same amount of coverage as whole or universal life insurance, but at a much lower cost. Getting the best benefit for the lowest price is a

---

1. 1979 United States Federal Trade Commission Staff Report.

major consideration in the purchase of any product, and life insurance is no exception. Purchasing term insurance instead of any other type of life insurance may save you tens of thousands of dollars in premium payments over a certain number of years.

For example, if you are 25 years old and need $250,000 worth of life insurance coverage, you can either pay about $400 a year for it in the form of level premium term insurance, or you can pay approximately $2,400 a year for it in the form of whole life or universal life insurance. You pay a lot more money for exactly the same amount of coverage with whole life insurance. Whether you die after one year or ten years, your beneficiary still only receives $250,000, no matter how much you have paid in premiums over the years. In the above example, if you can save $2,000 a year in premium costs and redirect that money toward your financial freedom fund, you are taking a giant step toward financial independence.

#5 Realign Your Assets

In order to increase your net worth and enhance the value of what you already own, you should realign (move) your assets from low-yielding bank savings accounts, certificates of deposit, gold bullion, raw land, and other static (no or low-yielding) possessions to high-yielding, liquid, and safe no-load stock and bond mutual funds. If your intention is to reap potentially greater rewards, you should position your money to obtain the best possible return without jeopardizing your capital.

One of the best ways to increase your profits is to eliminate any intermediary between your money and its potential return. Whenever any financial institution guarantees you a certain return for the use of your money, you should understand that it probably makes twice that amount from loaning it out to others. For instance, if a bank guarantees you a 4% interest on your deposit, it must be able to get a much higher return in order to remain profitable. If not, it won't be in business for long.

In 1993, U.S. banks were paying between 2% to 4% interest on deposits (savings accounts, certificates of deposit, etc.). The bank, in turn, loaned this money to someone else (maybe even back to you) in the form of credit (as in a Mastercard or Visa credit card, usually at about 18% interest); or it loaned this money to someone who was purchasing a home, usually charging about 8% interest; or to someone buying a used car for about 13% interest. Banks also invested these deposits in the stock and bond market and made between 8% to 25% return. As you can see, any financial institution which guarantees you a certain interest rate must be able to invest your money and get a higher return. This is basic business sense. The point of this illustration is to show that banks are intermediaries between your money and its potential return. By taking your deposits, for which the bank guarantees to pay you a certain interest rate, it lends your money to someone else and charges them a much higher interest rate or invests your money in the global market place.

It is evident from the above figures that the bank's profit from using your money is not only doubled, but in some cases even quadrupled from your guaranteed interest rate. And since a bank usually requires a borrower to provide some type of collateral before transacting business, there is very little chance that it will lose your principal or its profit to the borrower. Like other financial institutions, such as credit unions, saving and loans, and life insurance companies, banks profit greatly as middlemen from the use of our money. If we plan on becoming financially independent, we should strive to realign our personal finances by becoming an owner of assets (an investor), instead of a loaner of money (a depositor). If we become satisfied with a guaranteed interest rate, we are usually overlooking some higher and generally safe returns. Short of establishing our own bank, we can invest our money in the global market and receive an excellent return.

#6 Earn Additional Income

One of the best ways to get enough money to reach the goal of financial independence is to earn additional income through a part-time job. The income requirements for creating a good source of revenue for funding an investment program are minimal, since every dollar we earn from working part-time can be invested in our financial freedom fund.

Some people say they have no spare time for part-time work; however, if we spend hours watching TV, we have enough time to work at a temporary job. If our desire and commitment to being financially independent are strong enough, we will find the necessary strength to work part-time, no matter how difficult it may seem. If we have a specialized skill that is in demand and easily marketable, our temporary employment in that line of work to earn extra money will be that much easier. Instead of working for someone else, we may wish to set up a small business of our own or provide some service in our off-hours. Even if we work for minimum wage, we can still earn enough to become financially independent. By working ten hours per week for five dollars per hour, we can invest an additional $200 per month toward our financial freedom fund. If we do this for only five years and get an average annual return of 15% on our money, we will have accumulated $17,700 during this five-year period.[1] Of course, by itself this amount doesn't make us financially independent. However, if we quit our part-time job and never add to our $17,700, yet continue to receive the same return as during the first five years, it will take another 27 years for this amount by itself to grow into $1,000,000. This is in addition to the amount we may

---

1. From 1988 to 1993, one-in-six mutual funds with a five-year history did better than a 15% average annual return for this period.

already be investing by paying ourselves first from our regular incomes. The point is that becoming a millionaire is well within our reach if we apply some of these success-proven methods.

Another source of extra income which can be contributed to your investment portfolio is the additional money you may periodically receive from a promotion, a bonus, or a salary increase. Instead of spending this money on a new car, new clothes, new stereo, a nicer vacation, or any number of the other wonderful things you would like to buy with this extra money, you could use it to increase the amount of money in your financial freedom fund. Even if your pay raises are really cost-of-living increases, you could add all or most of this amount to your investment program for a number of years without seriously diminishing your standard of living.

There are other legitimate ways of adding extra money to your investment funds. For example, if your company matches you dollar-for-dollar when you invest in its retirement program, it would be foolish for you not to take advantage of this golden opportunity. Not only will your portion come directly out of your paycheck so that you don't even see it, but you will also be receiving a guaranteed 100% return on your money at no risk to you (this is because of the company's matching-dollar portion). Even if you cannot immediately contribute the maximum amount allowed by the company, usually between 6% to 16% of your gross income, at the very least, you should try to contribute the matching-dollar portion.

If you are in a tax-free plan or a plan which defers taxes until you retire, you should contribute the maximum amount allowable, since this will save you about 30% in non-collectible taxes on your profit every year. Also, if you receive an income tax refund, you could invest all or part of it in your financial freedom fund. Any windfall you receive can be contributed to increasing the amount in your investment portfolio. As will be seen in Chapter 9, "Utilizing the Magic of Compound Interest," even small amounts of money can multiply into far greater amounts if given sufficient time.

Chapter 8

Providing For Your Family

A good man leaveth an inheritance to his children's children.
—Proverbs 13:22

Many people are unaware that they should make plans for both living and dying. Your living estate, known as your financial freedom fund, is the money you are currently accumulating through investments in order to provide a sufficient income for yourself and your family upon retirement. It forms the basis of your net worth at the end of your working career. Your death estate, in the form of life insurance, is the money which will support your family should you die too soon. Your death estate supplements your living estate and is usually created well before you achieve financial independence. When the monetary requirements of your death estate are met by the accumulated money in your living estate, your family no longer needs the temporary financial security provided by life insurance. When this occurs, you can cancel your life insurance policy and use the premiums to strengthen your living estate. The starting point for creating a living estate begins by determining your net worth, since this will show you the amount of progress that needs to be made in order to achieve financial independence.

Calculating Your Net Worth

You should never equate income with wealth. Income is simply what you make at any given time, whereas wealth is determined by what you own. Earning a large income does not automatically make you a wealthy person; it only provides you with a better opportunity for becoming wealthy, not a guarantee that you will. Admittedly, it can propel you toward the attainment of financial freedom much faster, but only if you have the necessary self-discipline and commitment to invest in your future well-being.

Experience has shown that people's living expenses usually equal, and in many cases exceed, their available income, no matter what that level of income may be. Making sure that your expenses are under control is the key to slowing the drain on your financial resources. Of course, the person who makes a large income would be smart to invest more than the required minimum of 10% of his gross earnings, if he can avoid the temptation to live extravagantly. Practicing self-discipline by living within your means will greatly increase the sum of your net worth and quickly help you reach the goal of financial independence.

In its simplest form, "net worth" is a formula which equals the value of your total assets minus the remaining debt of your total liabilities. When you estimate the real value of your possessions (their appraised or purchase price), then subtract what is left to pay on these possessions (the debt), the resulting figure is your net worth. Net worth is simply a financial tool for measuring your monetary situation or level of prosperity at any given point in time. It provides a snapshot of your current financial situation and will fluctuate, either up or down, as your monetary situation changes over time. The following is the formula for determining your net worth:

ASSETS minus LIABILITIES equals NET WORTH (A − L = NW)

Assets fall into two major categories—liquid and illiquid. Your liquid assets consist of cash and those things which are easily convertible to cash. All bank accounts, money market accounts, certificates of deposit, stock and bond mutual fund accounts, and other such easily convertible possessions are considered liquid assets. Various precious metals, such as gold and silver coins or bars, are also considered liquid assets. A good rule of thumb for determining the liquidity of an asset is its easy convertibility to cash. The further removed an asset is from being convertible to cash, the less liquid it is. In most cases, the more liquid your assets, the stronger and more secure your financial position. The saying "cash is king" is just as true today as it was many years ago.

Illiquid assets would be anything else that is not readily convertible to cash, but could be given enough time, such as a house or other real estate property, jewelry, automobiles, artwork and other collectibles, appliances and other household goods, and any other tangible assets needing to be sold in order to be converted into cash. Although these assets can be converted to cash, it usually takes a certain amount of time and extra effort to accomplish.

By separating your liquid from your illiquid assets, you can determine the relative strength of your net worth and your flexibility in the event of a financial emergency. Such emergencies usually require the fluidity and immediacy of cash for their resolution. Because of this, it may be inappropriate to shackle your assets with too much illiquidity. In any event, emergencies should not be funded by selling off illiquid assets as this plays havoc with your financial stability and destroys the long-term purpose for owning these assets. Of course, you should include both your liquid and illiquid assets when determining your net worth.

Your liabilities are determined by what you owe or have left to pay on your assets (these are invariably illiquid assets), otherwise known as your debts. What you have left to pay on your house, automobile, credit cards, appliances, college loans, and any other debts are considered your liabilities. The total amount of these debts are subtracted from the total value of your assets for determining your net worth. At least once a year, you should re-evaluate your illiquid assets (price them approximately to what you can sell them for) and adjust your net worth accordingly. Figure 8.1 below provides an example of how to figure your net worth.

Assets	Value	Liabilities	Debts
House	$150,000	Mortgage	$100,000
Car Values	$25,000	Car Loans	$13,500
Raw Land	$10,000	Raw Land	$8,000
Jewelry	$4,000	Credit Cards	$1,500
Savings	$12,800	College Loan	$2,000
College Fund	$30,100	Total	$125,000
Retirement	$82,200		
Stereo	$2,500		
Clothes	$3,000		
Misc. Goods	$2,000		
Bank Account	$400		
Total	$322,000		

Figure 8.1 Calculating Your Net Worth.

As you can see from Figure 8.1, all of your assets are listed on the left side and all of your liabilities on the right side. To figure your net worth, you must take the total value of your assets (which amount to $322,000 in this example), then subtract the total amount of your liabilities (which equal $125,000) to get your net worth figure ($197,000). The computation would look like this:

$$\text{Assets} - \text{Liabilities} = \text{Net Worth}$$
$$\$322,000 - \$125,000 = \$197,000$$

Financially, this is how much you are worth on the day you calculate these figures. Notice that $43,300 (in your savings and bank accounts as well as the children's college money) or about 22% of your net worth can be considered liquid. You would not necessarily count the $82,200 in your tax-deferred retirement funds as being liquid, since its accessibility is conditioned by the payment of taxes and penalties, both of which would probably amount to nearly 40% of the amount withdrawn, if it were cashed-in prematurely (assuming you could liquidate this pension money before retirement without needing it for an emergency). Of course, for an emergency situation as defined by the government, you would be allowed to liquidate this money; otherwise, for practical purposes, just think of all tax-deferred retirement monies as being illiquid until maturity.

As seen in the above illustration, just over 25% of your net worth is tied up in the equity of your home ($50,000 out of $197,000). In order to utilize this money you would have to either sell your house or refinance that portion of your home. If you refinanced, you are simply borrowing money, which adds to your liabilities, and the value of your new asset would then be determined by what you did with this borrowed money. If you reinvested the money, your net worth would initially remain the same; but if you spent this money on depreciating material items, vacations, or other such things, your net worth would decrease proportionally. What you do with this money will determine its relative value and overall benefit for increasing your net worth.

In order to increase your net worth, you must either reduce your debts or increase the value of your assets or both. The direction and movement of your net worth is dependent upon the increase or decrease in the value of each asset and liability. If the value of your assets are depreciating instead of appreciating, it will reduce the value of your living estate and reflect a proportional change in the value of your net worth. Also, as you add to your savings and investments, it will increase the value of your assets. The more money you can put into assets that appreciate in value, or grow through compound interest, the greater will be the amount of your net worth—as long as your liabilities (debts) are under control and being reduced or eliminated.

When you determine your net worth and can see how liquid you are in relation to your other assets, you will have information on the financial direction you are heading and what you will need to do in order to improve your financial situation. Although you may spend your money on consumer products, creature comforts, and other similar things, they should not constitute the bulk of your assets, since they depreciate in value. Real worth is decreed by how much an asset appreciates in value or produces in income. Such assets should comprise the major portion of your portfolio. Remember, your net worth is just a barometer for measuring the direction and distance of your wealth acquisition activity. It can also act as a source of encouragement for achieving your financial goals once you start putting into practice the principles outlined in this book.

Figure 8.2 below provides an example of how to calculate the liquid portion of your family's net worth on a monthly basis. Using this one-page outline will not only allow you to keep track of the value of the most important portion of your living estate, but also assist in monitoring your progress toward financial freedom. It is meant to help you focus on the investment portion of your family's finances. This has a twofold effect. The first is that if you are using the paying yourself first method, the value of your investment portfolio will increase more rapidly from month-to-month; and secondly, by focusing your attention on the increasing value of your liquid investments, instead of the often decreasing value of your illiquid material possessions, you are more likely to gravitate toward investing, thereby improving your overall financial stability.

FAMILY NET WORTH STATEMENT
End of Month: Date

	$ PAID $	#SHARES	VALUE
FATHER			
IRA in (name of Stock Mutual Fund)	$10,000.00	2100.916	$18,100.00
IRA in (name of Bond Mutual Fund)	$10,000.00	1250.556	$13,000.00
401k Pension Plan at work	$23,500.00	1220.589	$32,000.00
TOTAL CONTRIBUTED	$43,500.00	VALUE	$63,100.00
MOTHER			
IRA in (name of Stock Mutual Fund)	$12,000.00	900.916	$20,100.00
401k Pension Plan at work	$4,500.00	220.589	$9,000.00
TOTAL CONTRIBUTED	$16,500.00	VALUE	$29,100.00
EACH CHILD [list each child separately]			
College Savings in (name of Mutual Fund)	$10,000.00	2100.916	$30,000.00
Savings Bonds	$500.00	5.000	$1,000.00
TOTAL CONTRIBUTED	$10,500.00	VALUE	$31,000.00
JOINT FAMILY ACCOUNT (including Emergency Funds)			
Money Market Emergency Account	$9,000.00	n/a	$10,700.00
Credit Union Savings Account	$2,000.00	n/a	$2,100.00
Bank Checking Account	$400.00	n/a	$400.00
TOTAL CONTRIBUTED	$11,400.00	VALUE	$13,200.00
GRAND TOTALS	$81,900.00		$136,400.00

TOTAL OF ALL INVESTMENT FUNDS
All Funds, Latest Value: 136,400.00 [this value will change every month]
All Funds, Total Contributed: $81,900.00 [changes w/each additional contribution]
DIFFERENCE or Profit/Loss: $54,500.00 [gain of 66.5% on contributed amount]

TOTAL VALUE AMOUNTS AND PERCENTAGE IN [the three investment categories]:

STOCKS:	$109,200.00	80.0%	[stocks or stock mutual funds]
BONDS:	$14,000.00	10.3%	[bonds or bond mutual funds]
CASH	$13,200.00	9.7%	[cash in bank and money market accounts]
	136,400.00	100.0%	

NET WORTH FIGURES:

ASSETS:	$322,000	[total value of all material possessions and investments]
LIABILITIES:	$125,000	[total debt, or what you have left to pay, on all assets]
NET WORTH:	$197,000	[total money available after liquidating assets and paying off liabilities]

NET WORTH CALCULATIONS: Ratio = 2.58 to 1 [This ratio signifies that for every $2.58 in assets, you have $1.00 in liabilities. The higher the ratio, the better off you are financially.]

Net Worth at the End of Last Year: $190,000.00 [calculated at the end of last year]
Difference from the End of Last Year: +$7,000.00 [progress made so far this year]
Difference from the End of Last Month: $1,100.00 [amount of increase in one month]

Figure 8.2 Example of a Family's Financial Net Worth Statement.

The first thing to do in completing the above statement is to list all family members who have investments; then list the specific investment under each person's name, i.e., the particular stock or bond mutual fund and what type of funds they happen to be, e.g., IRA (Individual Retirement Account), UGMA (Uniform Gifts to Minors Act),

401k, and even non-retirement or non-tax-deferred funds; next, list how much out-of-pocket money was invested in each fund, then how many shares each fund currently has, and what the current value of those shares equal at the end of any given month.

Second, determine the total value of all the funds combined, then subtract the total amount originally contributed to all of these same funds. This will give you the difference (profit or loss) of the collective value of all of the family's investments. Next, divide this difference by the original amount contributed and you will see by what percentage you are ahead (or behind). By figuring the percentage of gain (or loss) in your investment portfolio, you will be able to gauge the progress your family is making toward financial independence.

Third, determine the amount and percentage of your family's total value in the three main areas of investments—stocks, bonds, and cash (this is usually in money market, saving, or bank accounts)—then record these figures by category. This will help you gauge the relative stability of your investment portfolio and help you determine the extent of your diversification. You may also wish to subcategorize each stock mutual fund category into conservative, moderate, or aggressive in order to pinpoint the extent of your diversification even further.

Fourth, use the formula and categories in Figure 8.1 for determining your total assets and total liabilities in order to calculate your total net worth figure. This figure will also include the illiquid portion of your net worth. The statement of your net worth, as illustrated in Figure 8.2, deals primarily with the liquid and retirement portions of your portfolio.

Fifth, by calculating the increase or decrease in your total net worth from last year, as well as from last month, you will be able to chart your progress toward financial freedom. You may also wish to include the value of your net worth from previous years as you track it annually.

In addition to this general statement, you may also wish to update the specific information contained in each family member's file, such as their name and social security number, the fund's account number, company address, telephone number, current value of each account, and number of shares—any and all data you may find useful for keeping accurate financial information on each person.

Establishing an Emergency Fund

There are two types of emergency funds that a family should establish: the first is for unexpected expenses, while the second is for those expenses which are expected, but only occur periodically throughout the year. These funds should not be commingled in one account. Each fund has a singular purpose, so it is advisable to keep them in two separate accounts. These accounts should be in short-term money market, bank (or credit union) savings, or checking accounts which pay interest. The most important thing in establishing an emergency fund is not its rate of return, but its completely risk-free preservation of principal and instant liquidity. Stock and bond mutual funds usually fluctuate too much in price to be of practical use and do not guarantee the value of the principal. An emergency fund is not meant to be a long-term investment vehicle, just a short-term guaranteed preserver of your capital for when you need instant access to it. Creating two separate emergency funds will help facilitate your control over your money.

Emergency Fund for Unexpected Expenses

The primary purpose of this emergency fund is to establish a financial cushion for protecting your family from unanticipated expenses. This should provide you with some maneuvering room in the event you need ready cash in an emergency situation. When establishing an emergency fund for unexpected expenses, most financial planners recommend setting aside the equivalent of three to six months worth of net income. Your actual living expenses are considered your net income, since that is what you specifically live on or spend each month. Therefore, your primary emergency fund should contain a minimum of three months of net or spendable income, though the closer you can get to having six months worth set aside, the better off you will be.

Examples of emergency situations for unexpected expenses would include such things as the boiler breaking down and needing replacement, the car blowing an engine and needing to be overhauled, an unexpected death in the family where you would have to fly to the funeral, or any number of other large item expenses which cannot be anticipated as part of your general operating cash flow.

The ultimate emergency would be if you lost your job. Hopefully, you would be eligible to receive unemployment compensation. However, losing a job and the resulting decrease in income would cause a crisis in your financial well-being. This situation would cause you to use the cash in your emergency account to cover most of your living expenses until you became reemployed. Depending on your particular situation, three to six months is usually enough time to find another job. Of course, whatever money you use from your emergency account should be replaced as quickly as possible for other unanticipated future expenses, since emergencies have a tendency to occur more than once per lifetime.

Emergency Fund for Periodic Expenses

The purpose of this second emergency fund is to establish a reserve for those occasional, though anticipated, expenses for which you are saving monthly to pay. Establishing this account will allow you to accumulate enough money to preempt your large periodic payments or save for a large item expense in the future.

When establishing an emergency fund for your periodic expenses, you should take into consideration all quarterly, semi-annual, and annual payments which will come due during the year. These anticipated large item expenses might include such things as an annual life insurance premium, a semi-annual automobile insurance premium, or a quarterly medical insurance premium. This account may also include the savings for a down payment on a house, or money for buying a new car for which you wish to make monthly payments now (to your fund) in order to pay cash for the automobile later and remain debt-free. By accumulating enough money on a monthly basis to cover these periodic expenses when they come due, you can preserve the money in your other emergency fund that has been set aside for your unexpected expenses. This is an example of sound financial planning.

Building Your Living Estate

Your living estate is the total value of your financial resources or the collective wealth that you have acquired over the years. Its primary purpose is to provide you with sufficient income during your retirement years. The exact amount of money needed in your living estate will be determined by your own personal requirements for a dignified, comfortable, and on-going retirement. If you have faithfully followed the principles of wealth acquisition leading to financial independence as outlined in this book, you will have little trouble reaching your desired goal.

In regard to a mandatory retirement age for Bahá'ís, the Kitáb-i-Aqdas states: "Concerning the retirement from work for individuals who have reached a certain age, Shoghi Effendi in a letter written on his behalf stated that 'this is a matter on which the International House of Justice will have to legislate as there are no provisions in the Aqdas concerning it'." [1] As of this writing, no age limit has been set by the Universal House of Justice for retiring from work. Therefore, until such time that the House of Justice determines this matter, it is left up to the discretion of the individual to determine when he or she feels ready to retire.

Determining the correct age to retire is really a subjective point of perceived cognitive and physical ability. While some would do well to retire at age 30, such as the players of certain professional sports, other people in different careers can function well into their 90s, such as people in the arts and entertainment. Ideally, everyone should be allowed to continue working in their chosen profession for as long as they wish to and are capable. In reality, this is not always the case, since most businesses and government agencies have a mandatory retirement age, usually age 65 or 70, were the worker has no choice

---

1. Kitáb-i-Aqdas, n56, p. 193.

but to retire. Some employers may provide an early retirement option, starting at age 55 or younger. One drawback of retiring early is that early retirees may not be eligible to receive their full retirement benefits until a later date or until they reach a certain age. However, if you are not totally dependent on your company retirement benefits for survival, this will not be a drawback for you.

In any job where you are working for someone else, you have very little say in determining your retirement age or when you can utilize your retirement benefits. However, the more control you have over your own finances, as well as the more money you have invested in your financial freedom fund, the more control you will have over your retirement options, both in benefits and age. Of course, if you own a business, then it is your prerogative to decide when you will retire.

Every individual has unique abilities and talents which should be utilized and developed. However, due to injustice, economic disparity, and other limiting factors in the material world, many people are unable to fully utilize their special talents. As long as people have to worry about the basic necessities—such as food, shelter, clothing, and paying bills—it is unlikely that they will be able to develop the full potential of their inner reality. When the basic necessities of life are no longer a financial concern, people can concentrate more fully on developing their inner reality and help to carry forward an ever-advancing civilization. This is a strong motivator for creating a substantial living estate.

Creating a Death Estate

The financial protection provided by life insurance is the backbone of nearly every death estate. Although a general overview of life insurance was touched upon in the last chapter as a means for reducing expenses and generating extra cash for investments, a more detailed discussion on life insurance is presented in this chapter with the goal of helping the reader determine which type of life insurance coverage is the most appropriate for creating a death estate.

A death estate is composed of two separate things: the amount of one's life insurance and the value of one's net worth. Most young families have an insufficient net worth (the value of their living estate) to provide adequate financial support upon the premature death of the breadwinner, especially if very few assets are liquid. And since it is not really feasible to completely liquidate one's living estate in order to support surviving family members, the purchase of adequate life insurance coverage becomes an even greater financial necessity in the event of the breadwinner's premature death.

There are four major reasons for creating a death estate through the purchase of life insurance. These reasons are not theoretical, but are practical economic realities which may apply to your own family's financial situation in the event of your premature death. They are as follows:

1. To maintain your family's current standard of living without the benefit of your income;
2. To keep your spouse and your children from becoming destitute for lack of adequate financial resources;
3. To prevent financial hardship on your spouse in raising your children as a single parent;
4. To give your spouse the option of not having to remarry just to feed your children and make ends meet.

If the potential money available to your family in your current death estate is not adequate to meet the challenges of any one of these four possibilities, then you may wish to increase your life insurance coverage. Likewise, if none of these conditions apply to your current family situation, you may wish to reduce or even eliminate the life insurance you do carry. The only exception would be to cover a large estate-tax burden or some other business liability upon your death, but this is a condition which applies primarily to the rich or to independent business people and may not be germane to your situation at this stage in your life.

Although everyone should establish a death estate, not everyone needs life insurance. A family with young children, a house mortgage, and other debts would be the most likely candidates for life insurance, since the death of the breadwinner would be financially devastating to the family. On the other hand, a young adult just out of college with no debts would need only enough money for funeral expenses in the event of premature death, since no other financial obligations exist for that person. It is the extent of our financial responsibilities which determines our specific need for life insurance.

There are general guidelines for determining the amount of money required by the deceased breadwinner's surviving family members in order for them to maintain their standard of living, prevent financial hardship, and stay solvent for many years afterwards. The amount of money needed from a life insurance policy rests on fulfilling the financial requirements of five death estate costs. These expenses include:

1. The cost of replacing the breadwinner's income for a certain number of years, which pays for food, utilities, clothing, and all other expenses.[1]

---

1. You may also wish to consider the cost of replacing your spouse's income for a certain period of time in the event of his/her premature death in order to help defray some of the costs associated with his/her contributions to the household finances. Many life insurance policies can add a spouse as a "rider" to the main policy. This will save the cost of the administrative fees associated with having an additional policy. Also, any reputable company should be able to offer you one policy which will cover both the husband and wife.

2. The cost of maintaining the monthly mortgage payment or paying it off entirely, which would allow the family to keep their place of residence and not be forced to sell or move.
3. The cost of eliminating or reducing all other debts, such as auto loans, credit card balances, college loans, and department store obligations.
4. The cost of a funeral, burial, cemetery plot, and other related expenses.
5. The cost of a college education or trade school training for each child when they reach the age of maturity, which would give them a better start in life.

Without adequate life insurance to cover these potential costs, your spouse would be forced to liquidate your assets in order to survive financially. By determining the total cash requirements for establishing your death estate from these five cost items, you will have a fair estimate of the amount of life insurance needed to cover your financial responsibilities.

Buying the Right Life Insurance

As explained briefly in the last chapter, term life insurance is the only form of life insurance which should be purchased. However, for those who harbor any lingering doubts, a description of the so-called benefits of whole life insurance and what is involved in purchasing any other kind of life insurance will be useful.

In the first place, life insurance should be thought of like any other commodity. You pay a certain amount of money and expect to receive a certain product or level of service. In the case of life insurance, you are paying (a premium) for a specific amount of cash (the face value or death benefit) to be paid to your spouse (the beneficiary) by the life insurance company (the insurer) in the event of your death. It seems reasonable that you should pay the least amount of money for the most amount of coverage needed by your family to survive financially. Only term insurance fits this category.

Term Insurance

Term insurance is life insurance that is sold without any gimmicks, has no savings or investment features, and is very cheap relative to every other type of commercial life insurance. It is strictly and purely life insurance coverage. Like all life insurance, the cost of term is based on statistical mortality tables. Statistical mortality tables are based on the actual death rates of people by age, gender, and physique over a specific period of time. Insurance companies use these tables and the law of averages to estimate life expectancy or the probability of certain people dying during any particular year. The difference between term and the other forms of individual life insurance is that term insurance has no added features which substantially add to the cost of the coverage. When the name of the life insurance coverage changes to something other than term, it causes a substantial increase in the price of the policy, though the life expectancy data has not changed at all. Term is the pure cost of insuring a life based on statistical information.

Term insurance is temporary insurance in that it only last for a certain period of time or "term." The term can be for one year, five years, ten years, or even twenty years, and the cost for this insurance during the prescribed term is based on the average life expectancy for that period of time. As you grow older, the odds increase that you will die sooner, hence, the cost of insuring your life goes up. Whatever the statistical mortality tables indicate, the cost for term insurance is based on it. Other types of life insurance coverage are much more expensive because they contain additional features which have nothing to do with establishing a death estate.

Whole Life Insurance

One of the most popular kinds of life insurance is called "whole life" or "ordinary life" insurance, which is sometimes known as "permanent" life insurance, because the premium payments are figured to your 100th birthday. Although whole life insurance has been the mainstay of the life insurance industry for over a century, newcomers to the insurance field, such as universal life and single-premium life insurance can be a riskier proposition than whole life and will be briefly explained below.

The basic premise of whole life insurance is that it can provide an individual with both a death benefit and a "savings account" (known as the cash surrender value) and is sold as much as an investment vehicle, or a forced savings plan, as it is a form of death protection. As recently as January 1994, a well known international business magazine featured an investigation of insurance industry salesmen who use misleading sales tactics to deceive the public on the value of life insurance as an investment. Agents were "tempted to misrepresent whole life policies as retirement or savings plans,"[1] since the sale of investments have more appeal to consumers than the sale of life insurance. Obviously, life insurance policies are not investment plans, since their purpose is to provide a death estate, not a living estate.

The so-called investment theory of whole life insurance is that as you pay your premiums every year, your policy will accumulate a "cash value" which will eventually grow to replace your coverage (death benefit), usually at age 100. Of course, most people die before becoming a centenarian, so your beneficiary never sees this accumulated cash value, only the death benefit, and only if you keep the policy in-force until you die, which most people never do after discov-

---

1. "Policies of Deception? Investigations of Misleading Sales Tactics Rock Insurance Industry," *Business Week* (International Edition), January 17, 1994, p. 26.

ering how inefficient and expensive this type of life insurance really is. In the event a policyholder does reach his 100th birthday, the insurance company will pay him the cash value, which should at least equal the face amount of the policy, and cancel his coverage, since the policy is considered "endowed." As silly as this concept seems, it is seriously sold to millions of unsuspecting and misinformed people every year to the tune of hundreds of billions of dollars.[1]

As will be detailed below, the basic problem with whole life insurance is precisely this theory of trying to combine insurance with investments. The two are incongruous and highly-priced when blended together. The main purpose of life insurance is the creation of a death estate for people with large financial responsibilities and little money; while investments are indispensable for building a living estate and are the conduit leading to financial independence. Life insurance is a temporary stopgap for averting financial disaster, while investing is a permanent pipeline for producing perpetual abundance. For this reason, we should never combine the function of life insurance with the benefits of investing.

To illustrate how detrimental this combination can be, a simple review of the so-called benefits of a whole life policy will suffice. When you purchase a whole life policy, you are actually paying for three different things, but are only allowed to receive one of them at a time. This situation is like going into a clothing store and paying for a customized three-piece suit. Later, when you return to the store to collect your new custom-fitted suit, the salesman asks which of the three pieces you would like to have—the vest, the pants, or the jacket. Of course, you laugh and say there's been some mistake, since you have already paid for the entire suit, not for just one of its three pieces. Besides, what good is only one piece of a three-piece suit, you ask? The salesman smiles benignly, but replies that it is store policy to allow the use of only one piece of a suit at a time, and although he acknowledges that you did pay for all three items, you are still entitled to use only one of them at a time. He again asks which one of the three pieces you would like to have. You can't believe this is happening and ask to see the manager. When the manager arrives, he also repeats the store's inflexible policy and unashamedly awaits your decision on which piece you would like to wear. You soon become angry and frustrated, but are left with no option except to cut your losses and leave the store. No other legal option is available since you did sign the contract and accept the policy of your own free will.

Like the story of the three-piece suit, the three things you pay for when you buy a whole life policy are expensive protection, an inadequate emergency fund, and a dismal retirement income. How-

1. Over 155 million Americans carry life insurance having a total face value of more than $6 trillion ($6,000,000,000,000) and nearly 80% of all policies issued by the life insurance industry contain some whole life.

ever, you are allowed to utilize only one of these three features at a time. It is precisely because of this incompatibility in mixing insurance with investments that you should never buy any life insurance policy which contains so-called savings or investments as part of the policy. In order to understand the inherent problems of whole life insurance, we must look more closely at each of its three dysfunctional features.

Problems with Whole Life Insurance

The first problem with whole life is its exorbitant cost. Although it does provide protection in the form of a death benefit, it is usually much more expensive, normally five or six times more expensive, than term insurance. And because it is so expensive, most people cannot afford to buy enough coverage to sufficiently protect their family from financial disaster in the event of the breadwinner's death. It is true that the premium payments are level and do not increase from year-to-year, but you are obligated to pay for this coverage until age 100, if you hold the policy that long, or unless you have been sold an even more expensive policy, usually called some form of "endowment," in which the premium payments end at age 65, or some other point before your 100th birthday.

Another way of determining the cost of whole life is by factoring in the number of years required for paying your premiums. Although the premium for a 25 year old will be less than that of a 35 year old, whose premium will be less than that a 45 year old, and so on, when you add up the total cost of these premiums over a period of years and factor in the time-value of money, it actually costs more for a young person to own whole life at a lower premium for many years than it does for a middle-aged or older person to own it at a higher premium for a shorter period of time. This is an example of how compound interest works in reverse and where the insurance company is the one that profits.

The second problem with whole life concerns the cash value itself. The cash value is purported to be an emergency fund for the policyholder, but you are required to borrow this cash from the life insurance company and pay between 5% to 8% interest on it if you decide to use it. This is like having $1,000 in your bank savings account and having to pay the bank interest whenever you decide to withdraw it. Unfortunately, during the first year or two that the policy is in force, you usually have no cash value accumulated, so there's no money available to borrow against during an emergency anyway. And when the policy does begin to accumulate cash, it usually takes many decades for it to accrue more than just a marginal amount of money.

Another oddity is that the cash value in a life insurance policy actually belongs to the insurance company, not to you, the policyholder. Of course, this should be evident from the fact that when you withdraw it, you have to borrow and pay interest on the amount withdrawn. If the cash value were truly yours, you could simply withdraw it from your account without paying interest. Another fact which may help dispel the notion that the cash value is actually your money, is that the insurance company can legally deny you access to the cash in your policy for up to six months after you request it. This provision is standard in the legal contract (called the policy) that you must sign with the company whenever you purchase any type of cash value life insurance. It doesn't make much sense to have a so-called emergency fund when it could take up to six months before you receive the money.

However, the greatest oddity concerning a policy's cash value is that it is considered part-and-parcel of the face amount and not in addition to the death benefit. For example, if a policyholder dies with a $100,000 death benefit (face amount) and an accumulated cash value of $25,000, the beneficiary of the policyholder only receives the face amount ($100,000), not both the face amount and the cash value ($125,000). The insurance company considers the cash value to be part of the death benefit, not something which is extra. At least when your investments are separated from your life insurance coverage, your beneficiary will receive both the face amount of the insurance policy and the separate savings account which is invested elsewhere. This may be the best reason for never combining life insurance with investments.

The third problem with whole life is that the accumulated cash value is touted as being a source of income during retirement. However, since very little cash is actually being accumulated over the years, due to a very low rate of return, which averages about 1.3% per year (at this rate, it would take over 55 years for your money to double), life insurance as a retirement vehicle is completely inadequate and unsuitable for accumulating sufficient retirement monies.

Also, once you redeem all of the cash in your policy, you no longer have any coverage, since the policy is canceled. If you do decide you want to keep the policy and use the cash value, then you must borrow it from the insurance company and pay interest on it. And when you borrow all of your cash value to use as a source of retirement income, you not only pay interest on this borrowed amount, but you must also continue to make the premium payments in order to keep the policy from being canceled. This large outlay of money is usually very difficult for retirees on a fixed income. Furthermore, if you happen to die while there is an outstanding cash value loan, the insurance company will simply deduct this debt from the policy's face amount and pay your beneficiary what is left. This is a no-win situation for the policyholder.

The greatest flaw with owning whole life or permanent insurance is that a retiree normally does not need any life insurance when he no longer has any financial responsibilities. Usually at age 65, his family is grown, his house is paid for, and he no longer has any debts to repay. What is needed at retirement is plenty of cash to last for the next 15 to 20 years, not an insurance policy which cannot be used for living expenses while the retiree is still alive. The reasons for owning life insurance normally don't apply when you are near retirement age, since you have few, if any, financial obligations at the end of your working career. The only exception would be to cover a large tax liability on your estate after your death, but this should be covered with term insurance, too.

Life insurance, as an investment, is not designed to provide you with a sufficient amount of money during your retirement, and certainly not enough for achieving financial independence. Try finding someone who is living comfortably on the cash value of their life insurance policy. No such person exists. However, true investments, such as mutual funds, are intended to achieve financial freedom by generating an independent source of income for life. Many people have already achieved this state of financial independence, some well before reaching mandatory retirement age.

Universal Life Insurance

Concerning universal life insurance, it has all of the problems associated with whole life and a few more. Although the extra money you pay for universal life can go toward legitimate investments, you still have to pay up-front fees and commission charges which can evaporate nearly 30% of your initial annual premium payment. There is also the problem of big surrender or back-end fees which can substantially reduce the investment benefit, especially during the first few years of owning such a policy. However, the worst problem may be the hidden charges within the premium itself. Although your premium payment usually remains the same, it is divided differently each year with more going toward the insurance coverage and less being used for the investment portion. This is standard procedure, since your age increases every year and it costs more money to insure you.

Another problem with universal life concerns the guaranteed interest rate, which normally applies to only the first year of the policy; thereafter, the interest rate is not guaranteed and is generally lower than that of the first year. Of course, the first year also happens to be the time when the least amount of your money goes toward the investment portion because of all the initial costs associated with getting into the program. Unlike whole life though, universal life does not even guarantee a minimal amount of cash value. You could lose everything if the investments chosen by the insurance company are high risk and fail. Variable life, a variation of universal life, is the riskiest of all permanent life insurances, because its managers are allowed much more latitude in choosing which investment options to use.

Single-Premium Life Insurance

Single-premium life insurance is simply another form of whole life, but in this case, you pay for it all immediately, in one large single premium, instead of over many years in gradual increments. With this type of insurance, you are really losing the power inherent in the time-value of money, since you pay for everything up-front (although at a discount) instead of gradually over time. Remember that inflation makes money less valuable as time goes by, so it is better to pay later with money that will be worth less tomorrow, than it is to pay now with money that is worth more today. Besides, even with a discount, by paying all of your premiums up-front, the insurance company has complete use and control of your money immediately. If you die after just one year, your family will get only the face amount of the policy. So never pay more in advance than is absolutely necessary.

Furthermore, single-premium life insurance is touted as being a tax-sheltered investment with the major benefit being that you can borrow money from it tax free. The truth of the matter is that you can borrow money from anywhere tax free, since no income taxes are levied on borrowed money. This tax-free borrowing of the cash value is just another gimmick by which life insurance companies try to get you to purchase their products. Always beware of such gimmicks and read the fine print before transferring money from your pocket to someone else's.

In the final analysis, it is best to stay away from anything which combines life insurance with investments, for in both the long and short run, you will most likely end up the loser. It is worth remembering that whenever you take the time and expend the effort to educate yourself on the best places to invest your money, you and your family usually end up the winner, especially if it is invested outside the life insurance industry.

Managing Finances is a Family Endeavor

The basic unit of society is the family. Although most families in the modern world have gone from extended to nuclear, the family is still "the bedrock of the whole structure of human society."[1] The family relationship is based on both its spiritual unity and material resources. Achieving success in both areas will create a stable family environment.

One of the most sensitive areas of family life is its financial condition. The flow, control, and management of money can be a critical pressure point to its stability. If a family does not incorporate the principles of prosperity as part of its daily endeavor, it will suffer from a chronic lack of material resources. This lack of money, or its poor management, can have a devastating effect on family survival. Financially, running a household is similar to running a business: the family should live within its means; be accountable for its purchasing, debt, and investment decisions; and establish short- and long-term plans for

1. *The Kitáb-i-Aqdas*, n134, p. 223.

improving its monetary well-being. This idea is reflected in one of the most explicit Biblical admonitions in Christianity on family finances: "But if any provide not for his own, and specially for those of his own house, he hath denied the faith, and is worse than an infidel." [1] Proper management of family finances is an important aspect of spirituality.

When family members demonstrate a healthy attitude toward money, it usually demonstrates a family with a balanced and moderate lifestyle. Feeling secure and peaceful about money is a result of properly handling household finances. This attitude reflects the spiritual values under which the family operates. If the members of a family work together by taking collective responsibility for their financial situation, these lessons will be transferred to the community as well. If service, sharing, and self-discipline are the primary ingredients for the smooth operation of a family household, then these qualities can be extended to improving a nation's economic system. 'Abdu'l-Bahá says that *"a family is a nation in miniature"* and *"nations are but an aggregate of families."* [2]

Also, the family's financial condition and attitude is the matrix in which a child's material attitudes are formulated and financial values are defined. Families who have control over their finances usually raise children with fewer financial problems than those families who are out of control. The parent's attitude toward money and the level of consultation the family shares on financial matters are the keys to successfully rearing financially cognizant children. [3]

It is wise to involve all family members in the consultative process whenever any major financial decisions have to be made. Unless children are too young to understand, they should also be included in consultations involving major decisions. As members of the family, children have the right to be consulted on financial matters, especially when they are personally effected by the results. If we do not involve our children in such consultations, how can we expect them to understand the underlying spiritual principles involved in solving problems or the importance of carrying out the final decision of the family? It is these examples of family consultation which provide a healthy environment for children to imitate as they grow into adulthood. If children are not allowed to participate in family consultations concerning finances, this may breed attitudes of indifference or neglect concerning material means later in life.

There are certain things parents can do to insure a smooth transition for their children when they begin life on their own. The first

---

1. 1st Timothy 5:8.
2. *Lights of Guidance*, no. 740, p. 222.
3. An execellent book devoted to the subject of giving your children "a basic financial education; a healthy, responsible attitude toward money, and a sound understanding of it," is Jean Ross Peterson's *It Doesn't Grow on Trees* (Crozet, Virginia: Better Way Publications, 1988).

thing is being a good example to our children, since this is the most important factor for acquiring a proper financial education. When we begin teaching the Cause of God, we should prepare by first teaching our own selves. In like manner, teaching through example is needed to convey sound financial practices to our children. If we exercise control over our finances by wisely investing a certain portion of our monthly income, regularly contribute to the Bahá'í funds, make payments to Huqúqu'lláh, avoid indebtedness, especially to finance our indulgences, and make important financial decisions a matter of open consultation within the family, then we are cultivating the appropriate soil for producing financially well-balanced and prosperity-oriented children. Unless we utilize these principles and demonstrate the benefits of abiding by them, we will not be able to influence our children to do the same.

Another expression of this family endeavor is in the role of the primary breadwinner vis-a-vis the primary homemaker. The breadwinner's major function is to provide an income for the family, while the homemaker's primary concern is to manage the household. Although these roles are not automatically defined by gender, they are complementary and integral to the family's stability. Both husband and wife must operate as a team in doing what is best for the family. There should not be any selfishness involved in financial matters that affect the welfare of the family, either by the one providing most of the money, or by the one providing most of the domestic service. The family should think of itself as an analogue of the human body. Each organ performs a different, but necessary, function for the benefit of the entire organism. All family members are essential contributing components to the body of the family. Unless decreed by law, such as when establishing a pension plan, there should be very few "mine and your" situations when it comes to generating wealth for the family. Family wealth should mostly be a matter of "ours." Exceptions might include an inheritance or a dowry, which would be the sole property of the receiver.

To further illustrate this point of sharing and cooperation, the Universal House of Justice, in its 1990 Ridván message, likened the teaching activities of the Faith to "a condition in which different individuals will concentrate on different activities, appreciating the salutary effect of the aggregate...because each person cannot do everything and all persons cannot do the same thing." [1] Likewise, the wholesome endeavor of each family member contributes to the collective well-being of that particular family, similar to what we are asked to do as members of the Bahá'í community. Whenever we operate on the premise of the whole taking precedence over the individual, harmony and unity are maintained. Whenever the individual takes precedence over the whole, the stability of the unit is undermined and incapaci-

---

1. *A Wider Horizon: Selected Messages of the Universal House of Justice, 1983-1992,* p. 80.

tated. Obedience should not be coerced by an act of force, but should result from the detachment and self-discipline of the individual concerned. Until individual submission to the welfare of the whole is realized, family structure will continue to crumble and collapse. The example of the Administrative Order, as envisioned by Bahá'u'lláh, should be our standard for the functioning of a healthy family.

Another beneficial action of a unified family occurs when the parents set aside, from birth, a certain portion of their monthly income for their children's college education or for some other worthwhile purpose. Such a healthy financial outlook implies that it is better to remain debt-free by paying for our children's college education now, through investing small sums of money during their growing years, than it is to go into debt all at once later in life and spend many years repaying this debt. By using the time-value of money to create a college fund for our children, we may also be giving them an opportunity to start life debt-free. Beginning a career or marriage debt-free can greatly improve our children's opportunity for advancement in their chosen field. This is another example of using the Paying Yourself First principle to good advantage.

Finally, it is important for a family to think long-term when applying the principles of sound financial management. A family's perennial fortune can be insured by following the principles of prosperity. Family wealth need not be confined to only the present generation, but can be extended to future generations. It is possible for us to create a vast fortune for the perpetual support of the Bahá'í Fund as well as for the education and training of many future generations of Bahá'í family members by applying the principles of wealth acquisition to our lives now and passing this knowledge on to our children and our children's children. Part of what it means to carry forward an ever-advancing civilization may be found in the dynamics of a family fortune tempered by spiritual discipline and obligation.

Chapter 9

Utilizing the Magic of Compound Interest

Whoso keepeth the fig tree shall eat the fruit thereof.
—Proverbs 27:18

It is reputed that Albert Einstein, after receiving a warm welcome on his arrival to the shores of the United States in 1933, was asked by a reporter to identify the most powerful force in the universe. After a thoughtful pause, he is said to have responded "compound interest." The world's greatest physicist was not far off the mark. Compound interest is one of the most powerful mathematical concepts ever discovered by the mind of man. Effectively applying this concept to your wealth accumulation plan will guarantee success in achieving financial independence, provided you have sufficient time and enough patience for it to work properly on your behalf. Understanding the impact of doubling your money within an acceptable time frame is paramount to achieving the expeditious growth of wealth within your working lifetime. The earnings which are generated from your investments, and which are continuously reinvested to earn further gains, are not only the sum and substance of compound interest, but also the means for building your fortune. It is your capital (usually the money from your income that you set aside to invest each month) and the growth of your capital (through the compounding effect of reinvesting what your money earns) which can create wealth far beyond what most people expect.

A Token of Favor

In this Dispensation, it is not only lawful, but also necessary for people to charge or receive interest for the use of their money. In other words, it is both permissible and proper that we gain a profit on our investments. In His Tablet of Ishráqát (Splendors), Bahá'u'lláh states:

> If there were no prospect for gaining interest, the affairs of men would suffer collapse or dislocation....Therefore as a token of favor towards men We have prescribed that interest on money should be treated like other business transactions that are current amongst men. Thus, now that this lucid commandment hath descended from the heaven of the Will of God, it is lawful and proper to charge interest on money...even as He had made it unlawful in the past.[1]

As we can see from the above passage, it is perfectly acceptable to earn interest on our money. Although Bahá'u'lláh has refrained from establishing any limits on the amount of interest which would be considered as illicit gains or usury, He has warned us against such practices. To this end, Bahá'u'lláh says that *"moderation and fairness"* are necessary in determining interest rates. Also, He advises His followers *"to observe justice and fairness and to show forth love and contentment"* as well as *"to do that which would prompt the friends of God to evince tender mercy and compassion towards each other."*[2] Furthermore, Bahá'u'lláh promises to *"double their portion through the heaven of His bounty"*[3] if people faithfully follow His teachings in this matter. So, although it is permissible to receive or charge interest, it is not permissible to do so usuriously.

The Rule of 72

Since Bahá'u'lláh has permitted us to earn interest, we should endeavor to understand how interest works and properly utilize it to increase our wealth. The compounding effect that interest has is one of the keys to riches and is simply known as the Rule of 72. In order to assure our financial success, we must not only understand this rule, but also be prepared to utilize its magiclike qualities in all of our financial endeavors.

The Rule of 72 is a formula for measuring the effects of compound interest. It does this by ascertaining the length of time needed for doubling money. For instance, dividing 72 by the percent of interest will determine how long it takes money to double in value. If you earn 6% a year, your money will double every 12 years ($72 \div 6 = 12$);

1. *Tablets of Bahá'u'lláh*, p. 133.
2. Ibid. p. 134.
3. Ibid.

but if you are able to earn 18% interest, your money will double every 4 years (72÷18=4). For those being exposed to this idea for the first time, this difference may not seem like much, but by reviewing Figure 9.1 below, you can see that over time, getting a higher rate of return makes a large difference in the growth of your money. In this example, only $1,000 is invested. The results show the dymanic power of compound interest.

	At 6% money doubles every 12 yrs	At 12% money doubles every 6 yrs	At 18% money doubles every 4 yrs
After 12 Years	$2,000	$4,000	$8,000
After 24 Years	$4,000	$16,000	$64,000
After 36 Years	$8,000	$64,000	$512,000

Figure 9.1 The Compounding Effect of the Rule of 72.

In the above table, although 18% interest is three times more than 6% interest, at the end of 12 years (1st row) you would have four times the amount of money in your account by getting the highest rate of return; after 24 years (2nd row), you would have 16 times more money at 18% than at 6%; and after 36 years (3rd row), your money at 18% interest would be 64 times the amount compounded at the 6% rate. As can be seen, the shorter the time needed to double your money, the larger the amount of money accumulated in the long term. The importance of investing your money at a higher rate of return is paramount for success.

Some financial experts have recently stated that the Rule of 72 is technically inaccurate for determining the compounding effect of money in stock mutual funds, because this rule really reflects the compounding effect on interest received monthly, such as with bond mutual funds and bank savings accounts. Many other mutual funds receive dividends and capital gains either quarterly or only once a year, therefore, the Rule of 72 does not apply accurately to these types of mutual funds. In cases such as these, the Rule of 72 has been renamed by these experts as the Rule of 76. All this means is that it will take a little longer for the money to double, since whenever the value of either the divisor or the dividend changes, the quotient will also change. However, although the Rule of 72 may not be exactly correct in every case, it is the most popular expression of the idea of compound interest and is close enough for our purpose.

Regardless of which Rule you go by to measure your progress, the critical point is to utilize the concept of compound interest in order to substantially increase your wealth. Since the time frame for accomplishing your goal normally spans decades, knowing the exact number of months for its realization is not that important. Having a general idea of the number of years it will take to reach your goal is sufficient. The most important thing is knowing what to do in order to reach your goal of financial independence. While you are able, you should employ this most powerful of financial tools so that the value of your living estate will reach a level where it can replace your paycheck.

Doubling Your Money

Money is your best employee. It works for you 24 hours a day, 7 days a week, 365 days a year, and never takes a vacation or a sick day. Money will diligently labor for anyone who is willing to find profitable employment for it. This is done primarily through investments, which utilize compound interest to multiply your capital many times over. Compound interest is the internal mechanism for determining the growth rate of money and will double its value whenever the opportunity presents itself.

Eventually, nearly all of us will be forced to substitute the return from our investments for the income from our employment in order to support ourselves during retirement. We must ask ourselves if this future income will be sufficient to replace the earnings from our current labor. If not, we will experience serious financial difficulties.

For those who have already begun their own plan for financial independence, the exponential growth of money through compounding is already taking effect. As the years pass, and with a good rate of return, their money will rapidly multiply. This multiplication of money is nothing short of staggering. If you have patience (letting enough time elapse), self-discipline (consistently investing a certain percentage of your income), and remain committed to your long-range plan for financial freedom (not touching this money until it has reached its stated purpose), your money can blossom into a fortune. We should also realize that working smarter (using compound interest), instead of harder (getting a higher paying job) is what will greatly increase our wealth. It does not matter as much what we are worth today as how we plan to use the money we will earn during our future working years. By utilizing time, practicing consistency, and receiving a good rate of return, compound interest will do the work for us.

Although no one has an unlimited amount of time for building a fortune, most of us have access to the power of compound interest. The rate of compounding will determine the time and speed for achieving results. Leaving money in low interest bearing instruments and getting a low rate of return can generate wealth, but it takes a long time. You could invest $100 per month at 3% interest and still become wealthy, but you would have to wait 109 years, since the lower the rate of return, the slower the compounding effect. Furthermore, the hardest part of this waiting period would be the first hundred years, since the rate of compound interest is based on a logarithmic formula which realizes exponential growth only after the elapse of a certain period of time.

Most of us, however, want to enjoy our wealth while still alive, so we should be prepared to invest in those vehicles which can double our money much sooner than the slower compounding effect of those vehicles with low interest rates. This is why investments which generally provide a higher rate of return are recommended.

As you can see from the figures in the table below, the larger your rate of return, the shorter the number of years needed for doubling your money. The number of years have been rounded to the nearest tenth and are based on the Rule of 72.

Rate of Return	4%	5%	6%	7%	8%	9%	10%	12%
Number of Years	18.0	14.4	12.0	10.3	9.0	8.0	7.2	6.0

Rate of Return	14%	15%	18%	20%	21%	24%	28%	30%
Number of Years	5.1	4.8	4.0	3.6	3.4	3.0	2.6	2.4

Figure 9.2 Investment Time Required to Double Your Money.

As safely as possible, you should double your money within the shortest period of time in order to reach your goal at the fastest possible speed. However, you must always be sure that you are putting your money into legitimate investment vehicles. Abiding by this cautionary note is very important for retaining your principal, since any investment giving an unrealistic or unusually high rate of return may be suspect or even fraudulent.

Although the rate of return will determine the doubling power of your money, many investment vehicles can fluctuate in value. The degree of fluctuation is technically known as "investment volatility" and may dissuade some investors from putting their money into some investments. Due to this volatility, a mutual fund will record its growth in two ways: as a cumulative return (the total return over a certain period of time) and as an average annual return.

Procrastination is Costly

If we delay in implementing an investment strategy, we are losing precious time that cannot be made up or relived. Once time passes, it is gone forever. If time is not working for us, it is probably working against us. We should do everything we can to put time on our side by utilizing it to help make our fortune. Procrastination is simply failure in the installment plan which inhibits the time-value of money.

Figure 9.3 below shows how procrastination can effect your investments. The figures in this chart are based on a fully-funded IRA of $2,000 per year ($167 per month) which receives a 15% rate of return per year. These figures reflect the reinvestment of all capital gains and dividends without the payment of taxes, since an IRA is a tax-deferred investment vehicle. The chart not only shows a long period of time (30 years) until the commencement of retirement, but also the high cost of waiting before taking action toward investing for the future. The "Cost of Delay" column is that money which fails to get included in the retirement fund because of procrastination.

When Beginning	Future Value	Cost of Delay
Start Today	$1,153,800	Zero
Start in 1 year	$992,200	-$161,600
Start in 2 years	$852,900	-$300,900
Start in 3 years	$732,900	-$420,900
Start in 4 years	$629,600	-$524,200
Start in 5 years	$540,500	-$613,000
Start in 6 years	$463,800	-$690,000
Start in 7 years	$397,700	-$756,100
Start in 8 years	$340,800	-$813,000
Start in 9 years	$291,800	-$862,000
Start in 10 years	$249,500	-$904,300
Start in 15 years	$111,400	-$1,042,400
Start in 20 years	$45,800	-$1,108,000
Start in 25 years	$14,700	-$1,139,100
Start in 30 years	None	-$1,153,800

Figure 9.3 The High Cost of Waiting to Invest.

It is amazing how much money is lost through procrastination. The above chart clearly shows the time-value of money. As you can see in this example, by waiting only one year to get started, you will lose $161,600. This figure represents the compounding effect of $2,000 over 29 years at 15% interest. For each passing year that you delay in getting started with your investment program, you lose the value of what your money could have made over this time period. Failure to take advantage of time is costly and reflects the essence of the saying "time is money."

Figure 9.4 below shows another way of looking at procrastination and its stranglehold on the ability of money to compound. All dollar amounts represent an average annual return of 12% interest. In our hypothetical illustration, Martha decides to invest $100 per month ($1,200 per year) in an IRA starting on her 25th birthday. She does this for six years until her 31th birthday, at which time she decides to quit investing. During this six year period, the $7,200 ($100 per month for six years) she has contributed to her investment fund has grown in value to $10,470. For the next 34 years, until she retires at age 65, she will simply let this money compound without adding another dollar to it.

Her friend Sally, who has been delaying her plans to contribute toward her retirement fund, finally decides she is able to begin her investment program on her 31st birthday and does so by contributing $100 per month to her own IRA. Sally continues to invest $100 per month ($1,200 per year) for the next 34 years until she reaches her

65th birthday (the last time she contributes before retiring). The following table shows the costly effects of procrastination:

Age	Martha	Sally	Age	Martha	Sally
25	$1200	$0	46	$0	$1200
26	$1200	$0	47	$0	$1200
27	$1200	$0	48	$0	$1200
28	$1200	$0	49	$0	$1200
29	$1200	$0	50	$0	$1200
30	$1200	$0	51	$0	$1200
31	$0	$1200	52	$0	$1200
32	$0	$1200	53	$0	$1200
33	$0	$1200	54	$0	$1200
34	$0	$1200	55	$0	$1200
35	$0	$1200	56	$0	$1200
36	$0	$1200	57	$0	$1200
37	$0	$1200	58	$0	$1200
38	$0	$1200	59	$0	$1200
39	$0	$1200	60	$0	$1200
40	$0	$1200	61	$0	$1200
41	$0	$1200	62	$0	$1200
42	$0	$1200	63	$0	$1200
43	$0	$1200	64	$0	$1200
44	$0	$1200	65	$0	$1200
45	$0	$1200	Total Value:	$606,800	$569,600

Figure 9.4 The Costly Effect of Procrastination.

A delay of only six years in Sally's investment program has prevented her from catching up to Martha during the remaining 34 years of her working career. Although Martha quit contributing on her 31st birthday, Sally began at age 31 and continued her contributions until her 65th birthday. Additionally, Sally's total outlay of cash for this 34-year period was $40,800, compared with Martha's six-year outlay of only $7,200. The truly amazing part of this illustration is that with only six years of contributions, Martha ended up with $606,800 at retirement, while Sally contributed more than five times that amount over three decades and ended up with $569,600, or $37,200 less than Martha at retirement. If nothing else, the power of compound interest should convince everyone to start their investment program early in life. Even if it is too late to recapture your early investment years, you can still begin a retirement fund now. Don't let even more procrastination rob you of the remaining years you have left to invest.

For those who are curious to find out what Martha could have accumulated in her retirement fund had she continued to invest $100 per month (within the same parameter as Sally), the answer is found by adding Martha's $606,800 to Sally's $569,600 for a total of

$1,176,400. Furthermore, had Martha continued with her contributions and received an average annual return of three percent higher, or 15% return, her $100 per month investment would have grown to nearly $3,101,000 during the 40-year period. Additionally, if her monthly contribution reflected 10% of her gross income, then her annual earnings would equal $12,000 per year for the entire 40-year period. Although this is a ridiculously low salary in the United States, and unlikely to remain unchanged over the entire 40-year time period, it is used here to demonstrate the power of investing small sums of money over long periods of time to achieve wealth.

If Martha had contributed to her retirement fund during the entire 40-year period of her working career, she would have retired as a millionaire. Furthermore, if her $100 per month contribution reflected less than 10% of her gross annual income, then she not only undernourished her financial freedom fund, but she became wealthy by investing less than 10% of her gross income. Also, her total outlay of cash during this 40-year period would have been $48,000 ($1,200 x 40), which equals about 4% of the total accumulated amount of $1,176,400. In other words, in this example, Martha's millionaire status would have resulted from 4% capital and 96% compound interest. The immense power of compound interest should never be underestimated when investing a portion of your earnings every month in your attempt to become financially independent.

Excuses for Not Investing Now

Since before the Great Crash of 1929, there have been any number of excuses for why people should not invest their money in the stock market. Every year there is some major crisis or special concern which could possibly lead to another major crisis, which has prevented people from investing in the stock market and participating in the ever-expanding profitability of many national economies within the international economic system. The fear of a downturn in the economy, usually brought about by some major crisis, is what keeps most people from investing in the stock market.

For example, since 1950, exactly half-way through this turbulent century, there have been any number of major worldwide crises. Of course, each crisis passed as a new one took its place, which caused even further procrastination as people expected this new crisis to lead to still greater economic instability and political turmoil. Meanwhile, although there have been fluctuations in the price of every company's stock, the stock market as a whole, as represented by the Dow Jones Industrial Average (and to a certain degree by other indexes), has steadily maintained its upward trend during the latter half of this century.

The following outline, representing 45 years from 1950 to 1995, shows some of the world's significant economic and political highlights. When reviewing this list of successive crises, we should ask ourselves if any of them would have prevented us from investing in the stock market at that time. Looking back, they should have been opportunities for buying into the market, not situations for keeping us out of the market. They are as follows:

1950 - Korean War begins; Dow Jones Industrial Average (DJIA) reaches 235.

1951 - Six European countries form a competitive coal and steel coalition; China enters Korean War.

1952 - USA explodes world's first H-bomb; Dwight Eisenhower elected president.

1953 - USSR explodes H-bomb; Korean War ends in stalemate.

1954 - French defeated in Indo-China; Vietnam divided.

1955 - Warsaw Pact formed by Eastern-bloc countries.

1956 - Suez Canal crisis; USSR invades Hungary.

1957 - USSR launches Sputnik satellite.

1958 - USA launches Explorer satellite; DJIA tops 500-market considered "too high."

1959 - Castro seizes power in Cuba; Alaska and Hawaii join the USA as 49th and 50th States.

1960 - Decolonization of Africa begins; John F. Kennedy elected president.

1961 - Berlin Wall erected; Bay of Pigs invasion of Cuba; first Soviet manned space flight.

1962 - Cuban missile crisis; Telstar, first communications satellite, launched.

1963 - Nuclear Test Ban Treaty signed; President Kennedy assassinated.

1964 - China explodes nuclear bomb; Lyndon Johnson elected president; War on poverty begins in USA.

1965 - War in Vietnam escalates as USA sends in regular ground troops.

1966 - France leaves NATO; China's Cultural Revolution begins.

1967 - Six-Day War in the Middle East; Suez canal closed.

1968 - USSR invades Czechoslovakia; Martin Luther King and Robert Kennedy assassinated; Richard Nixon elected president.

1969 - USA astronauts walk on the moon; Sino-Soviet border clashes.

1970 - President of Chile assassinated; USA resumes bombing of North Vietnam.

1971 - USA currency devalued due to massive deficit; Pakistan civil war; China joins UN.

1972 - Nixon visits China; Equal Rights Amendment passes; DJIA tops 1000-market "too high."

1973 - USA withdraws from Vietnam; Yom Kippur War in Middle East; Arab oil embargo and worldwide energy crisis.

1974 - Nixon resigns after Watergate scandal; OPEC quadruples oil prices; USA goes into recession.

1975 - Suez canal reopens; Communist victory in Vietnam and Cambodia.

1976 - USA and USSR sign disarmament treaty; Jimmy Carter elected president.

1977 - Egyptian president Sadat visits Israel; saccharin (a sugar substitute) considered cancer-causing.

1978 - Middle East peace plan signed between Israel and Egypt at Camp David; Iranian Islamic Revolution begins.

1979 - USSR invades Afghanistan; Shah deposed in Iran; American hostages held in Tehran; interest rates soar in USA.

1980 - Iran-Iraq war begins; gold reaches a high of $850 per ounce; high inflation in USA; Ronald Reagan elected president.

1981 - Sadat of Egypt killed; attempted assassinations of President Reagan and Pope John Paul II.

1982 - Falkland Islands war between England and Argentina; worldwide oil glut; Israel invades Lebanon; largest tax-hike in U.S. history.

1983 - USA invades Grenada; drought in Africa triggers massive famine; hundreds of U.S. marines killed in Beirut car bombing.

1984 - Prime Minister Indira Gandhi of India assassinated.

1985 - Gorbachev assumes power in USSR; DJIA tops 1500–market "too high."

1986 - Chernobyl nuclear accident in USSR; USA bombs Libya; space shuttle Challenger explodes; record deficit in USA.

1987 - DJIA tops 2000 & 2500 before crashing 22% in one day; Iran-Contra scandal in USA.

1988 - Cease-fire in Iran-Iraq war; USSR withdraws from Afghanistan; George Bush elected president.

1989 - USA invades Panama; Communist governments collapse in Eastern Europe; Berlin Wall falls.

1990 - Iraq invades Kuwait; Nelson Mandela of South Africa freed; recession in USA.

1991 - Persian Gulf war against Iraq; break-up of the Soviet Union; DJIA tops 3000–market "too high."

1992 - Gorbachev ousted by Boris Yeltsin in Russia; Bill Clinton elected president.

1993 - North American Free Trade Agreement ratified; DJIA tops 3500–market "too high."

1994 - DJIA reaches 3978 in February before falling 10%; Mandela elected president of South Africa.

1995 - Earthquake destroys much of Kobe, Japan; U.S. dollar slips 10% to 20% against world currencies; DJIA tops 4700 in July, market considered "too high."

Although the world has experienced a number of political and economic crises during the latter half of this century, not one has caused a permanent loss of money, if the money was kept in the market for the next couple of years after the crisis. Even after the crash of 1987, when the DJIA dropped 500 points in one day, no money was lost if it remained invested for the next two years. All temporary losses were regained.

For example, in 1987, the DJIA reached an all-time high of 2722 on August 25th, then fell 984 points to 1738 by October 19th. However, over the next two years, the DJIA reached another all-time high on October 9, 1989, when it closed at 2791. In 1991, the DJIA topped the 3000 mark and almost gained another 800 points by December 1993. In the first part of 1994, the DJIA was less than 22 points away from breaking through the 4000 barrier, before falling 10% in a long-expected correction. A year later, the DJIA broke through the 4000 barrier, and in early July 1995, the DJIA surpassed the 4700 mark. Some analysts predict the DJIA could be around the 6000 point level by the end of this decade, while more aggressive analysts say it will reach 7000 by early 1998.

Year	1981	1982	1983	1984	1985	1986	1987
High	1024	1070	1287	1286	1553	1955	2722
Low	824	776	1027	1086	1184	1502	1738

Year	1988	1989	1990	1991	1992	1993	1994
High	2183	2791	2999	3168	3413	3794	3978
Low	1879	2144	2365	2470	3136	3241	3593

Figure 9.5 Yearly High and Low of the DJIA from 1981 to 1994.

Each One Teach One

In 1969, during the mid-point of the Nine Year Plan, the Universal House of Justice, in trying to encourage the establishment of individual teaching goals, recommended using the "admonition of 'Abdu'l-Bahá to lead at least one new soul to the Faith each year." [1] This admonition pertained to a certain teaching method referred to by 'Abdu'l-Bahá when He said: *"If by this method every one of the friends of God were to try to lead one soul to the right path, the number of the believers would be doubled every year."* [2] This is an example of using the power of compounding to greatly increase the number of new believers entering the Faith every year.

In December 1975, during the second year of the Five Year Plan, the National Spiritual Assembly of the United States published a pamphlet entitled "Each One Teach One: A Call to the Individual Believer." The purpose of this booklet was "to help the individual Bahá'í understand the importance of teaching the Faith to at least one person each year and to assist him in his teaching efforts." [3] For

1. *Messages from the Universal House of Justice: 1968–1973*, p. 35.
2. *Bahá'í World Faith*, p. 386.
3. *The American Bahá'í*, December 1975, p. 14.

the first time in American Bahá'í history, the National Spiritual Assembly officially applied the concept of compounding to teaching the Faith. This method became the rallying cry for the American friends in teaching the masses and was supported by teaching conferences held in New York, California, and Illinois in 1976. Upon the success of this project rested the hopes of the Universal House of Justice in initiating the long sought after "entry by troops" on the American continent.[1]

Think for a moment of the powerful effects that can result from compounding our efforts. It is theoretically possible for a small number of dedicated believers to achieve complete victory (i.e., for every man, woman, and child on the planet to become a Bahá'í) in only 20 years using this method. In 1994, there were approximately five million Bahá'ís throughout the world. From this population of Bahá'ís, if a core of only 10,000 committed believers were organized to focus their entire attention on bringing into the Faith just one new person every year, and those whom they brought into the Faith also did the same (taught and enrolled one new person in the Faith every year), and this continued for the next 20 years, then every person on the planet would be a Bahá'í by the year 2014 (assuming a world population of over 10 billion within the next 20 years). By doubling its number every year, it is mathematically possible for this core group of 10,000 Bahá'ís to transform the world in just 20 years.

An interesting detail, which is pivotal to understanding the concept of compounding, is that the greatest effects of these doubling efforts would not be noticeable until near the end of the time period calculated for its completion. For instance, it would take 17 years for this 10,000-member core group to equal 12.5% of the world's population by doubling itself every year; in the 18th year, 25% of the world's population would be Bahá'í; and after 19 years, one-half of the world's population would be enrolled in the Faith. However, at the end of the last year, the other half of the world's population would be enrolled. Theoretically, this is how compounding works. The mathematical sequence of compounding starts out slowly, then gradually accelerates to higher speeds after a certain period of time, until finally, carried by the weight of its own momentum, it assumes astronomical proportions.

It should be noted that the limited success of America's Each One Teach One program was due to a lack of sustainable enthusiasm and consistency in carrying out the project. This lack of focus fragmented the compounding effects of the teaching campaign, which made it almost impossible to reach fruition. The same thing can happen to our financial freedom fund if we fail to be consistent in our contributions or cease to focus our thoughts on achieving the goal of financial independence. Once we have compound interest working for us, we should never allow it to leave our employ.

---

1. *The American Bahá'í*, December 1975, p. 14.

Chapter 10

The Dazzling Prospects of Self-Transformation

For as he thinketh in his heart, so is he.—Proverbs 23:7

Prosperity, both in the form of material wealth and affluence, and as reflected in spiritual blessings and happiness, is the ultimate goal of self-transformation. However, the realization of this personal change cannot be achieved without the inculcation of a positive mental attitude reflected through a positive self-image. If we are unable to view ourselves as persons who are richly created by a bountiful God, then we will have little hope of attaining the spiritual qualities and material benefits provided by a loving Creator. 'Abdu'l-Bahá indicated that He desired a special kind of distinction for Bahá'ís, not the common types of recognition prevalent in the world today, such as scientific, commercial, industrial, and even financial, which, though important for civilization's advancement, will eventually pass away and be no more. 'Abdu'l-Bahá hoped that the servants of God would achieve *"spiritual distinction"* and become known *"for justice and fidelity, for firmness and steadfastness, for philanthropic deeds and service to the human world...for removing prejudices and promoting international peace."* [1] By not undergoing self-transformation we may be undermining the foundation of our spiritual progress in the subsequent worlds of God: *"True loss is for him whose days have been spent in utter ignorance of his self."* [2] Therefore, the

---

1. *The Promulgation of Universal Peace*, p. 190.
2. *Tablets of Bahá'u'lláh*, p. 156.

discovery of one's self through transformation is necessary for acquiring spiritual attributes and qualities.

The Treasury of the Mind

All material wealth is created from the mind of man. It is the human mind, through the application of its creative powers, that has allowed man to discover and utilize the laws of God to his advantage. All of man's inventions, discoveries, and knowledge emanate from his mind. The power of the human spirit is the mind of man: *"Mind is the perfection of spirit and is its essential quality, as the sun's rays are the essential necessity of the sun."* [1] The human mind is the *"supreme emblem of God"* which *"stands first in the order of creation and first in rank, taking precedence over all created things."* [2] Science is essentially the discovery and culmination of man's knowledge of the laws of God. Reduced to its simplest form, we might say that God created the universe, but man discovers it. 'Abdu'l-Bahá, when describing this *"supreme endowment"* of man, said: *"Consider carefully: all these highly varied phenomena, these concepts, this knowledge, these technical procedures and philosophical systems, these sciences, arts, industries and inventions— all are emanations of the human mind."* [3] The mind of man is on an eternal journey of discovery and exploration of God's creation.

In discovering the laws of the physical creation, especially since the inception of the Bahá'í Faith, human advancement has been propelled to previously unimaginable heights. Human beings have changed the physical face of the planet through the very weight of their civilization; they have revolutionized technology through the use of inventions, including, more recently, advancements in computers, artificial intelligence, telecommunications, and travel; they have achieved monumental breakthroughs in medicine, including the eradication of many virulent diseases which have plagued human society for centuries. Ultimately, it is the quickening power released by the revelations of the Manifestations of God that is responsible for this advancement:

> Is not the object of every Revelation to effect a transformation in the whole character of mankind, a transformation that shall manifest itself, both outwardly and inwardly, that shall affect both its inner life and external conditions? For if the character of mankind be not changed, the futility of God's universal Manifestations would be apparent. [4]

---

1. 'Abdu'l-Bahá, *Some Answered Questions*, chapter 55, p. 209.
2. 'Abdu'l-Bahá, *The Secret of Divine Civilization*, p. 1.
3. Ibid., p. 2.
4. Bahá'u'lláh, *Kitáb-i-Íqán*, pp. 240-241.

It is an irony of history that mankind has accomplished all of these material changes while still in a state of disunity and mortal conflict with his fellow human beings. So far, we can only imagine the heights of man's advancement were he to become completely unified and totally at peace with all the members of his species.

Through the blessings and power of God, man is no longer chained to the limitations of his material being. The advent of the Revelation of Bahá'u'lláh has signalized the *"coming of age of the entire human race."* [1] By letting loose the floodgates containing the mind's creativity, man has the potential to transform both his physical and spiritual reality into that of a noble being and the planet into a garden of paradise. It is now materially possible for the life of man to be occupied in pursuing the mysteries of God's creation. The future path of human nobility stretches out ahead; the way is now open for man's complete refinement through the transforming power of thought emanating from the treasury of his mind.

The Secret of Success

The secret of all success, be it financial or spiritual, can be stated in one all-powerful word—SERVICE. Service is the starting point of all success and all success is dependent upon service. The priceless opportunity for acquiring wealth comes from our ability to provide service to others. Through such actions, we automatically increase our potential for receiving wealth, since *every* seed of service we sow will multiply and come back to us in great abundance. It is the giving of service before receiving a reward which reinforces one of life's most basic laws—the impossibility of receiving something for nothing. Money is a commodity which can easily be lost in the real world, but since the mind is the true treasury of our wealth, and the quality of our service is one of the surest means for acquiring this wealth, we can replace nearly any amount of money with additional or renewed service. There are virtually no limits to the number of ways for acquiring wealth when it comes to providing useful or needed service to others. However, in order to pursue the highest standard necessary for success in any field of endeavor, you must be willing to apply your MATE to the problem. MATE is an acronym standing for Mind, Ability, Talent, and Enthusiasm. It is a measure of the quality of your service.

Mind: The mind is the vehicle through which you can simultaneously imagine your future prospects while ignoring your present or temporary setbacks. It enables you to visualize a better future. By having faith and a strong belief in your ability to achieve ultimate victory, you can remain positive through the many difficulties which may plague you along the way to success. Those who view difficulties

1. Shoghi Effendi, *The World Order of Bahá'u'lláh*, p. 163.

as stepping stones to success cannot be easily defeated and will eventually achieve victory; while those who view difficulties as a sign to give up pursuing their goals will fail and rarely achieve anything worthwhile in life. How your mind perceives problems and difficulties will determine the extent of your success. Therefore, by firmly establishing in your mind a vision of success, and through unwavering persistence in reaching your goal, you will ultimately be able to achieve victory.

Ability: In the same way that coal is transformed into diamond, you can vastly increase your compensation through your ability to provide a needed service to others. Your willingness and ability to provide such service will determine the value of your reward. In terms of defining the relationship between money and service, Earl Nightingale, a noted speaker and motivator of human ability, once said: "The amount of money you receive will always be in direct proportion to the demand for what you do, your ability to do it, and the difficulty of replacing you." [1] If the skills for the service you provide are in high demand, and you are one of the top experts in your field, and these skills have taken many years to learn, either through education or experience, you will be highly compensated for your ability to perform such a service. This is the outcome of the law of compensation as it applies to your skills and abilities. Your career goals should incorporate the potential for providing such excellence of service to others.

Talent: Natural talent is the innate ability you have for performing a task without the benefit of learning or training. Beyond your natural ability lies what you can achieve through experience and education, which demands perfection before it can continue to be called talent. Talent is generally 90% preparation and 10% performance. The person who is identified as being talented makes performing a task seem simple because of all the preparatory work involved in perfecting his skills. The skills you possess are simply the perfection of your talent through practice and training. The more education or experience you have in doing a particular job, and the more in demand it is, the greater will be the amount of your compensation.

Enthusiasm: The value of enthusiasm in your quest for success is incalculable, since it provides a zest for living which finds expression in being excited about whatever you do in life. Enthusiasm is the amount of energy and effort you are willing to put into your service. Your motivation is the primary source of your enthusiasm, but it is your enthusiasm which will determine whether or not you go the extra mile in providing quality service for others. Those who lack enthusiasm, who go about their work in a half-hearted manner, or who are bored by their work, will rarely achieve success. If you cannot get excited about what you are doing in life, it might be better for you

---

1. Kimbro and Hill, *Think and Grow Rich: A Black Choice*, p. 264.

not to do it. Either get excited about your present job, or find something you enjoy doing and stick with it. When you do get excited about your work, you will always succeed at it. The key to getting the most out of any job is determining the amount of enthusiasm you are willing to put into it.

Furthermore, by studying the lives of successful people and deepening on the moral values proclaimed by the Manifestations of God, we can begin the process of self-transformation leading to ultimate success. A good example of this process is found in the life of William Sutherland Maxwell, the architect of the Shrine of the Báb, who was not only spiritually blessed by being offered this unique task, but was also afforded the rarest of all professional opportunities when he had "the chance to pour out the mature wine of his talent and life-long experience in a worthy expression of his genius"[1] by designing a befitting sepulcher for the Báb on "the very spot which Bahá'u'lláh Himself had designated...and had blessed with His presence."[2] The style of the Shrine of the Báb, as conceived by Mr. Maxwell, and approved by Shoghi Effendi, is both majestic and beautiful. Similar to that of Mr. Maxwell, our service should be an example of our genius or uniqueness.

Shoghi Effendi, in a letter written on his behalf, defined the meaning of successful service by saying: "What the Cause needs is...ardent and self-sacrificing servants and not lukewarm followers who are ready to reap the fruit but unwilling to take a part in winning that victory."[3] The type of people who are needed in the Cause of God are "not passive admirers but active servants of the New World Order,"[4] who are ready to sacrifice everything in the path of God. It is this condition of service, as first exemplified by the Dawn-Breakers, which is the true measure of love and willingness to succeed.

Keys to Successful Living

The measure of success in life is not simply a matter of how much money we possess; it is also based on the spiritual quality of our lives and the extent of our peace of mind. The truly fortunate are those who have developed a sense of purpose in life and are actively pursuing it. In an open and free society, where there is a choice in the type of work an individual does, that person is the arbiter of his own destiny. In reality, you are the president and chief executive of your own company, which, of course, is your own self. Your success or failure is dependent upon what you do or accomplish in life and is measured by the degree of your self-satisfaction.

1. Rúhíyyih Rabbaní, *The Priceless Pearl*, p. 239.
2. Shoghi Effendi, *Guidance for Today and Tomorrow*, p. 50.
3. *Lights of Guidance*, no. 384, p. 113.
4. Ibid.

By measuring your success in life in the same way that a company evaluates its ability to stay in business, you are able to gauge the extent of your progress. Reduced to its simplest form, there are four basic areas in which every company should excel, regardless of its size and complexity, if it intends to remain in business. These areas include sound financial and accounting practices, successful production and marketing strategies, efficient customer sales and services, and on-going research and development. When applied to the personal realm, these four areas can be viewed as keys to successful living and include the following: money management, creative output, service orientation, and progressive perfection. You can achieve greater success, become more fruitful, and produce better results when you implement these basic strategies in your personal life.

Money Management: Sound money management shows respect for the source of your livelihood as well as for the ultimate Source of all wealth. This is critical to financial survival, since true prosperity eschews wastefulness and selfishness and rejects hoarding and miserliness. In the same way that every company should employ sound financial and accounting practices, your personal financial survival depends on your ability to manage your cash flow. The successful handling of money is more a matter of learning skills and employing common sense than of innate knowledge. By exerting enough effort to acquire sufficient financial education and investment information, nearly everyone can become a successful manager of his or her own money.

Creative Output: Creative output is your ability to produce worthwhile endeavors in life. The factors comprising your creative output are a combination of the unique skills, talents, energy, and knowledge that you can offer to the world of humanity. Just as you should strive for both inner and outer perfection, you should also utilize your God-given abilities to create a more productive civilization, especially since you were born to fulfill some special purpose in life. Your unique gifts and creative abilities are the keys to developing your own personal success story and they should be used to the fullest extent possible.

Service Orientation: As previously stated, the attainment of all wealth and prosperity is based on service. Without sincerely serving others, people will not be motivated to spend their money on your products or services. By providing a needed service or product for others, you can tremendously increase your prospects for prosperity. As in the material world, the spiritual world also attracts wealth to those who provide service to others. For example, Shoghi Effendi, in a letter written on his behalf, defined the value of service in the Faith by saying:

> There is nothing that brings success in the Faith like service. Service is the magnet which draws the Divine Confirmations. Thus, when a person is active, they are blessed by the Holy

Spirit. When they are inactive, the Holy Spirit cannot find a repository in their being, and thus they are deprived of its healing and quickening rays.[1]

It is one of the laws of God that before a person can receive anything, he must first give something. By giving something first, we make room for receiving something else. For example, you cannot get heat from a stove without first providing it with fuel. This is the only way a stove will produce warmth. Thus, we should always strive to be of service to others, since service is the fuel of success and a magnet attracting heavenly blessings and material benefits.

Progressive Perfection: The last area for creating a successful business, ongoing research and development, permits a company to stay viable by allowing it to discover ways for improving its service or product line. In any endeavor to improve ourselves, we should strive for perfection through training and education. Professionals recognize the critical need to keep abreast of the latest information and advances in their chosen field. Even the worker who is not a college graduate must undergo periodic training if he wishes to maintain a certain level of competence in his work, and more so if he desires to advance in his specialty. Therefore, similar to the reasons Bahá'u'lláh has given for daily deepening in the Writings, the acquisition of knowledge is critical to our progressive perfection and should be a permanent part of our career development.

Finding One's Purpose in Life

Without a purpose in life, a person has no motivation or reason for existing. Whether or not your purpose is consciously or unconsciously chosen, hidden away or clearly manifested, the pattern of your life is a direct expression of your aspirations. If asked, most people probably could not give a specific reason why they get up every morning, for they have never taken the time to clearly define their purpose in life, much less establish goals for achieving that purpose. Many people have no idea why they exist; they simply plod along the highway of time, thoughtlessly using up the precious moments of their lives. Ben Franklin once said: "Lost time is never found again, and what we call time enough always proves little enough. Let us then be up and doing, and doing to a purpose." If we lack purpose, we lack having clearly defined goals.

Setting and reaching achievable goals will not only empower you to define your purpose in life, but will also help you transform yourself into better a person. By centering your life around your goals, you will be able to better reflect your unique talents and abilities and give yourself an opportunity to create something worthwhile for yourself and others. Although most success is based on the progressive

1. *Lights of Guidance*, no. 405, p. 118.

realization of worthwhile and achievable goals, many people would rather complain about what they lack than create the necessary tools for attaining what they want in life. Your first priority should be to discover your own personal aspirations, then make plans for achieving them. They may include a wide range of desires for improving yourself and your abilities, including advancements in spiritual development, social refinement, business savvy, monetary gain, physical stamina, intellectual acuity, or anything else that will increase your feelings of success and self-worth. The attainment of all wishes begins with the formation of goals.

Goals are as integral to the success of the Bahá'í Faith as the sun is to life on this planet. Since the time of the Báb, when He first addressed and gave specific instructions to the Letters of the Living, the Cause of God has been directed by various goals and plans. Bahá'u'lláh established specific guidelines for establishing the Most Great Peace, not only for application by His immediate followers, but by the kings and rulers of the earth, and by future generations of mankind. In His *Will and Testament*, 'Abdu'l-Bahá outlined the goals which needed immediate attention to further the Plan of God; and in His *Tablets of the Divine Plan*, He established specific objectives for bringing about the progressive spiritualization of the planet. Shoghi Effendi initiated various worldwide teaching plans of certain duration with specific goals, the last of which was the Ten Year Crusade. And finally, the Universal House of Justice has guided the Bahá'í community through a series of additional teaching plans, which contain specific goals and objectives for spreading and consolidating the Bahá'í Faith throughout the world. The entire history of the Bahá'í Faith has been marked by a series of achievable goals and objectives intended to bring about the spiritual regeneration of humankind.

Individual Bahá'ís should also establish personal goals for directing their own lives. For example, everyone must work, but the teachings do not tell each individual specifically what kind of work he or she should do in order to earn a livelihood. 'Abdu'l-Bahá does provide general guidance when He says that we should study those arts and sciences which are beneficial to society, but He does not name all of these sciences. He simply says that *"the individual should, prior to engaging in the study of any subject, ask himself what its uses are and what fruit and result will derive from it. If it is a useful branch of knowledge, that is, if society will gain important benefits from it, then he should certainly pursue it with all his heart."*[1] Since your career decision is based on many factors—your interests, where you can be of greatest service to the Cause, the amount of education or technical skill required to do the job, the availability of such work, the amount of money it pays, and many

---

1. *The Secret of Divine Civilization*, p. 106.

other factors—it is important to develop your primary interests early in life. As you discover your God-given talents, it is critical to establish appropriate goals. By pursuing your specific interests, you will eventually find personal happiness and fulfillment in your chosen profession.

Reaching Achievable Goals

All goals contain four components which are necessary for achieving success, otherwise they are usually unreachable or unworthy. These four elements have been identified by many experts as being critical for achieving goals and are as follows: goals must be meaningful, they must be exceptional, they must be measurable, and they must be manageable. Each of these elements is briefly described below.

#1 Goals Must be Meaningful: A meaningful goal is a worthwhile goal. Since you will be spending a major portion of your life accomplishing your goals, they must be worthy enough for you to devote the precious days of your life to them. First, determine how much of your life you are willing to give in order to achieve your dreams. Once you have a clear idea of the extent of sacrifice needed to fulfill your goals, then you can judge their true value. This is essential for determining the meaningfulness of a goal. Many situations in life require you to weigh each thing and choose that which you desire most. Only you can judge the ultimate merit and worthiness of your particular choice.

#2 Goals Must be Exceptional: An exceptional goal is a richly-rewarding goal. It has the power to transform your life and the lives of others. A goal should convey a sense of wonderment and far-reaching possibilities. Set your standards high. Your plans for the future should require excellence and involve effort. For example, one of the primary goals of the Bahá'í Faith, and "the pivot round which all the teachings of Bahá'u'lláh revolve," [1] is the establishment of the oneness of mankind. Not only is this an exceptional goal for Bahá'ís, but one which has staggering implications for changing the structure of human society. Achieving such a goal will not be easy, especially since it will be impossible to realize without a spiritual transformation first taking place in the hearts of men; but it is a worthwhile goal, especially for the sake of those future generations as yet unborn. Our personal goals should also convey a similar sense of exceptional vision and worthiness. Life will usually give us what we desire, so we should not sell ourselves short with uninspiring goals.

#3 Goals Must be Measurable: A measurable goal is a specific goal, one which is precisely defined. Any goal which is not specific is not measurable, and therefore, is basically useless. Ambiguity in goal setting is fatal to its success. The more specific you can be in

1. Shoghi Effendi, *The World Order of Bahá'u'lláh*, p. 42.

defining your goal, the more real and attainable it will be to you. Exactness is a virtue when it comes to goal setting.

#4 Goals Must be Manageable: A manageable goal is a responsible goal. It can be regulated and controlled. Whenever you exercise control over the resources needed to reach your goal, you can better manage the outcome of that goal. By regulating and maximizing both your material and spiritual resources, you are better able to minimize any wastefulness associated with achieving your goal. Prayer is also a valuable form of management when it comes to attaining goals. Supplication to God when you decide to succeed at something attracts divine confirmation, partially because your ability and capacity will increase with prayer.[1] Other resources include the time, effort, and money you expend on your goal. Any area of your goal which is not under your direct control has the potential of derailing your progress. Thus, it is important to manage every possible resource that can have an effect on the outcome of your ultimate objective.

Not surprisingly, Shoghi Effendi has used similar criteria to set goals for the Bahá'í community. When explaining the parameters under which the Bahá'í administrative order operates, he said: "We should be elastic in details and rigid in principles."[2] What matters most in goal setting is adhering to the fundamentals. Being elastic in detail, as it applies to goal setting, means that you are open to the many opportunities which will inevitably manifest themselves in the pursuit of your fundamental purpose. This elasticity has nothing to do with changing your basic aim, though it may expand the parameters of your original objective.

In addition to learning these four components for achieving success, following the seven steps described below will also prove useful to setting and achieving realizable goals. Although you may see variations of these steps in other books on success, the differences are minor.

Goals

1. Be Very Specific
2. Establish Deadline
3. Write Out Your Goal
4. Develop a Plan of Action
5. Decide on the Price to Pay
6. Recite Your Goal Twice Daily
7. Review Goal on a Regular Basis

Figure 10.1 Seven Steps for Measuring Goals.

Step One: Be specific. Every goal must be stated in precise terms, since no goal can be measured if it is ambiguous. The more specific you are in defining and detailing the parameters of your goal,

1. 'Abdu'l-Bahá in *Bahá'u'lláh and the New Era* by J. E. Esslemont, p. 93.
2. *Dawn of a New Day*, p. 123.

the clearer it will be in your mind, and the greater its chance of being achieved. Concerning this subject, 'Abdu'l-Bahá says: *"So long as the thoughts of an individual are scattered he will achieve no results, but if his thinking be concentrated on a single point wonderful will be the fruits thereof. Thus is it necessary to focus one's thinking on a single point so that it will become an effective force."* [1]

Step Two: Have a precise time frame or deadline in which to achieve your goal. Designating a specific amount of time for accomplishing your stated purpose will not only give your goal structure, but will also provide a tool for measuring your progress. By giving yourself a deadline for completing your goal, you will eliminate any temptation to procrastinate or prolong its accomplishment. Also, having a deadline is a good way to generate enough enthusiasm to ensure its completion.

Step Three: Write out your goal. The act of writing out your goal makes it seem more official and provides it with a certain kind of power. A written goal transforms itself from a vague notion to a concrete reality; from a theoretical possibility to a realistic probability. Putting your goal in writing will also enable you to identify any of its inherent ambiguities, to refine it, and to think more clearly about its realization.

Step Four: Develop a specific plan of action for achieving your goal. In other words, outline the steps and time frames needed for reaching your goal. Consider your plan of action as your personal road map to success. In order to reach your goal, you must know where you are, what your next checkpoint along the way is, how long it will take you to get there, to what extent you have traveled so far (the effort expended), and if you are ahead or behind schedule in reaching your desired destination. Without a specific plan for monitoring the course of your actions, not only will it be difficult to keep going in the right direction, but your desires will probably never become a reality. Every captain who travels from safe harbor to safe harbor knows how to plan his route; otherwise, his ship would end up a derelict on some rocky shoreline.

Step Five: Decide the price you are willing to pay to achieve your goal. This involves a willingness to sacrifice. Sacrifice is giving up something of value in order to obtain something considered to be of greater value. The price is usually measured by the amount of energy, time, and money needed to achieve it. For example, if your goal is to get a university degree, you must apply and get accepted at a university (having already pre-qualified by passing certain academic tests), put in the required number of years by attending and passing an appropriate number of classes, and pay a certain amount of money *before* you can receive your diploma. Being close or almost

1. *Selections from the Writings of 'Abdu'l-Bahá*, no. 73, pp.110-111.

there does not qualify, since you have not yet paid the full price for achieving a university degree. When the price is paid in full, you will then receive your reward, but not beforehand. Although we may learn from our experiences, reaching our goals is an all-or-nothing proposition—we either reach them or we don't. Therefore, we should be very careful in choosing a goal, since the price required for success may be more than we are willing to pay for its achievement.

Step Six: Think about reaching your goal every day. Each morning and evening, repeat your written goal aloud to yourself in private. In between the times you recite your written goal, let your mind think about it throughout the day. This activity will not only allow you to keep your goal at the forefront of your thoughts, but will also inspire your subconscious mind to discover ways for achieving your goal. This principle works in the same way as the recitation of the sacred Writings. By keeping the counsels of Bahá'u'lláh foremost in your thoughts, your subconscious mind will seek ways to put them into practice. Goal achievement, like spiritual regeneration, is a daily endeavor requiring constant effort. Faithfully reciting your goal two or three times a day will assist you to reach it.

Step Seven: Review your progress regularly, if not on a daily basis, then at least on a weekly one. Being on the right track is essential for success. Getting off-track is a sure sign of failure. Adjusting to any new situation which may occasionally occur in pursuit of your goal (being elastic in detail) is vital for evaluating your progress. In the same way that we should bring ourselves to account each day when reviewing our spiritual progress, we can also apply this technique to evaluating the progress of our personal goals. Similar to a ship's navigator, when we constantly check and realign our position relative to our starting point and ultimate destination, we can be sure of reaching our destination safely.

Once you have applied these seven steps to your own situation and mastered the four components of goal setting, you will be well on your way to achieving success in whatever endeavor you choose. Progress requires daily effort, and just as the completion of a successful teaching plan is nothing more than a string of successful years, and a successful year nothing more than a string of successful months, and a successful month nothing more than a string of successful days, and so on until the goal is reached, your own plans should be viewed in a similar light. By working on your goal each day, you will accomplish a lot over the long run, but if you neglect to work on your goals, you will be in the same situation next year as you are in now. The point is to advance daily, since the seemingly imperceptible progress of each day will look like great leaps forward over the years.

The establishment of the Most Great Peace is considered by many Bahá'ís as the ultimate strategic goal of the Bahá'í Faith. Many phases, eras, and periods of development must be achieved before this supreme goal can be realized. Every plan from the Universal House of Justice is one step closer to the establishment of this supreme purpose. Our personal vision of the future should encompass this highest goal of mankind, especially since we are able to play a part, however small, in its successful realization.

The next section of this book will provide specific methods for becoming wealthy and an opportunity to work on your goal for achieving financial independence. All that has been said so far is merely preparation for taking action to achieve financial success. Nothing succeeds like success, so begin today, whatever your level of preparedness. Only through action will you discover what great results you can attain.

Part Three
Practical Principles

Chapter 11

Paying Yourself First

In the house of the wise are stores of choice food and oil, but a foolish man devours all he has.—Proverbs 21:20

The first principle of prosperity is to save and invest at least 10% from every source of revenue you receive. Ten percent is the minimum, but you will reach your goal of financial independence much faster if you can save more than 10%. This principle is known as "paying yourself first" and is the seed money for virtually all wealth. So important is this first principle to your financial well-being that if you fail to apply it throughout your working career, it is almost impossible for you to achieve wealth of any kind. A Chinese proverb says that every journey, no matter how distant, begins with the first step. The initial step on your journey to financial independence begins with paying yourself first. This chapter will show that paying yourself first is the surest method for turning the minor money of today's paycheck into the major wealth of tomorrow's financial freedom fund.

Your First Priority

Just as there are laws of God which govern all created things, there are also laws or principles which govern the building of wealth. Even as far back as biblical times it was recognized as unwise and irresponsible to consume everything one earned or received. If you have not succeeded in acquiring sufficient wealth over the years, it is because you have either never learned these principles or else you do not observe them. The first principle governing the acquisition of wealth, and the heart and soul of *every* investment program, is to save and invest a certain portion of *every* dollar you earn. Paying yourself first means that whenever you receive any money, you must take a certain portion or percentage of it and invest it for your future *before* you spend it on anything else. Taking this first step on the road to achieving wealth is absolutely essential for becoming financially independent. Conversely, without taking this first step, your chances for building wealth and reaching a state of financial freedom are remote. Therefore, your first priority, without exception, must be to pay yourself first.

Most competent financial planners recommend saving a minimum of 10% of your gross earnings. There is a logical reason for using your gross earnings, instead of your net or take-home pay, as the basis for determining your investment savings. Your gross income represents your true earnings, while your net pay is simply what remains of your spendable income after deductions, such as federal, state and local taxes, unemployment insurance, loan repayments, union dues, pension plan savings, and anything else that is taken out of your paycheck before you see it.

After the government and others have taken this money from your gross earnings, the amount remaining is what you take home every payday. But the dwindling of your paycheck does not stop here. Once you deposit your net pay in the bank, you then have other bills which need to be paid: the rent or mortgage, utilities, food, clothing, credit cards, and all of your other expenses. It is only after everyone else gets paid that most people think about keeping something for themselves. However, there is usually nothing left at the end of the month to contribute to an investment program. Even if there were some money remaining after paying your bills, there is normally a strong urge to spend this remaining money on yourself or on various things you feel you need, everything except saving and investing for a future retirement income when it will be needed most.

This concept of being the last in line to receive a portion of your own paycheck can be called "paying yourself last." However, since there never seems to be any money left at the end of the month for investing, using this method is both unrealistic and inappropriate for achieving financial independence. This condition of having more month than money left at the end of each paycheck is one which is caused by the cycle of consumerism and leads to potential poverty. Without planning and investing for a prosperous future, we tend to squander our resources on spontaneous and wasteful spending in the present. Furthermore, the advent of each payday again triggers the cycle of paying everyone else first before paying yourself. It is this cycle which causes the onslaught of retirement poverty and must be broken.

In order to begin your wealth acquisition plan, you must reverse what you have been doing (paying yourself last) and start doing its opposite (paying yourself first). By using the same method as employed by the government for deducting money from your paycheck, you can always ensure that there will be enough money to invest for your future. Notice that the government *always* makes sure they receive their portion (taxes) *before* your money even gets to you. It bases the taxes you owe on your gross income, not your net income. It is your gross income, minus exemptions, on which your share of taxes is based. By employing this same method to your own financial freedom program, you will be equally as successful as the government in getting money from your paycheck.

Also, the government is absolutely consistent in keeping a portion of everything you earn. It does not matter how much or how little you make during any given month, the government still receives its share of your paycheck. No matter how tough times are or how many emergencies occur within any month, the government will always take its portion. There are no exceptions to this policy.

In order to be as successful as the government in retaining a portion of your income, you must apply this same technique to yourself. Starting with your next paycheck, tax yourself 10% of your gross income and establish your financial freedom fund. In other words, pay yourself first. Even if you do not as yet understand anything about investing, you can always put this money into a temporary bank savings account until such time as you know how to invest it. The important thing is to get started immediately with paying yourself first. Only then can you begin the process of building a future income for yourself and your family.

In order to maintain the necessary self-discipline required for paying yourself first, you must be firm and strict on this point. Nothing should interfere with your efforts. Every other financial obligation you have is secondary to paying yourself first. Every other bill gets paid *after* you have paid yourself. The obligation you have to your future and your family should not be minimized, forgotten, or take second place. Therefore, at all times and under all conditions, pay yourself first. If you want this technique to work, be totally committed to its success.

An Unselfish Concept

Paying yourself first demonstrates a willingness to improve your financial well-being in order to ultimately better serve the Faith. It has nothing to do with the negative side of the ego or any of the other selfish tendencies that have been discouraged by Bahá'u'lláh. Paying yourself first is simply the most practical method available for most people to fulfill 'Abdu'l-Bahá's criteria for becoming wealthy: *"Wealth is praiseworthy in the highest degree, if it is acquired by an individual's own efforts"* and *"wealth*

is most commendable, provided the entire population is wealthy." [1]
This second condition represents the collective goal of wealth acquisition, that is, raising the standard of living of the whole community.

By investing a portion of all we earn, we are striving to play our part in raising the standard of living of the entire population. When this occurs, civilization in general, and our families in particular, advance in prosperity. Fortunately, nearly everyone who receives money can improve their material well-being by following this simple principle of paying yourself first. Through regular and consistent endeavor, most people can appreciably improve their financial condition. The more people embark on the road to becoming wealthy, the more the entire population will advance in that direction.

As a dedicated Bahá'í, you may feel a certain sense of discomfort in paying yourself before contributing to the Bahá'í Fund. This is understandable and even laudable, but it should not prevent you from applying this principle to your plan for financial independence. Since the underlying theme of paying yourself first reinforces the concept of regularly contributing to the Bahá'í Fund, the solution is really very simple: Every payday concurrently write two checks—one to the Bahá'í Fund and one to your financial freedom fund. This collateral action will not only secure your own financial well-being, but regularly support the lifeblood of the Cause of God. Furthermore, this method of regularly contributing to the Fund each payday has the added advantage of ensuring that your contributions to the Fund are not dependent upon your attendance at Feast. Many of us have fallen into the habit of using the Nineteen Day Feast as a convenient vehicle for making our contributions to the Bahá'í Fund, but by applying the pay yourself first method to the Fund, our contributions will be made whether or not we are able to attend the Feast during any given month.

Irrespective of the amount you have decided to contribute to the Bahá'í Fund, it is important to maintain the 10% minimum to your financial freedom fund. If you feel the necessity of increasing your contributions to the Bahá'í Fund, then you should search for ways to sacrifice *without* touching the contributions destined for your financial freedom fund. You may decide to cut down on any number of other pleasures or expenses which drain the financial resources of the other 90% of your income, but do not reduce or suspend your 10% contributions to your future retirement fund. If you do, you will defeat the purpose for its existence.

The Seed Money of Wealth

The money you set aside for paying yourself first is the seed money for producing a rich harvest during your golden years. Those

---

1. *The Secret of Divine Civilization,* p. 24.

who are willing to consistently save and invest at least 10% of their earnings throughout their lifetime create a rich and abundant estate for their future needs. And the greater the percentage of your income you can earmark for investing, the faster your estate will grow. The money you invest earns additional money, and its earnings produce even more money, and so on, until eventually your small sum swells into a vast reservoir of wealth for use during your non-earning years.

The process of building wealth during your lifetime can be compared with the life of a fruit-bearing tree. When you plant seeds in the ground, they are usually tiny, seemingly lifeless, and do not appear to have the capacity to become large trees. How small are orange and apple seeds, yet look at the capacity contained within each one of them. All they need is a chance to grow in good soil, with a little water and warm sunlight, in order to provide you with an abundant and continuous source of food for the rest of your life. This is one of the basic laws of nature. The same concept applies to the growth of money and the acquisition of wealth. You must plant your seed money now if you intend to reap the future rewards of financial prosperity. Similar to the seeds of an apple or orange tree, the 10% savings or seed money you withhold now from your paycheck doesn't look like much, certainly not the foundation for financial independence, but with a little nurturing (consistency) in good soil (sound investment vehicles) these seeds will eventually grow (through compound interest) into fruit-bearing trees (your financial freedom fund) with an abundance of fruit (lots of cash). Becoming wealthy by following this money management principle requires even less effort than that of a fruit farmer and his orchard.

Any one of us can become a financial farmer if we learn the basic principles governing wealth and its growth. It is an amazing revelation to discover that although people earn different incomes, all seem to be equally broke. When considering the state of your current income, it is important to understand a very subtle, but crucial point: what you do with what you earn is more important than how much you earn. In other words, it's not what you earn that counts, it's what you keep. This fact should demonstrate that your ultimate wealth is not based on the amount of income you currently earn, but on the amount of income you actually retain and invest. Acquiring tomorrow's retirement income is a deliberate act of saving and investing a certain portion of your present-day earnings.

'Abdu'l-Bahá recommended saving for retirement. When commenting on the subject of capital and labor, He said that management should provide sufficient benefits for those workers who, because of old age, become feeble or helpless and can no longer support themselves; but, if this is not possible, then *"wages should be high enough to satisfy the workmen with the amount they receive so that they may themselves be able to put a little aside for days of want and helplessness* [and] *will no longer be submitted to the worst privations at the end of their life."* [1] Since most company pension plans are usually insufficient for providing a comfortable retirement, it is wise to save and invest a portion of your wages for your future retirement income in order to avoid the severe privations spoken of by 'Abdu'l-Bahá.

Another reason favoring financial independence is biological in nature. As you age, your body becomes less reliable and does not function as well, and your ability to endure the stress and strain of doing without certain material conveniences begins to diminish. If you are also burdened with the worry and trauma of financial uncertainty, then you could suffer further physical deterioration, which could pull you farther down the path of aging and financial instability. The cure for this malaise is to begin your financial freedom fund immediately by investing at least 10% of your current earnings. After a few years of continuously contributing to your financial freedom fund, you will be surprised at how much better you feel as your investments begin to multiply and the burden of financial stress is lessened.

Furthermore, once your investments produce a satisfactory income to meet your daily needs, your labor will no longer be required for sustaining your livelihood. At that point, you will be financially independent and can pursue whatever activities your investment income will allow. On the other hand, if you have no substantial income from your investments, then you will be relegated to a lifestyle commensurate with whatever the government, your former company, or some charity is able to give you. Therefore, it is critical to build the foundation of your wealth with your current income.

An additional benefit of financial stability is that it can give us renewed confidence and allow us to be more creative in our field of service or work. The greater our financial independence, the greater our personal freedom; and the greater our personal freedom, the more opportunities we will have for doing whatever we enjoy most, including teaching the Faith and participating in its activities. When we manifest the positive attitudes associated with being created rich, our confidence and potency in performing our work substantially increases, since financial independence not only improves our working ability, but may also lead to job security. It is an unwritten rule of business ethics that employers would rather retain financially successful employees than employees who are impoverished, living from paycheck to paycheck. One reason is that financially successful employees are more conscientious of the bottom line and are therefore more likely to manifest these qualities at work.

We will earn only a limited amount of money during our lifetimes, and no matter what that monetary figure is, ethically we should

---

1. *Some Answered Questions*, chapter 78, p. 275.

only spend that amount and no more. The same limitation applies to what we have available to invest during our lifetimes. If we have not developed the habit of regularly saving a portion of our earnings, then we are losing an invaluable source of income—we are not planting seeds for our future orchard of fruit-bearing trees. The younger you are when you begin investing for your future, the more you will have when that future arrives. The longer you wait, the more money you must invest to reach a comparable goal. However, because time is of the essence, there will come a point when it will be too late for you to achieve your goal. Since wealth is not made instantly, but needs time to grow, we should not delay but start now to plant the seeds of our future financial independence.

The Law of Tenfold Return

This chapter would not be complete without mentioning the law of tenfold return and the role it plays in achieving financial prosperity. The law of tenfold return is an ancient law of God which simply promises to return to the donor ten times the value of his donation. It is a promise that one's contributions, if given in a spirit of service and detachment, will be blessed, and, by some means or other, returned in multiples of ten. 'Abdu'l-Bahá has said: *"In brief, O ye friends of God, rest assured that in place of this contribution, your commerce, your agriculture and industries shall be blessed many times."* [1] In another place, 'Abdu'l-Bahá specifically mentions a tenfold return as the reward for being generous: *"Whosoever comes with one good act, God will give him tenfold. There is no doubt that the living Lord shall assist and confirm the generous soul."* [2] Likewise, we may not see the immediate benefits of paying ourselves first, but the rich reward for our current sacrifices will be certain in the end. The same principle is applicable to many areas of spiritual responsibility, such as daily prayer, reading the Writings twice a day, teaching the Cause, regularly attending Bahá'í feasts and holy days, and so forth.

Our faith, in terms of receiving a tenfold return, is continually being tested by the principle of giving. Faith is the key to the realization of every goal and the secret of most success, so have faith in your endeavors, whether in fulfilling your obligations as a spiritual being or in becoming financially independent. And if you cannot find faith in yourself, at least have faith in these principles, for they are guaranteed not to fail.

---

1. In *Lights of Guidance*, no. 840, p. 250.
2. Ibid., no. 836, p. 249.

Chapter 12

Controlling Your Expenditures

The rich ruleth over the poor, and the borrower is servant to the lender.—Proverbs 22:7

The second principle of prosperity is the controlling of expenditures by curbing wasteful spending and trimming excessive consumption. This will redirect your cash flow away from squandering to investing. It is an important aspect of personal financial streamlining and is partially accomplished through the use of a cash flow management system, otherwise known as budgeting your income. Its most important feature is freedom from debt, especially credit card and other consumer-related debt. Concerning thriftiness and the control of one's expenditures, 'Abdu'l-Bahá said: *"Economy is the foundation of human prosperity. The spendthrift is always in trouble. Prodigality on the part of any person is an unpardonable sin."* [1]

Freedom From Indebtedness

All debt is a form of financial slavery. Being in debt is like being in financial bondage—you are shackled by its repayment. The repayment of debt is a spiritual obligation from which you will never be free until the liability is satisfied. Every borrower is a slave to his lender, and as long as you are not free from indebtedness, you are not free at all. Most consumer debt results from a lack of self-discipline and not having a plan for reaching financial independence.

---

1. In *Bahá'u'lláh and the New Era*, by J. E. Esslemont, p. 102.

So harmful is debt to our financial well-being that Shoghi Effendi "more than once refused to permit an individual to make the pilgrimage who he knew was in debt, saying he must first pay his debts." [1] The Guardian advised against indebtedness as a means for supporting the lifeblood of the Cause. The reason is quite profound and should always be considered whenever we are tempted to go into debt for any reason. When asked if Bahá'ís should incur debts for the purpose of contributing to the Fund, the Guardian responded through a letter written on his behalf, which states:

Even though Shoghi Effendi would urge every believer to sacrifice as much as possible for the sake of contributing towards the fund...yet he would discourage the friends to incur debts for that purpose. We are asked to give what we have, not what we do not possess, especially if such an act causes suffering to others. [2]

Since we are not asked to give what we do not possess, conversely, how can we go into debt to possess that which we do not own? All indebtedness is really just a promise to pay for a product or service. Every time you borrow money to buy something via a credit card and do not pay for it before incurring a monthly interest charge, you possess something you do not own. The individual or business which loans you this money is trusting that you will repay it. By borrowing money on your credit card, you are allowing someone else, in this case the bank or a credit card company, to pay for your possession without having earned enough money to pay for it yourself. Although such a promise binds you with a legal and moral obligation to repay your debt, this debt is an additional financial burden on your family for which you and they are ultimately responsible.

Most consumer indebtedness is a condition which causes suffering to families, since it is an acute form of financial bondage. The elimination of this unnecessary burden usually causes happiness in the family, since it diminishes a family's financial stress level. A rise in the level of a family's financial well-being is in direct proportion to a decrease in the level of its debt. A major part of controlling your expenditures is complete freedom from the burden of all debt, especially consumer related debt. So important is this condition of being debt-free, that Bahá'u'lláh has said that the *"settlement of debts is a most important command set forth in the Book. Well is it with him who ascendeth unto God, without any obligations to Huqúqu'lláh and to His servants."* [3] The repayment of debt is such a weighty spiritual obligation that it even takes precedence over the payment of Huqúqu'lláh upon the death of the believer.

---

1. Rúhíyyih Rabbaní, *The Priceless Pearl*, p. 131.
2. *Lights of Guidance*, no. 842, p. 250.
3. *Huqúqu'lláh: The Right of God*, no. 22, p. 7.

Not only do most people consume, squander, or spend everything they earn, but they frequently go beyond this by incurring debts to satisfy their indulgences. No matter how much money a person earns, it seems that his necessary expenses will usually equal, and in some cases exceed, his income. The best way to get out of this trap is by controlling your expenditures through self-discipline and being committed to a plan for financial freedom.

When you have a clear understanding of the difference between your most cherished desires (what you want most in life) and your casual wishes (those spur-of-the-moment impulses), you are more able to discipline yourself to invest for the realization of those dreams, instead of squandering your money on some passing trifle. Knowing your limits and being prepared to live within its bounds are two conditions for remaining free from debt. By referring daily to your written financial freedom goal and understanding that any major purchase which does not further this goal is money wasted, you will have a good chance of reaching financial independence. We should fine tune our desires to reflect exactly what we want in life and discard all other impulses. This is an important key to controlling our expenditures.

A good example of controlling the expenses of the Bahá'í Fund is found in the building of the first African House of Worship in Uganda and the development of the Bahá'í World Centre properties in Israel. When building the first Temple on the African continent, Shoghi Effendi urged the responsible national spiritual assembly to carefully control and monitor its expenditures. To demonstrate the importance of this point, the Guardian described how indispensable it was for him to control and supervise the Fund's expenditures in building and developing the Bahá'í World Centre properties in Haifa and Bahjí. As all who have visited the Bahá'í properties in the Holy Land can acclaim, it was Shoghi Effendi's attention to detail which made the completion of such a vast and monumental project possible.

> It is only through a wise economy, the elimination of nonessentials, concentration on essentials and a careful supervision, that the Guardian himself has been able to build the Shrine and the International Archives at the World Centre, and surround the Holy Places here by what appear in the eyes of the public to be lavish gardens, but are in reality the result of rigorous and economical planning.[1]

If, through attention to detail and economical planning, it was possible to control the expenditures of a major project like the one at the Bahá'í World Centre, then it should be a relatively simple matter to control our own expenses, which merely represent a financial project on an individual or family scale. The need for employing a wise

---

1. *Bahá'í Funds: Contributions and Administration*, p. 14.

economy in administering personal finances should be apparent to anyone desiring to consolidate their limited resources.

Avoiding Consumer Debt

Since most debt results from a lack of self-discipline in the use of money, there is a need to implement various techniques to limit the spending of money by prioritizing its allocation. This topic was partially covered in Chapter 7; however, since this is such an important subject for controlling one's expenditures, the specifics for avoiding consumer debt will be presented in this section.

Consumer debt occurs when you borrow money on credit and make periodic payments to finance your purchases. It also occurs when you use credit cards to pay for goods and services for which you have no immediate means to repay. You may have good intentions of repaying this money, but at the moment of purchase, you are not able to pay cash for these goods or services. This action may ensnare you into having to make long-term debt payments—a situation which runs counter to achieving financial independence. Long-term consumer debt can be defined as making monthly payments beyond six months duration.

The typical American consumer has an average of 12 credit cards and, in the aggregate, Americans were $250 billion in credit card debt in 1993. The result of such indebtedness not only places you in a vicious circle of living from paycheck to paycheck, but is a foolish way to indulge yourself, since it may lead to financial enslavement for many years or even decades to come. When the burden of consumer debt becomes overwhelming, it can lead to personal bankruptcy and all of the other horrors associated with this debilitating condition.

Credit cards are financial time-bombs by which many people, unwittingly or not, kill their future prosperity. Therefore, restraint should be employed whenever you are tempted to use a credit card. Credit is never free. You pay dearly for your indebtedness. Credit cards not only promote wasteful spending, but they also encourage people to lose caution in managing their money. Credit cards give a false sense of security while destroying your self-discipline by making you feel that it is okay to postpone your payment until a later date. A misused credit card is a guaranteed way to dig your economic grave. Always evaluate credit in terms of how it contributes to your future financial well-being.

Whenever you desire to buy anything, use the following criteria when considering its cost: first, its price in terms of how many hours of work it took you to earn this money; second, its ability to give you a high level of pleasure at that price; and third, its utilitarian or long-term value in relation to its cost. If the object you desire is within the limits of this value criteria, then you should go ahead and purchase it (with cash). However, if the item under question does not meet this criteria, then do not purchase it. Shoghi Effendi did not purchase anything that he considered too expensive or did not meet with his strict sense of economy:

> More than once, when a beautiful ornament for the Shrines, Archives, or gardens was too expensive, and the seller could not or would not meet the Guardian's price, he would not buy it even though he wanted it and had the money. He just considered it wrong and would not do it.[1]

This story of how the Guardian operated to keep his expenses (and those of the Faith) under control should inspire us to follow the same example whenever we desire to purchase something. Even if we have the money to purchase something and the reason for wanting to buy it is a good one, we should still apply the three value criteria when evaluating its cost. And we should never purchase anything with a credit card (except in an emergency situation) unless we can pay for it in full when the bill comes due at the end of the month.

Another method for controlling expenditures is in the purchase of quality items. It is always better to pay more for something which lasts, than to pay less for something which keeps needing repair or replacement. Items which are constantly discarded may also overburden the environment. Furthermore, since substandard products require constant replacement, they usually end up costing more money in the long run than quality products. There really is no substitute for quality. The amount of immediate savings cannot relieve the frustration associated with the constant breakdown of inferior products; nor should the higher costs and ultimate savings associated with quality products be considered extravagant. Quality is an ingredient which should find expression in everything we do.

Methods for Eliminating Debt

There are various methods for eliminating most debt, especially consumer debt, from your life forever. Since the condition of indebtedness is similar to that of being an addict, only in this case our addiction is to materialism, the elimination of debt may require some stringent recovery techniques for it to be effective. Keep in mind that the deeper you are in debt, the stronger the medicine needed to ensure your recovery.

The very first step in controlling your expenses and preventing your debts from rising is to stop borrowing money! This obvious solution may sound too simple, but it is the best way to begin the process of curing the addiction to indebtedness. Each day, with great conviction, just say "NO" to debt and refuse to borrow any money on

---

1. Rúhíyyih Rabbaní, *The Priceless Pearl*, p. 131.

that day. Every day, without fail, promise yourself not to borrow any more money today. Don't worry about borrowing money tomorrow. Your immediate concern is to not borrow any money today. By taking it one step at a time, you can eliminate the burden of new debt. If you can do this each and every day of your life, or until you are cured of your indebtedness, you will be completely free from the painful addiction of debt.

The next step is to put yourself on a strict diet of reducing, and finally eliminating, your remaining debts. There is a simple technique which many financial experts use to accomplish this feat. First, write down your debts (to whom you owe money), the total amount still owed (your balance), the expected monthly payment amount, and the interest rate on this debt. Next, put these figures in ascending order by the amount of money left to pay on them with the smallest balance first, then the next largest, and so on, until the last figure listed is the largest loan balance outstanding (this is usually your mortgage balance). At the moment, don't worry about the interest rate. Your main concern is the balance left to pay. Your list might look something like this:

Item	Total Balance	Monthly Payments	Interest Rate
Visa	$400	$55	18%
Dept Store	$500	$60	18%
Mastercard	$900	$90	18%
Pesonal Loan	$1,000	$50	15%
Car Repair	$1,500	$85	18%
Student Loan	$5,000	$150	6%
Auto Loan	$7,000	$300	13%
Mortgage	$90,000	$950	8%
	$106,300	$1,740	

Figure 12.1 Paying Off Your Outstanding Debt.

To start, make an extra payment or earn extra cash through a garage sale (or from some other source) and add this money to the regular payment on your first debt (in this example, your Visa credit card). If possible, continue making extra payments until this first debt is completely paid off. If this is not possible, make whatever additional payments you can until it is satisfied. Once the Visa debt is completely paid, you then take the $55 you were paying to Visa and apply it as an extra payment to reduce your department store debt. Next, after the department store debt is paid in full, take this extra $115 per month ($55 that you were paying to Visa and $60 previously paid to the department store) and use it, in addition to your regular payment of $90, and pay your Mastercard bill. Provided you do not incur any new debts, this method should quickly eliminate all of your consumer or personal loan debts, until all you have left to pay is your mortgage debt.

By using the method in the above illustration, nearly half your debts would be paid in one year, and in about three years, you would have nothing but your mortgage obligation left to pay. This system works well if you incur no further debts and combine the amounts from the previously paid balances to reduce the balance of the next debt on your list. You can save years of payments and thousands of dollars in interest charges by reducing your debts with this method. Eliminating a credit card debt on which you are paying 18% interest is equivalent to earning 18% on your money, since that is how much you are saving by not paying this high interest.

When you utilize the above system to eliminate your consumer debts (except for the mortgage) within a relatively short period of time, it will free up a large amount of money which can be used for your future investments. According to the above illustration, this freed up money would amount to $790 per month. By not incurring any new debt, which primarily helps large financial institutions become rich on the interest you pay them, you can now take this extra $790 per month and apply it to your own plan for financial independence. In ten years, $790 per month would grow to $181,700 (at 12% average annual return); in twenty years, it would grow to $781,500; and if you continue to invest this money (which would normally go to repay your debts) for another two years, it would grow into a million dollars. It does not take much imagination to see the amazing results which can occur when you redirect your money away from consumer debt and toward investing.

While using the above system to eliminate your debts, you can also use a second method to further reduce your interest rate charges on your credit card accounts. This procedure requires you to replace your high-interest credit cards with low-interest ones. Most banks issuing Mastercard and Visa cards charge their customers about 18% interest or higher. However, there are a number of other banks which charge a much lower interest rate, even down to a few points above the prime rate.[1] If you could reduce by half the interest rate charges on your credit card debts, more of your monthly payments would go to reduce the principal and less of it would go to pay the interest. Were this to occur, the amount of time needed to eliminate your debts would be substantially reduced. Many popular personal financial magazines provide the addresses and telephone numbers of those banks which issue low-interest credit cards. Once you receive your new low-interest credit card, use it only to get a cash advance to pay-off the balance on your high-interest credit card. By using the credit card in this way, you are basically transferring your debt from a high-interest one to a low-interest one.

---

1. The prime rate, which was 6% in 1993 and rose to 9% in 1995, is what banks charge their best customers, usually Fortune 500 companies.

WARNING! Do not use these low-interest cards to incur additional debt. Their purpose should be strictly to replace high-interest debt with low-interest debt, not to increase the burden of your indebtedness. Used correctly, these low-interest credit cards can sharply reduce your interest payments and the time it takes to eliminate your remaining debt. Also, once you have received your low-interest card and transferred the balance from your high-interest card onto it, cancel the high-interest card immediately in order to avoid any temptation to incur further debt.

Finally, once you have only the mortgage left to pay (it should be the only liability on your net worth statement unless you also have investment property with an outstanding mortgage), you can reduce the number of years left to pay on it by making one extra mortgage payment per year which is entirely applied to the principal. This will reduce the remaining balance on the mortgage loan principal (possibly saving you tens of thousands of dollars in interest payments) and reduce the number of years left to pay on the loan by shortening the life of your mortgage.

These are just some of the positive benefits associated with controlling your expenditures and redirecting the outflow of your money to improve your financial well-being. The next section will discuss specific methods for avoiding the trap of easy consumer credit, and its wasted opportunities, through the establishment of a cash flow management system.

Cash Flow Management System

In order to obey the law of Huqúqu'lláh, it is important to subtract your necessary expenses before calculating what is owed to God. In its broadest sense, this procedure requires a system for determining the flow and management of your income. Such a process, called a Cash Flow Management System (CFMS), is popularly known as establishing a budget, though a CFMS is simpler to use, since its purpose is to make it easier for you to pinpoint and control the flow of your money.

A CFMS allows you to see exactly how much money comes in and where it flows out; it is considered a general budgetary device, not an exact and detailed accounting system (which may help dissuade you from abandoning it after using it for only a short period of time). Determining where your money goes should be informative, not tedious, since the main purpose for gathering this information is to identify and direct your cash flow. Another important feature of a CFMS is that it can be custom designed to fit your exact needs.

A cash flow management system basically consists of two parts: income and expenses. Expenses are further categorized as being either fixed or flexible. A fixed expense would be one that does not fluctuate over a certain period of time, usually about one year or more. Your mortgage or rental payments are usually an example of a fixed expense. Your investments should also be considered as a fixed expense, since they reflect a percentage, or a fixed dollar amount, of your annual income. Designating a certain percentage or set dollar amount for the Bahá'í Fund would also be considered a fixed expense.

Flexible expenses are those which fluctuate from month-to-month, such as food, personal items, medical bills, and utility bills, although some utility companies are now estimating a yearly use factor and billing customers based on a monthly average. Once a year the billing is adjusted according to the actual usage. This may be convenient for those who own their homes and prefer having fixed amounts to pay each month. If this is your particular situation, be sure that any underpayments accruing throughout the year are covered by sufficient monies in your emergency fund account.

Figure 12.2 below is a compact outline of the various categories in a CFMS and can be used as a guide for developing your own system. By using this form as a monthly record of your cash flow, you should have accurate information concerning your money patterns at the end of the year. This information can assist you in managing your cash flow by identifying the type and amount of your expenditures during the year.

INCOME: (List separately the monies received from the husband, wife, property rental, and any other sources. Do not include any distributions that are reinvested from your tax-deferred retirement accounts.)

EXPENSES: Outflow from the following sources or categories.

    Investments (Total should equal a minimum of 10% of your gross income.)

        Retirement (List each person and his or her accounts separately.)

        College Fund for Children (List each child and his or her accounts separately.)

    Emergency Funds

        Unexpected (This should equal 3 to 6 months of net income.)

        Expected (List each quarterly, semi-annual, or annual payment, such as all insurances and any monies for replacing material items such as furniture and automobile or money being saved to buy a house or some other large item expense.)[1]

---

1. An excellent method for acquiring sufficient money for pilgrimage to the Bahá'í holy places would be to establish a separate pilgrimage fund for yourself and

Huqúqu'lláh (Record yearly payments and keep account of what has been purified.)

Bahá'í Funds (List separately the local, national, continental, international, and arc funds.)

Mortgage or Rent (List any second mortgage as well.)

Utilities (List separately electric, water, sewer, gas, garbage, cable TV, and telephone charges, including fax and electronic mail charges as well as long distance calls if so desired.)

Food (List separate categories for grocery stores, restaurants, and business lunches.)

Clothing (List each adult and child separately; include dry cleaning expenses.)

Transportation (List separately automobile payments, oil and gas, tires and repair, taxis and public transport, and miscellaneous expenses. List any travel, including air fare, which might be for vacation.)

Medical-Health (List visits to doctor, dentist, optometrist, chiropractor, and any other health care provider separately; include a category for drugs and prescriptions not covered by insurance.)

Personal (This may be a long list which includes life insurance premiums [unless paid other than monthly], child care services, beauty and hair care, subscriptions, school supplies, tuition, child support outside the immediate household, alimony, gifts for Ayyám-i-Há or birthdays, entertainment, allowances where each person is listed separately, vacations, and any miscellaneous expenses.)

Debts (Hopefully, this will equal zero, but if not, then list separately all credit cards in order of lowest to highest balance. Begin paying off all Visa, Mastercard, Discover Card, Diner's Card, American Express, gasoline cards, department store cards, student loans, and any other loans.)

Figure 12.2 Categories of a Cash Flow Management System.

Each individual or family unit will have a different priority for determining the appropriate category and amount of expenditures within their particular CFMS. Except for what has already been said about the minimum requirements for investing in your future financial

---

your family. By contributing to this fund every month, you would be able to meet the financial responsibility of paying for this expected expense without having to go into debt. And since it takes many years from the time you apply for pilgrimage to when you actually go on pilgrimage, there is plenty of time to accumulate the necessary funds to partake of this most precious of spiritual obligations.

well-being, as well as for payments of Huqúqu'lláh and the money you want to contribute to the Bahá'í Fund, there are no set standards for how much should be designated for each category.

Another method for simplifying the use of a CFMS is to put any expenditures which normally require cash, such as personal allowances, food, and restaurant monies, into an envelope and draw on it during the month. This will allow you to physically control what you can spend during any particular month. If you run out of cash, you won't be able to spend any more money in this category until the next month; and if you have money left over, you can either add it to next month's amount or use it somewhere else (be sure you record this transaction). Once you work out the details for finding the right amount of money required for each category (this normally takes about three to four months), then it will be much easier for you to live within your means. One of the positive effects of using a cash flow management system is that it eliminates the guilt one may feel concerning money, since it validates your expenditures within each category.

If you own a computer, it will be helpful to purchase cash flow management or personal financial software which can be used to keep track of these categories and automatically do the calculations for you. Tracking this information on a computer will greatly simplify this procedure. Some software packages even include charts to help analyze the information.

Finally, since we have a limited amount of income, we need to be very judicious in designating a sum of money for each category. Although we should stay within the limits of our CFMS categories, we should not squeeze ourselves so tightly that we won't be able to enjoy life. Moderation is needed here as it is in everything else. It's okay to suffer to reach our goals, or sacrifice to get where we want to be, provided we are not miserable in the process. In living, we should always feel good about what we are doing and practice moderation whenever possible.

Chapter 13

Maximizing Your Investments

He that hath a bountiful eye shall be blessed.—Proverbs 22:9

The third principle of prosperity is to maximize your investment potential by eliminating any obstacles on the road to financial success. This may include breaking the patterns of outdated and outmoded forms of financial management and following a new paradigm of money management. It calls for no less than a total rethinking of what you may have been taught about the traditional methods of investing money as well as obtaining selected professional advice when needed. In order to maximize the growth of your money, it will be necessary to acquire some basic financial and investment knowledge and take personal responsibility for your investment decisions, since you are, or should be, the best guardian of your wealth. Whenever you are able to maximize your investments to reach their full potential, you will attain financial independence that much sooner.

Guarding Your Treasure from Loss

There is a proportional correlation between reward and risk. Generally speaking, the greater the potential reward, the greater the potential risk. Conversely, the lower the potential risk, the lower the potential reward. Balancing the reward and risk factor means applying the principle of guarding your treasure from unwarranted loss. The major point of this principle is that although your money should be able to withstand a certain degree of calculated risk, your money management philosophy needs to be tempered by common sense. Learning to protect your money from the hazards of unnecessary loss include avoiding games of chance and schemes which promise to give something for nothing. It means staying away from anything which sounds like inside information for getting rich quickly, especially if it has the slightest taint of being illegal or unethical. For all practical purposes, there is no such thing as getting something for nothing; and participating in such schemes is not worth it. There are many legitimate ways to acquire wealth without compromising your values.

Although you may be tempted to make instantaneous wealth through get-rich-quick schemes that purportedly have no possibility of failing, you should not be misled. Wealth is usually made gradually, over a period of time, through the application of self-discipline, saving a certain portion of your earnings, and utilizing the concept of compound interest. When you stop trying to get rich quickly and start applying the principles of prosperity to your life, you will be surprised at how fast you can achieve financial success. Patience, as well as having a goal for your potential wealth, is also an essential ingredient for success.

There is wisdom in the adage which says that you must first learn to secure and protect small amounts of money before you can be entrusted with the use and protection of larger sums. Inheriting a large fortune, receiving a huge windfall, or making an enormous amount of money before learning how to handle the responsibilities associated with this increased wealth can be disastrous. The shock of becoming an instant millionaire without first having to work for it can actually be harmful to your present lifestyle, your relationship with others, and your work ethic. Wealth of any kind, but especially instant wealth, can be a severe test.

Becoming rich gradually through your own efforts, without disrupting the equilibrium of your life, is beneficial to your growth and well-being. Regardless of how well you think you can handle instant wealth, there are very few people who are so detached from the world that they can maintain their equilibrium under such pressure. It is only after many years of working to build one's investments that an individual can truly be said to be prepared to handle the obligations associated with such escalating wealth.

In guarding your treasure from loss, you should also eliminate all unrealistic desires for huge profits from your investments. This includes the temptation of trying to get a speculative rate of return on your money. A relative or a friend might try to persuade you to buy into a "ground floor opportunity" which can make you rich in a very short time. Always be sensible when reviewing the specifics of any proposal where your money is at stake. Use caution, even if the person making the proposal is a fellow Bahá'í or a family member, for ignorance and greed are universally present, even among the best of us. Your guiding principle should be: "If it sounds too good to be true, it probably is."

As you can see, guarding your treasure from loss requires regular vigilance. Never lightly relinquish your money to someone else without first determining the exact nature of the risks involved. If you feel you need to get the opinion of others, including professionals, do so. If you know people who are not involved in the scheme, but have done well financially, seek their advice and weigh their opinion against the proposal. Getting a second opinion may prevent the loss of your money and the emotional suffering which could follow such a tragedy. Never allow someone to pressure you into taking action quickly. It is better to seem the idiot with your money still intact than to profess brilliance and end up with an empty purse. Above all, stick to the guaranteed but secure way of becoming financially independent. This path may take years or even decades of sacrifice and self-discipline, but, in the end, you will have a much better chance of reaching your goal.

How Money Works

One of the major problems with the current financial system is that large companies in the financial services industry, such as banks and insurance companies, complicate what should be a relatively simple business, that of personal or family finances. These large financial institutions profit greatly from this artificial complexity and from the public's general lack of knowledge of how money works. Additionally, our unwillingness to acquire enough basic and accurate financial information, as well as our wasteful spending habits and settling for substandard returns on our money, play right into the hands of these financial institutions.

Since you are the captain of your own financial ship and carry the responsibility of your investment decisions, you should know how to navigate your ship through every type of fiscal weather. Putting most of your potential retirement money into fixed-income, short-term cash instruments while still many years away from retirement is usually inappropriate for reaching financial independence. At most, these so-called "safe" investment vehicles barely keep up with inflation.

Large financial institutions such as banks, credit unions, and life insurance companies currently pay between 1% to 6% interest on the money you deposit with them. Banks and credit unions call this return "earned interest." Life insurance companies call it "cash value." Neither is a particularly healthy way of investing and can literally cost you hundreds of thousands of dollars in lost profits during your lifetime. If an interest rate is guaranteed, then you are not getting the best or even an acceptable rate of return on your money. Only by increasing the potential for profit (without undue risk) in a non-guaranteed investment vehicle (such as a stock or bond mutual fund) can you get a better return on your money.

One of the methods used by large financial institutions for making huge profits with your money is through guaranteed or fixed income vehicles where you deposit your money and receive a regular return every month. By using the money you give them (your deposits) and paying you a fee for its use (guaranteed interest rate), financial institutions are able to loan your money to others and receive a much higher rate of return; or they invest your money in the stock and bond markets and make many times more profit than they pay you for its use. Banks and insurance companies, which provide most of these guaranteed investment vehicles, make a fortune using your money in this way.

Basically, this is how it works: Banks and credit unions loan money to their clients and charge them between 8% to 21% interest for mortgages, auto loans, and credit card usage. These institutions also use customer deposits to invest in the economic system and get between 8% to 25% return on this deposited money, while paying its customers a guaranteed rate of between 1% and 6% interest. All of this is legal, but because a bank is acting as the middleman in these financial transactions, it is able to benefit greatly from taking calculated risks with your money and pocketing a large portion of the profits it generates.

For example, let's say you put $10,000 in a bank Certificate of Deposit (CD) for five years at a guaranteed interest rate of 5%. At the end of five years, the bank will return to you $12,760 (all figures rounded). Now, let's say the bank loans your $10,000 to a client through a credit card charge and calculates the repayment of this money at the standard credit card interest rate of 18% over that same five year period. The result is that at the end of five years when the last credit card payment of $253.93 per month is made, the bank will receive $15,230 from this client—$10,000 in original principal and $5,230 in interest payments. At the end of five years, the bank returns your initial investment of $10,000 plus the guaranteed compound interest of 5%, or about $2,760, for a total of $12,760. You're happy because you've gotten a 5% return with no problems, but the bank also made $2,470 gross profit by using your money at no risk to them. Of the total profit made on the use of your money, you get to keep just over half of it, while the bank keeps the rest. Think of the profits that are made when millions of people loan hundreds of billions of dollars to these banks.

Now, let's say the bank invested your $10,000 in the stock market instead and made an annual return of 12% during this period. In five years, the money would grow to $18,160. The bank would still return $12,760 to you as agreed from guaranteeing you 5% interest, but this time it would keep $5,400 as profit or nearly twice what it paid to you for using your money. In the first scenario, where the bank loaned your money, it was amortized; in the second scenario, where the bank invested your money, it was compounded. This is why there is such a difference between the profits on your $10,000 at different rates of interest. As seen in the illustration below, these figures show what occurs when loaning your money to a middleman for a guaranteed rate of return.

**$10,000 Deposited in Bank CD for 5 Years at 5% Interest
(you are guaranteed a profit of $2,760)**

Bank loans your money to credit card customer at 18%

Original Principal	$10,000
Profit Received	$5,230
Total Gains	$15,230
Guaranteed Amount	$12,760
Bank's Profit	$2,470
Bank's % of profit	47.2%

Bank invests your money in stocks at 12% average annual return

Original Principal	$10,000
Profit Received	$8,160
Total Gains	$18,160
Guaranteed Amount	$12,760
Bank's Profit	$5,400
Bank's % of Profit	66.2%

Figure 13.1 How Banks Make Large Profits with Your Money.

Due to various laws and regulations, a financial institution can use a combination of investments and loans to generate profits for itself and its customers. However, it is important for these customers to realize that they can increase their profits by investing their money directly in the economic system themselves, instead of loaning it to financial institutions for lower guaranteed returns.

The insurance companies are even less restrained from making a profit with your money. Furthermore, insurance companies are also less generous in sharing the profits generated by the use of your money. As explained in Chapter 8, if you own a whole life insurance policy, you usually have nothing, no cash value, during the first two years of the policy. Additionally, the money insurance companies charge you for this type of policy is very expensive, usually five or six times more than the actual cost of the insurance itself.

Keeping the Lion's Share of Your Profits

For decades, people have minimized the growth of their investments by putting their money in conservative bank savings accounts, certificates of deposit, and cash value life insurance policies. Whenever a financial institution can guarantee you a minimum return on your money, you are guaranteed to lose the inflation-proof value of that money, since your profits will not be able to keep up with inflation.

The following illustration may be helpful in explaining why a guaranteed fixed return is not necessarily the best vehicle for achieving financial freedom. Let's say that you deposited $100 in a bank in January 1993 and received 3% interest on it. At the end of one year your account would have grown to $103, but since you must pay taxes on the three dollars you've earned (as it would be considered taxable income), you would lose one dollar in taxes to the government (at the 33% tax bracket), thus giving you a profit of only two dollars. But wait! If inflation for the year is 4%, then you've lost an additional four dollars in purchasing power and the true value of your $102 in January 1994 is really equal to only $98. Of course, you still have $102 in cash, but because prices have gone up by 4%, you would need $104 in January 1994 to buy exactly the same amount of goods that you were able to buy in January 1993 with just $100. And since you now have only $102, you would be two dollars poorer in equivalent purchasing power, since the original value of your money has actually declined over the past year due to inflation.

Notice that even if you were not taxed on this profit and kept the entire three dollars, you would still lose one dollar in value with inflation at 4%, since it is higher than your guaranteed return of 3% from the bank. In order to keep up with inflation, your money would have to earn at least 4% in non-taxable interest or at least 6% in taxable interest. It doesn't take much figuring to realize the long-term losing proposition of keeping your money in a bank, or any savings vehicle, which is unable to keep up with the inflation rate.

If you multiply the above figures many times over many years, you can see the impact inflation has on the value of your money. Although you have acquired more money over the years, it has not been enough to stay ahead of inflation. The value of your money (or purchasing power) has actually decreased because of inflation, since the same amount of money buys less goods and services today than it did a year ago or five years ago or whenever you first started saving your money.

Simply stated, inflation is generally defined as an increase in the price of goods and services. It is usually measured on a monthly basis, but described as an annual rate each year. Inflation is the usual result of a nation's economic growth. When workers receive more money, their buying power increases. This increases the competition for a limited number of available goods and services, which then causes businesses to raise prices in order to meet the higher market demand for the limited available supply. This is how inflation operates and effects the value of our money.

The only way to prevent inflation from decreasing the value of your money is by getting a higher rate of return than the current inflation rate. It is highly unlikely for you to beat inflation by keeping your money in the guaranteed interest rate vehicles so common to financial institutions. When your rate of return does not equal or exceed the inflation rate, you lose purchasing power, since the same amount of money will buy less goods and services now than it did in the past. Even a small rate of inflation is deadly to people on fixed incomes.

Part of the solution for avoiding impoverishment at retirement is to put your money in the same investment vehicles as these large financial institutions and earn between 8% and 25% return yourself. This can best be accomplished through investing wisely in a no-load mutual fund. When you bypass the middleman and take control of your own finances, you get to keep all the profits generated by your money. In terms of wealth, all of us are self-made, but it is usually only the successful who will admit it.

The Looming Retirement Crisis

Throughout much of North America, the so-called baby boomer generation can expect, within the next 20 to 30 years, a severe financial crisis as they begin to retire from their careers.[1] This crisis will be a lack of sufficient funds at retirement to provide them with enough money to carry them tranquilly through their golden years. The cause of this crisis springs from two major, related attitudes concerning money and the future. The first is complacency; in other words, retirement is considered too far off to be of any concern at the moment; the second is the excuse that no money can be spared right now for retirement investing. Both of these outlooks signalize a looming and potentially destructive crisis for retirees in the early decades of the twenty-first century.

In North America, there are three primary sources for receiving a retirement income. The first, social security or government benefits, you have no control over, since you simply get whatever the government decides to give you or has available to give you; the second, company-sponsored pension plans, you have limited control over, since your choice of an investment vehicle is limited by what the company can offer you; and the third, privately owned and funded retirement investments, you have complete control over, since you have nearly unlimited investment choices in diversity and growth. The most common example of this third option is an Individual Retirement Account (IRA), if you are an American, or a Registered Retirement Savings Plan (RRSP), if you are a Canadian. This third option, which is open to nearly every working person, should be considered as the only sure way of receiving sufficient income during retirement. All three options are discussed below.

Social Security or Government Benefits

In 1993, the *average* monthly social security check for a retired person in the United States was $653 (or $7,836 per year); while the *maximum* monthly social security benefit for a worker retiring at age

1. *Barron's*, April 26, 1993, pp. M6-M10.

65 was only $1,128 (or $13,536 per year).[1] Alone, these benefits are totally inadequate for a comfortable retirement almost anywhere in the developed world, especially if no other income is available. Additionally, no one in the United States can assume that future retirees will have the same level of benefits as current retirees. It may get a lot worse as the number of employees supporting one retiree continues to decrease over the next several decades.

This shrinking pool of workers for supporting one retiree should be of critical concern to every potential retiree, since it adversely effects their available benefits. The U. S. Social Security Administration does not invest the money it currently receives from the present work force for their future retirement; instead, it immediately pays this money out as benefits to current retirees. In other words, all the money that is being paid-in by the present work force is not being invested for them. It is being paid-out now as benefits to those who have already retired. Given this situation, it is unwise for working people to rely solely on social security benefits for their retirement income. Social security, as well as company pension plan benefits, should be considered as *supplemental* to one's other retirement monies, not as the main source.

Company-Sponsored Pension Plans

The potential problem with company-sponsored pension plans, the second possible source of retirement money, is in their rapid change from a defined-*benefit* system to a defined-*contribution* system. In a defined-benefit system, the company promises to pay the retired employee a certain income every month upon retirement. This amount is usually based on how much the retired employee has earned and how long he has been with the company. Generally, an employee of this system knows precisely the monthly amount of his retirement benefits. Additionally, the responsibility for generating this money rests with the company and the professional money manager it retains, not with the employee.

In a defined-contribution system, such as with 401(k), profit-sharing, or other similar plans, the responsibility for generating enough income for retirement rests with the employee. This situation is a mixed blessing for employees. The problem with this approach is that the employee, who must now take responsibility for his own financial well-being (the good news), is not necessarily prepared or educated to do so (the bad news). All too often, the employee limits himself to relatively low-yielding, fixed-income investments, such as certificates of deposit (CD), guaranteed investment contracts (funded through an insurance company), or money market funds, while putting few, if any, of his dollars to work in stock or bond mutual funds. According to recent financial news programs on CNN and CNBC,[2] it was estimated

---

1. U.S. Government Statistics, Social Security Administration, 1993.
2. Broadcasted as business news items in May 1994.

in 1993 that people between the ages of 35 to 45 were acquiring assets at only one-third the rate deemed necessary to generate the minimum nest egg needed for a retirement lifestyle consistent with their present one. The future does not bode well for those people who are currently approaching their peak earning years if they are not in a position to maximize the return on their investments.

As previously stated, the major problem with the defined-contribution system is that it places the responsibility for the growth of the employee's pension on the shoulders of that same, generally uninformed employee. Ignorance or lack of prudence on the part of the employee can prevent him from getting a good return on his self-directed investment program. Also a lack of company-sponsored employee education and information sessions for making intelligent decisions regarding retirement plans and goals is partially to blame for this ignorance.

Another reason many people shy away from investing in the stock market, by not purchasing either individual stocks or stock mutual funds, is their fear of the risks involved with this type of investing. Although it has been shown that over the long term stocks tend to do better than nearly all guaranteed-interest alternatives, many people are still hesitant to invest in something they know little about or feel is too complicated. Fortunately, you do not have to be a professional investor to put your money in a good mutual fund. The next chapter will provide you with enough information to get started in an investment program today.

To complicate matters, many financial institutions play on the fears of people by over-emphasizing the risks of the stock market. They take advantage of the individual investor's lack of financial acumen and end up keeping a sizable share of the profits for themselves. Ironically, it is the stock and bond market where many of these financial institutions make large profits from investing their depositor's money.

If investing in the stock market were as risky as certain financial institutions would lead us to believe, then why do so many of them make so much money from investing in this way? It seems obvious that if financial institutions can consistently make between 8% to 25% return with your money, while only paying you a guaranteed interest rate of 1% to 6%, then your money is not really at risk. Whether you deposit your money with these financial institutions or invest it yourself, your money is still being used to generate higher profits than what you are getting at the guaranteed rate. Never forget that no matter what the interest rate a financial institution guarantees to pay you, it must earn substantially more than that amount in order to stay in business.

Privately Owned Investments

Since the trend in today's business world seems to be toward having employees take responsibility for their own financial future, it makes sense to become thoroughly informed on the various options for retirement investing. Poor employee investment knowledge and habits can short-circuit the best intentions for a comfortable retirement. People should learn how to establish and achieve specific retirement goals, both in terms of how comfortably they want to live during retirement and how much money will be needed to do so.

If necessary, it may be helpful to get a professional opinion for determining the best financial vehicle available to attain your specific investment objective. Your first inclination might be to turn to a financial broker for help; however, financial brokers are really just professional salespeople who make their living selling stocks and bonds. Fortunately, a great deal of solid professional help can be obtained in many relatively inexpensive "how to" books on financial topics. The local library is an excellent source for basic financial information and materials. Business newspapers, or the business section of your local newspaper, as well as financial magazines, also have information on financial subjects ranging from the basic to the sophisticated. It pays to take advantage of every source of knowledge and information which can assist you in gaining a better understanding of how to protect and increase your retirement money. It is much cheaper to acquire basic information about investing through books and other sources than it is to trust a salesperson to give you objective and unbiased financial advice.

Ultimately, it is your responsibility to provide a secure source of income for your future retirement. Relying solely on social security benefits or company pension plan benefits for the majority of your income needs during retirement is unwise. Too many variables are out of your control when you rely on others for your primary source of income. Too many things can happen which may cause the loss or reduction in the value of your money. If you want to have a comfortable retirement income, you have no choice but to initiate your own private investment program, since it is estimated that 60% of your monetary needs during retirement will have to come from non-government sources. The simplest way to do this is to start an IRA (for Americans) or RRSP (for Canadians) in a mutual fund with an established no-load mutual fund company. Do not depend on the government or any employee retirement benefit program for your sole and continuous source of income. Consider government and company retirement benefits as strictly supplemental to your major source of retirement income—your own self-directed program for financial freedom. As many retirees can attest, retiring without sufficient money isn't living, it's lingering.

Owning Your Own Home

An important but lesser considered avenue for maximizing your investments is home ownership. Owning your home can be a profitable investment and a source for generating income which increases your net worth. The financial reasons for owning a home usually far outweigh the reasons for not owning one. The reasons are as follows: You are the owner of your property; the mortgage payment usually does not increase; your property may increase in value, thereby building equity; you have various tax deductions which can save you money; and you can sell the property and pocket whatever profit is made on it. These are some of the financial and psychological advantages for owning your home. Eventually, the property will be yours once the bank loan is satisfied. When your loan is paid off, you will be able to live rent-free for the rest of your life. Whenever people can save 20% to 30% of their income by not paying a mortgage (or rent), their investment potential skyrockets. And when you have no mortgage payments, and your debts are non-existent or under control, you need less money to live on.

Other benefits from owning your home include the following: if you decide to go pioneering and can rent your house for at least its mortgage payment, then someone else will be paying for your asset. This technique is called "using other people's money" and is basically offering a service or an item (in this case, the rental of your home) in exchange for money. You remain the owner of your home, but someone else is paying for it. If your situation is such that you receive a positive cash flow from its lease (receive more money from the rent payment than you pay in mortgage payments), then you have another source of income for increasing your investments. Ultimately, when your house is completely paid for and you have no outstanding mortgage loan, then everything you receive from your tenants is yours to keep and invest for your future. Of course, you will still have to pay taxes, insurance, and property maintenance costs. Looked at in another way, if you are receiving $1,000 a month in rent on a home which you own free and clear, it is like getting a 12% return on $100,000 in a mutual fund; or, at the 1993 bank savings rate of about 3%, it's like receiving interest on $400,000 in your bank account. This independent source of revenue can greatly supplement your income or may even totally support you at your pioneering post.

When you begin the process of buying a home, your payments will usually be figured on a 30-year mortgage. Ask to see the payment schedule on a 15-year mortgage as well. Depending on the interest rate, down payment, and financed portion of the loan, the monthly payment difference for a 15-year mortgage is only about 30% more than that for a 30-year mortgage, but the savings in interest payments by paying off the home in half the time are enormous. It may entail a little more sacrifice and self-discipline to make larger payments for a shorter period of time, but it is generally well worth it in the long run.

In addition to the purely financial advantages of property owner-ship, the non-financial benefits of owning your home are substantial and should be considered when deciding between owning and renting. The first of these non-financial benefits is peace of mind. When you own your home, you acquire a certain sense of comfort knowing that you have a place to call your own. Owning your home can bring a sense of stability to your family situation simply by knowing that you are not beholden to someone else for your family's place of resi-dence. There is also great comfort in knowing that your children are growing up in a dwelling they can call their own. Many marital rela-tionships improve after establishing a "nest" or permanent base of operation for the family, because putting down roots reduces stress.

Other worthwhile benefits include independence from others for your shelter and having more freedom to exercise your unique personal lifestyle. Within reason, you can do whatever you like in your own home. You have the freedom to decorate it anyway you wish, to add whatever improvements you want, and to enjoy a relatively hassle-free existence. This could be important if you enjoy hosting Bahá'í functions or holding weekly firesides where many people come and go.

Whenever you pay rent, regardless of the terms of your lease, it will always expire. And when it expires, it usually costs more money to renew it. If you have not prepared for this increase in rent and decide to move, you must uproot your family and cover the up-front costs of moving into another home or to another location. Moving is not only expensive, but also causes tremendous emotional stress. Spending time looking for a new place in a new neighborhood, pack-ing and physically moving, and changing your telephone number and address is often very stressful and physically tiring. Moving away from your neighbors and friends, even if it is only across town, can cause additional feelings of loneliness. You also never fully know the risks you are taking by moving to a new place until you have been there for awhile. And when the lease is up on your new place, you will be faced with the same dilemma if the rent is again increased.

There are some disadvantages to owning a home. The property may devalue (due to neighborhood decline or a drop in the real estate market); you may take a loss if you cannot sell your home above what you owe on it; you may want to transfer or move to another location and not be able to sell your home right away,[1] and the cost factors involved in owning a home may outweigh your ability to han-dle them, in which case, it is foolish to own such expensive property. For those who are not troubled by the disadvantages of property ownership, owning your home can be an excellent source for maxi-mizing your investments, stabilizing your family life, and increasing your net worth.

---

1. When you know for certain that you will only be living in a place for a short period of time, usually no more than two or three years, it may be better to rent.

Chapter 14

The Power of Mutual Funds

Wealth maketh many friends.—Proverbs 19:4

The fourth principle of prosperity concerns the utilization of one of the most powerful vehicles for achieving financial independence for the average person: mutual funds. Although other types of investment vehicles are available, such as real estate, individual stocks and bonds, and owning your own business, this chapter will concentrate on mutual funds as being the best all-around investment vehicle for the novice investor, especially for those who do not have the time, money, or inclination to study the alternatives. However, for those who want to supplement their mutual fund portfolio with other types of investments, there is no harm in doing so, provided they understand the intricacies of these vehicles.

The Optimum Investment Vehicle

Mutual fund investing is one of the most promising and easy-to-understand methods for becoming financially independent. Investing in a mutual fund allows you to become an active participant in the global economy. Owning shares of different companies in various industries is one way that a mutual fund can maximize your profit potential and reduce your risk exposure. Mutual funds also provide an excellent and inexpensive way for the self-directed investor to control his or her financial destiny. Mutual fund investing has grown to become the most preeminent investment method in the latter part of the twentieth century and looks to be as strong in the twenty-first century.

Not only are mutual funds the vehicle of choice for the average investor who desires to increase earnings and limit risks, but mutual funds are professionally managed to achieve maximum profit at minimum risk. A stock represents ownership in a company, while the stock market measures the strength of economic growth and activity. In order to wisely invest your money in individual stocks, you would have to spend many hours researching the best ones to choose for creating a diversified portfolio. When you invest in a stock mutual fund, a professional fund manager and the manager's team of staff assistants do this work for you. Individual stocks are normally sold in blocks of 100 or 1,000 (though some discount brokerage houses will sell you partial units), so it could cost a relatively large amount of money to purchase these shares. With mutual funds, once you have opened an account (the initial deposit usually ranges between $500 to $3,000, though some funds will accept much less for starting an Individual Retirement Account), your subsequent investments can be as low as $50 in many cases. This allows you to make monthly contributions to your financial freedom fund without having to save large amounts of money over long periods of time before making additional purchases, as would be the case with individual stocks. Furthermore, unless you have large amounts of money already invested, your portfolio cannot be very diversified through owning individual stocks.

Nearly everyone can benefit from investing in mutual funds, since they are the ideal investment vehicle for the average person desiring financial freedom. Originally created for the small investor, mutual funds have now become one of the largest financial service sectors in the world. The amount of new money from investors flowing into mutual funds is staggering. In 1990, $12.6 billion poured into the mutual fund industry; in 1991, $38.3 billion; in 1992, $78.1 billion; in 1993, nearly $123.1 billion; and in 1994, over $250 billion in new money was invested in U.S. mutual funds. With this increase in the amount of money being invested in mutual funds, the number of funds has grown substantially, too. In December 1993, there were 4,538 mutual funds. By July 1995, this figure had increased 50% to 6,832 mutual funds. As you will see in the section below on mutual fund categories, nearly every type of investment is available through a mutual fund, from safe and secure money market instruments (which include bank certificates of deposit in their portfolios) to highly volatile sector funds (one of the most speculative and potentially rewarding investment mutual fund categories). Whatever your investment temperament, with over 6,800 mutual funds to choose from, one or more should be compatible with your financial disposition.

Seven Reasons to Invest in Mutual Funds

There are at least seven good reasons why mutual funds are well suited to your investment needs. Although mutual funds are primarily bought for their ability to generate profits by accumulating valuable assets inexpensively, there are other factors to consider when using mutual funds as your primary investment vehicle. These reasons include professional management of the fund, diversification in the number of companies and industries, the convenience of accurate record keeping as well as the safekeeping of certificates and money, easy marketability and liquidity of shares, a variety of investment objectives to choose from, the flexibility of transferring between funds, and reports of all transactions which are easy to read.

Professional Management

Mutual funds are managed by professionals whose only job is to insure the steady growth and development of their particular fund. This gives the small investor a great advantage in that he does not have to spend his time and money analyzing which stocks or bonds to buy, sell, or hold in his portfolio. The fund manager does this work for him. Hiring a high-caliber, professional manager is expensive, but by pooling together the money of many thousands of small investors (the basic foundation of mutual funds), you receive this professional management expertise and experience for a fraction of the cost. Moreover, such expertise would normally be unavailable to a person with less than a million dollars to invest.

Diversification

One of the most appealing features of a mutual fund is its diversity. Putting all of your money in a few stocks can be very risky. If the price of the stock drops for any reason, you could end up losing most of your money. It is also expensive to buy a block of shares, since there is usually a minimum number that must be purchased, usually costing many thousands of dollars. A mutual fund, however, reduces investment risk by spreading the fund's assets over many different companies in a variety of industries. A stock mutual fund may have between 50 and 250 companies spread throughout numerous industries in its portfolio. If the stocks of a few companies in one industry decline, it is quite possible that the stocks of other companies in a different industry will increase in price. Thus, the negative effects of a selected downturn in one industry would be off-set by the positive effects of an upturn in another industry, thereby reducing your chances of loss.

Convenience

The mutual fund company assumes the time-consuming details of buying and selling stocks and bonds, the bookkeeping and administration of such transactions, and the safekeeping of your securities and cash that you would normally have to do yourself if you held a portfolio of individual stocks and bonds. Whenever you purchase or sell shares in your account, the mutual fund company sends you a statement confirming what has occurred. Even if there are no transactions during the year, the fund will still send you periodic statements updating the activity in your portfolio. On an annual basis, you will also receive a statement listing any distributions for the year. In addition to these features, mutual fund companies offer their clients other special services, such as limited check writing (usually only for money market funds), automatic reinvestment of dividends, transfer or investment of money by telephone, and automatic withdrawal plans.

Marketability

When you invest in mutual funds, your money is liquid and always available to you, since your shares can be sold anytime you wish. Should you decide to sell your shares, the fund will buy them back at the then current net asset value (NAV). This price may be more or less than your initial investment, since the price of mutual fund shares normally fluctuate daily. However, over time and through the reinvestment of your distributions, the value of your portfolio should be higher than when you first started. Whenever you request shares to be redeemed, the law requires that a mutual fund company mail your money within seven calendar days, though most companies will mail a check by the next business day. For this reason, mutual fund investments are considered liquid assets on your net worth statement.

Variety of Objectives

A mutual fund family (a combination of many types of mutual funds within one fund company) can offer you a variety of stock, bond, and money market instruments which range from the conservative to the aggressive and include short- to long-term investment objectives. Depending on the goal of your particular investment strategy, such as accumulating sufficient monies for a college education, retirement income, or some other purpose, you have a choice as to which vehicle is best suited to your specific needs. Only mutual funds offer such a wide variety of investment vehicles and these usually meet the objectives of most investors.

Flexibility

Mutual funds allow an investor to exchange all or part of his or her assets within a family of funds for only a minimal or no exchange fee. As your investment objectives change, or market conditions fluctuate, you can transfer your money between funds by telephone or mail. Upon the receipt of your request, the exchange will be made at the end of that business day. (If you call after business hours, the transaction will occur at the end of the next business day.) A mutual fund family which offers a variety of funds can be ideal to your investment strategy. This flexibility makes it possible to transfer money between stock, bond, and money market funds within the same family of funds without any inconvenience.

Reporting

Each time you invest money or receive a dividend or capital gains distribution, you will receive a complete and detailed statement that is easy to read showing these changes. This type of reporting is one of the major benefits of investing in mutual funds. You will also receive annual reports as well as regularly updated reviews on the progress of each fund. This makes it easy to track the value of your investments and provides you with an accurate accounting for tax purposes. In addition to annual reports, each fund will send you an updated prospectus with any changes in the objectives or policy of the fund. This information is useful for comparison between other funds in the event you desire to change funds.

Finally, investing in a mutual fund is many times safer than investing directly in stocks and bonds, primarily because of the greater diversity provided by mutual funds. Also, researching the potential rewards or hazards of purchasing individual stocks and bonds is time consuming and unfeasible to the average investor. Additionally, you always pay a sales commission when buying individual stocks and bonds. Paying sales commissions will lessen the impact of any good investment strategy. However, by using one of the many hundreds of no-load mutual funds, you not only avoid a sales commission, but you take some responsibility for managing your own money. You also have the freedom to switch funds without being penalized for changing your mind.

Mutual Fund Categories

Mutual funds are divided into various categories depending on their type, fees, and objectives. Although all mutual funds charge a fee for their managerial operations, some funds also charge a sales commission. Those funds charging a sales commission are called "load" funds, while those which don't are called "no-load" funds. The pros and cons of paying a sales commission will be discussed under the heading "Load versus No-Load Funds" below.

There are basically three types of mutual funds: stock funds, bond funds, and money market funds. Stock funds can be further subdivided into regular stock funds and specialty stock funds, although this designation is basically for the convenience of the investor (to easily identify the investment objectives of a particular fund). These subcategories are not all-inclusive, since mutual funds can be divided into even more specific subheadings. But for the sake of simplicity, the subcategories listed below cover most of the various types of mutual funds.

Load Versus No-Load Funds

As stated previously, a loaded fund is one with a sales commission, whereas a no-load fund has no sales commission. Both load and no-load funds buy the same kind of company stocks on the open market, so technically there should be no difference in the performance between the two types of funds. When you pay a sales commission to buy a loaded fund, you are not paying for financial advice from a professional portfolio manager, you are simply paying a salesperson a hefty fee to sell you shares in the fund, or, if you are already sold on it, to assist you in filling out an application for that particular fund. The salesperson, sometimes called a stock broker, or representative, or financial planner, can charge up to an 8.5% sales commission on the money you are investing, though most sales commissions today range between 4% to 6%. Furthermore, every time you purchase additional shares in the fund, you also pay a sales commission on the new money you invest, even if it is set up as an automatic withdrawal from your bank account. In other words, every new dollar you invest in a loaded fund is subject to a sales commission, whether or not you even see a salesperson. With a no-load fund, you never pay a sales commission, regardless of how often you decide to purchase shares in the fund.

For example, if you invested $10,000 in a loaded fund, it would cost you $850 in sales commissions (representing an 8.5% load), which means that only $9,150 of your money would actually be invested in the fund. In a no-load fund, the entire $10,000 would be invested, since no sales commission is charged for investing in the fund. Lest you think that $850 is not much money to pay someone for selling you shares in a fund, the table below demonstrates the potential lost revenue of this commission after a certain number of years. With all things being equal between both funds, the last column in Figure 14.1 below shows the amount of money that you would lose by paying a sales commission.

Time and Percent Return	No-Load Fund No Commission $10,000	Loaded Fund at 8.5% Commission $9,150	Differece or Money Loss Over Time
20 yrs @ 12%	$108,900	$99,650	$9,250
20 yrs @ 15%	$197,150	$180,400	$16,750
30 yrs @ 12%	$359,500	$328,900	$30,600
30 yrs @ 15%	$875,400	$801,000	$74,400

Figure 14.1 The Difference in Value Between a Load and No-Load Fund.

All mutual funds, whether load or no-load, charge a management fee, usually less than one percent of the fund's assets, for managing the fund. It is from this source of revenue that the fund managers and their assistants get paid. In addition to this standard fee, some funds may charge an extra fee, called a 12b-1, which can also be used to manage and operate the fund. For a complete explanation of mutual fund fees, charges, and expenses, see the next section of this chapter.

By eliminating the middleman or salesperson in mutual fund investing, you can save yourself many thousands of dollars as well as much frustration from feeling that you are squandering your money by paying unnecessary commissions and sales charges. The only time that it would make sense to pay additional fees, whether in the form of a sales commission or some other type of charge, is if a loaded fund greatly outperformed its no-load counterpart. However, historical data shows that whenever the load or sales commission is taken into consideration in performance calculations, loaded funds generally underperform no-load funds.

Another problem with buying loaded funds is that, once the sales commission is paid, you may feel an obligation to recoup or at least amortize the cost of the purchase before moving your investment elsewhere. Because of the up-front sales commission, loaded funds have a tendency to shackle your investment flexibility. This limited flexibility factor is also prevalent with back-end loaded funds, too. No-load funds are not burdened with this problem, since they allow you the freedom to move your money elsewhere at any time without penalty.

Regular Stock Mutual Funds

Regular stock mutual funds, consisting of the most popular types of mutual funds, including long-term growth, aggressive growth, growth and income, and equity income funds, are briefly explained here.

Long-term growth funds seek capital gains, often in large-company stocks with well-established histories and good prospects for growth. They are normally called growth funds and occasionally pay cash dividends. Growth funds generally mirror market cycles and will reflect these cyclical changes in their overall performance.

Aggressive growth funds seek maximum capital gains, often in small-company, growth-oriented stocks, which tend to be more volatile to market conditions. These funds may use leverage and other speculative techniques to increase profits. Generally, these funds have the best track record in a bull or up market with the reverse being true in a bear or down market.

Growth and income funds seek to combine capital growth with dividend paying or income stock companies. They generally tend to be less volatile to market conditions, since they emphasize safety and yield over capital appreciation by investing in the stocks of well-established, seasoned, dividend paying companies. These funds are generally considered conservative stock investments.

Equity income funds seek income over capital appreciation and are a mixture of large dividend-paying stock companies, usually known as "blue chip" companies, and bond funds. They are considered the most conservative of stock funds and usually have the poorest track record of regular stock mutual funds.

Specialty Stock Mutual Funds

Specialty stock mutual funds also consist primarily of common stocks of companies, but are usually more speculative and volatile than regular stock funds, since they specialize in specific areas of the market or employ techniques not commonly used in regular stock funds. Specialty funds are known by such names as balanced, sector, emerging growth, precious metal, index, and international or global funds.

Balanced funds seek a balance between stocks and bonds with a usual combination of 60% in stocks and 40% in bonds. These funds are not as concerned with producing income as are the equity income funds. The problem with balanced funds is that they are so over-diversified that they usually perform poorly in every economic climate.

Sector funds are invested in stocks concentrated in one particular industry or in one portion of the economy. This specificity has a tendency to increase their volatility by their limitation to that particular industry or economic area. Regardless of this limitation, certain sector funds have recorded some of the largest gains in recent years. Owning more than one sector fund within a mutual fund family can help ameliorate your diversity problem and increase your potential return.

Emerging growth funds are invested in the stocks of small and newly formed companies with good future potential, but they are highly volatile and risky, since they have virtually no proven track record by which to measure their success or failure. However, these funds usually do well after a recession when the economy is starting to pick-up and grow.

Precious metal funds are highly specialized sector funds whose portfolio consists of both foreign and domestic companies involved in the mining of gold, silver, platinum, and other precious metals, as well as holding gold and silver coins and bullion. Precious metal funds offer the investor more liquidity and diversity than purchasing gold and silver directly. During high inflationary periods, or tensions and instability in the world's political situation, these funds do well. However, these conditions create high volatility and severe fluctuations in share price.

Index funds theoretically mimic the performance of Standard & Poor's 500-stock Index or one of the other indexes. This parallel performance is achieved by owning shares in all of the companies which comprise a particular index. The problem with owning these funds is that they do not always accurately reflect the index. This may be good or bad depending on how much the index fund is above or below the actual index.

International or global stock funds are invested mostly in non-U.S. companies in various markets or regions around the world. They have their own special risk factors and volatility, and have the added problem of currency exchange fluctuations. The more economically dissimilar and independent these funds are to U.S. market conditions, the greater the potential diversification of these funds. Some of the problems with investing in non-U.S. stock markets could be blatant insider trading practices (illegal manipulation of stock prices) or lax enforcement of the country's securities (stock market) laws. However, for those willing to risk their money overseas, large returns can be garnered in international stock investing.

Bond Mutual Funds

A bond investment is a loan made by an investor to a corporation or government agency for a certain period of time at a specific rate of interest, though it can go up or down in value on a daily basis due to changes in interest rates and market conditions. A bond is basically an IOU (a promissory note to repay a debt) from a company or government which promises to pay back the borrowed money. It is similar to borrowing money from a bank. However, the less credit worthy a company is, the higher the interest rate it must pay to borrow money. For this reason, some bond funds are riskier than others. A bond mutual fund offers the investor diversification and liquidity, two components not readily available when buying bonds directly from a broker. Bond mutual funds consist of six types: fixed income, tax-exempt, GNMAs, government securities, international bonds, and high yield corporate bonds.

Fixed income bond funds emphasize safety by owning long-term, high-grade investment bonds. Tax-exempt bond funds emphasize safety by owning high-grade, federally tax-exempt municipal bonds. GNMA funds are invested in mortgage-backed securities that are issued by the U.S. Government National Mortgage Association. Government security bonds seek ownership of Treasury securities (T-bills) or those of federal agencies, including GNMAs. International bond funds are primarily invested in non-U.S. bonds offered by the governments of sovereign nations. High yield corporate bond funds seek higher yields by owning mostly lower-rated corporate and municipal bonds. These bonds have a higher risk of defaulting, so they must offer higher yields to compensate for this greater risk to the shareholder. High yield bonds are commonly known as "junk bonds," since they are somewhat riskier than other bond fund investments.

Money Market Funds

Money market funds are the safest of the three types of mutual funds, since they do not fluctuate in value on a daily basis, but simply accrue interest every month. Money markets are invested in short-term, interest-bearing, and conservative money instruments, such as U.S. government securities, large certificates of deposit, bankers' acceptances, and corporate commercial paper. A money market fund can be either regular or tax-exempt. A tax-exempt money market invests in municipal bonds which, because of their tax-exempt status, pay very low interest. Tax-exempt investments should only be used by those who have exhausted all other means for sheltering or deferring taxes, such as the very rich or those in the highest tax bracket.

Understanding Mutual Fund Terminology

There are certain terms and concepts basic to mutual fund investing. The most important of these terms include net asset value (NAV); prospectus; dollar cost averaging; distributions; expenses, fees and charges; industry groups; performance; average annual return; and cumulative return. By understanding the fundamental components of mutual funds, you will be able to determine those best suited to your needs.

Net Asset Value

Net asset value (NAV) represents the current dollar value of one mutual fund share. The NAV is determined by adding up the fund's assets (the value of all shares), subtracting its liabilities (any expenses and fees), and then dividing this figure by the number of outstanding shares. The NAV is computed at the end of each business day and usually fluctuates daily, since it reflects changes in the fund's investment income, expenses, gains, losses, and distributions. Many local American newspapers list the previous day's NAV of most mutual funds in the business section, which makes it easy to see how well each fund is doing on a daily basis.

Prospectus

Each mutual fund clearly states its objective in its prospectus. The prospectus is not a piece of sales literature, but a legal description of the factual, financial, and philosophical objectives of the fund. The prospectus is the official document of a mutual fund company describing its most important features, including the operation of the fund, its money management policies, procedures for investing and withdrawing money, the fund's expense structure, and the amount charged by the fund for fees and commissions (if any). Every mutual fund issues its own prospectus. Although most of the information contained in the prospectus is required by a U.S. government agency, the Securities and Exchange Commission (SEC), which oversees and regulates stock market transactions, the SEC does not recommend or give its approval to any individual prospectus or fund. It is wise to read the information contained in the prospectus in order to obtain an accurate understanding of the fund's policy and investment parameters.

Dollar Cost Averaging

This is a technique for reducing the cost of buying shares in a mutual fund by making fixed payments at regular intervals. This method allows you to buy shares in a mutual fund gradually, thereby averaging out your costs over time. For instance, when you buy mutual fund shares on a monthly or yearly basis using fixed dollar amounts, you can buy more shares when the price of the fund is down and fewer shares when the price is up. This method tends to reduce your average cost per share as the market fluctuates over time, because you buy more shares when the fund price is low and less shares when the fund price is high. The advantage of using this system is that as the share price fluctuates over a certain purchasing period, your average *cost* per share will usually be less than the fund's average *price* per share. In other words, by using this method in a fluctuating market, you will usually make a profit by selling your shares at a price above your average cost at some future date.

For example, if you had invested the maximum amount of your allowable IRA on the last day of each year from 1986 to 1990 in Scudder's Capital Growth Fund, the following would have resulted (see Figure 14.2 below). During this period, the average price of the fund's NAV was $18.15 per share (add the share price for the five year period and divide this total by the number of years), but your average cost for each share was just $17.74 (divide the total purchase amount by the number of shares that were actually purchased), for a savings of $.41 per share. For long-term or large-scale investors, this savings can be quite substantial.

Year of Purchase	Purchase Amount	Share Price	Number of Shares
1986	$2,000	$17.17	116.482
1987	$2,000	$20.41	97.991
1988	$2,000	$16.10	124.224
1989	$2,000	$22.30	89.686
1990	$2,000	$14.77	135.410
	$10,000	$90.75	563.793

The fund's average price per share = $18.15 ($90.75 ÷ 5)
Your average cost per share = $17.74 ($10,000 ÷ 563.793
Your savings per share = $.41 ($18.15 - $17.74)

Figure 14.2 Example of Dollar Cost Averaging.

Distributions

Distributions are payments to fund shareholders, usually at the end of the calendar year, of any interest, dividends, or capital gains that have accrued during the year after expenses have been deducted. The payments may be in the form of cash or additional shares of the fund. Since U.S. tax law requires that mutual fund earnings be distributed in the calendar year in which they are earned, a mutual fund company will distribute a proportional amount of any capital gains and income earnings to the individual investor's account at least once a year. After a fund distributes its profits, the NAV will decrease by the same amount as the distribution. Although the decrease in the NAV reflects the increased number of shares being added to the fund, or the money being paid out to the shareholders, the total assets of the fund remains the same. In other words, the dollar value of your fund remains the same, but because there are more shares being added to your account, the price of each share must decrease proportionally to the value of the total number of shares being added in order to keep the total amount (or value) of your account at the same level it was before the distribution. The value of the shareholder's account will remain the same until the NAV begins to change again. Throughout the year, the money being accumulated by the fund is reflected in its daily NAV. Anytime you purchase shares of a fund, the price you pay for each share already reflects the fund's profit or loss up to that point in time. The distribution is simply the transfer of profits from the fund's account to the account of each individual shareholder on a certain day of the year.

Expenses, Fees and Charges

The expenses of all funds normally include the investment advisory fee as well as various legal and accounting fees. Some funds may also charge a 12b-1 fee, which allows the fund advisor to use the assets of the fund to pay for advertising and sales literature, prospectuses and annual reports, as well as to legally pay commissions to brokers (though this is considered part of the fund's expenses and comes from the fund's assets). In addition to these charges, a loaded fund will include even more expenses, some that you pay directly out of your pocket, such as sales commission charges (which can range up to 8.5%), the fund's brokerage costs, and redemption fee charges or back-end loads (sales commissions paid when you exit the fund before a certain time period, normally five years). The prospectus will contain a detailed accounting of all fees, charges, and expenses as well as their impact on the fund's performance. It is always a good idea to thoroughly read the prospectus before deciding to invest money in any fund.

Industry Groups

There are many advantages to investing in a mutual fund, not the least of which is that it allows the small investor to be a shareholder in a number of industries that would normally be too expensive to acquire if bought separately. Figure 14.3 below lists many of the industries which comprise mutual fund shares. It should be pointed out that some of the larger corporations and conglomerates have branches or affiliates in more than one industry. By no means is this an exhaustive list of the available industries.

Advertising	Discount & Variety	Paper
Aerospace & Defense	Electric Equipment	Pharmaceuticals
Agribusiness	Electric Utilities	Photo Equipment
Airlines	Electronics, Components	Pollution Control
Aluminum	Electronics, Instruments	Printing
Apparel Manufacturers	Financial Services	Property Liability
Appliances	Food	Publishing

Automobiles	Food chain	Real Estate(REIT)
Auto Equipment	Health Care	Restaurants
Banking	Household Furnishings	Retail Dept Store
Broadcasting	Industrial Components	School Supplies
Building Supplies	Industrial Machinery	Soap Companies
Chemicals	Life Insurance	Soft Drink
Clothing Retail	Machine Tools	Steel
Communications	Metal & Mining	Telephone Utilities
Computer Manufacturers	Multi-Industry	Tobacco
Computer Software	Natural Gas	Toys
Containers & Packaging	Office Supplies	Trucking
Cosmetics & Toiletries	Oil	Water Utilities

Figure 14.3 Various Industry Groups Common to Many Mutual Funds.

Performance

This is a measure of how well or how poorly a fund has performed over a certain period of time. Performance is one of the methods used for comparing various mutual fund returns. Since the Securities and Exchange Commission tightened and standardized the rules for advertising mutual funds, all funds must now include a one-, three-, five-, and ten-year performance record in their advertisements. It is important to remember that past performance is no guarantee of future performance, though it does indicate a fund's historical track record.

Average Annual Return

Average annual return is a complicated formula for determining a fund's growth rate for one year or for every year over a certain period of time. Average annual returns have become the benchmark for determining a fund's investment performance by many investors, though again, it only indicates what has been, not what will occur.

Cumulative Return

Cumulative return is determined by adding up the fund's rate of growth over a certain number of years. It represents the cumulative growth of a fund over a defined period of time or since inception.

The Significance of Mutual Fund Track Records

Investors are privy to a great many statistical reports and reviews concerning mutual funds. Certain independently owned companies, such as Lipper Analytical Services, Morningstar Mutual Funds, the American Association of Individual Investors, and Donoghue's Money Fund Report, compile statistical data on the performance of most mutual funds. As a whole, mutual funds are so closely watched that it is almost impossible for any fund to hide a bad performance record.

On April 10, 1995, *Barron's* published its 1995 first quarter report on the statistical and performance data of 6,448 U.S. stock and bond mutual funds, both load and no-load. Of these funds, 667

Average Annual Return (AAR)	No. of funds above the AAR	Percent of funds above AAR	No. of funds below the AAR	Percent of funds below AAR
22%+	17	1.1%	1520	98.9%
20%+	27	1.8%	1510	98.2%
18%+	50	3.3%	1487	96.7%
16%+	87	5.7%	1450	94.3%
14%+	166	10.8%	1371	89.2%
13%+	230	15.0%	1307	85.0%
12%+	318	20.7%	1219	79.3%
11%+	455	29.6%	1082	70.4%
10%+	640	41.6%	897	58.4%
9%+	824	53.6%	713	46.4%
8%+	1041	67.7%	496	32.3%
7%+	1241	80.7%	296	19.3%
6%+	1359	88.4%	178	11.6%
5%+	1409	91.7%	128	8.3%

Figure 14.4 Five Year Average Annual Return of 1,537 Mutual Funds.

had a history going back at least ten years (from April 1, 1985 to March 31, 1995); 1,537 had a five-year history (from April 1, 1990 to March 31, 1995); and 2,078 had at least a three-year history (from April 1, 1992 to March 31, 1995) from which long-term average annual returns could be determined. The remaining 4,370 mutual funds in the survey had a history of less than three years, but whose returns may have been more or less than the average annual returns of those funds included here. The results of the five-year history of 1,537 mutual funds are shown in Figure 14.4 above. All of the data reflect total returns, including dividend and share-price appreciation, but not sales charges.

The above table shows that of the 1,537 mutual funds which had a minimum five-year history, just over 20% (or 318 of them) had at least a 12% average annual return for the entire five year period; almost 30% (or 455) had at least an 11% average annual return; over one-half of these funds (824) had better than a 9% average annual return; and that nearly 92% (or 1,409) of these funds had a return averaging better than 5% per year during this period. Just over 1.5% (or 24) of these funds lost money during this five-year period. Precious metal (such as gold), Japanese-oriented, international bond, and emerging market funds made up the majority of these twenty-four losers. Conversely, the top seven funds, mostly in the technology and computer fields, did better than a 25% average annual return during this same time period (one technology fund did better than a 27% average annual return for the entire period). Gaining an average annual return of 25% means that your money doubles every 2.9 years, or that an initial investment of $10,000 would grow to $34,400 at the end of five years and would become $1,000,000 after 18.7 years.

The results from figure 14.4 above show that the vast majority (over 92%) of stock and bond mutual funds, which had at least a five-year history, had safely outperformed bank savings accounts and certificates of deposit from April 1, 1990 through March 31, 1995. As can be seen from the above data, you had more than an excellent chance (12 to 1) of getting a better than average return on your money by investing in one of these mutual funds.

Vulnerability in Mutual Fund Investing

Regardless of all the positive benefits derived from mutual fund investing, there are three major areas of vulnerability that the average investor should be aware of. These include volatility in the market place, panic selling by shareholders in a down market, and the absence of federally insured protection by the government.

Market Volatility

The first area of vulnerability in mutual fund investing concerns the general volatility and occasional wild fluctuations in the stock and bond markets. Every bull market (rising bourses or market) is followed by a bear market (declining bourses) which is then followed by another bull market, and so on. This is, and has been, the natural course of stock and bond markets for over a hundred years. Since mutual funds are composed of individual stocks and bonds, volatility in the market will also effect the value of these mutual funds. As in physics, it is an inevitable aspect of investing that whatever goes up must also come down; but unlike this law of physics, history has shown that the overall direction or trend of most financial markets has been upward. If you are a long-term investor, the odds favor you doing well over time. However, if you are only investing for the short-term in order to make a quick profit, then individual stocks, instead of mutual funds, might be more suitable as an investment vehicle.

Shareholder Instability

The second area of vulnerability concerns shareholder fear and instability, especially in a down market. With the flow of hundreds of billions of dollars into the mutual fund industry during the last few years, mutual fund shareholders have become a major participant in the world's financial markets. The flow of these funds, either into or out of the world's various bourses, can upset any sector of the global market place. This is because mutual funds are subject to the short-term fears of individual shareholders and, like other investors, such as institutional pension funds, the market is vulnerable to the whims of these major participants. Whenever the market begins to fluctuate or decline, the greatest risk to the long-term investor comes from those shareholders who do not have a very long investment horizon and withdraw their money from mutual funds in panic. If too many shareholders decided to redeem their shares at the same time, fund managers would have no choice but to liquidate some of their holdings, possibly at a loss, which could lead to a debacle in the entire market. This type of panic selling by individual investors would have the same effect as a run on a bank. Banks normally retain only a small percentage of their assets in cash. The rest of depositors' money is loaned out or invested in various projects throughout the community. If most depositors tried redeeming their money from their bank accounts at the same time, it could debilitate the banking industry and the economy would suffer greatly. Although it is possible that such a situation could occur within the mutual fund industry, this prospect should not dissuade you from investing in mutual funds.

Lack of Governmental Guarantees

The third area of vulnerability concerns a lack of government protection through guarantees against losses incurred by the individual investor in a mutual fund. Many small investors believe that during a large decline in the market, their money is somehow protected by the government. This notion is untrue and is a misunderstanding of the risks involved in stock and bond investing. Money that is invested in mutual funds, or in the stock and bond market, is at risk to some degree. Although it is an unlikely scenario, it is conceivable that many investors could lose most of their money in an economic recession. The government does not insure against loss of any kind in the market. In a capitalist system, investors provide money or capital for private enterprises and businesses in order to gain a larger return than those offered by theoretically risk-free investments. Once you realize that there is no such thing as a totally risk-free investment, then you can more soberly evaluate your risk-reward potential and make only well-calculated investments which improve your financial situation.

Further Investment Considerations

Although this chapter briefly describes the fundamentals of mutual funds and the advantages of investing in such vehicles, it is beyond the scope of this book to give a full and detailed description of the entire field of mutual fund investing. It will be necessary for the self-directed investor to read other books and materials in order to gain a more detailed understanding of this subject. This chapter has only highlighted certain features of the mutual fund industry in order to give the reader a general understanding of one method for achieving financial independence. However, there are other investment concerns which also need addressing. They are as follows:

Bahá'í Economic Theory and Application

On the subject of Bahá'í economic theory and application as it relates to mutual fund investing, the Writings provide no specific guidance but only give general principles that may be applied to economics. It is left up to future Bahá'í economists to "evolve an economic system which will function in full conformity with the spirit and the exact provisions of the Cause."[1] Neither the capitalist nor socialist systems are fully compatible with the Bahá'í ideal, although elements from each will no doubt be adopted by future Bahá'í economists, as can be perceived in this statement written on behalf of Shoghi Effendi:

> Social inequality is the inevitable outcome of the natural inequality of men. Human beings are different in ability and should, therefore, be different in their social and economic standing. Extremes of wealth and poverty should, however, be totally abolished. Those whose brains have contributed to the creation and improvement of the means of production must be fairly rewarded, though these means may be owned and controlled by others.[2]

The elimination of the extremes of wealth and poverty is a fundamental Bahá'í principle, as is an individual's obligation to work (except in the case of people who are physically or mentally incapable). Shoghi Effendi also refers to "profit-sharing...as a solution to one form of economic problems."[3] This would seem to indicate, among other things, that individual Bahá'í investors have a legitimate right to share in the expanding profits of the world economic system by investing in it through mutual funds and other suitable investment vehicles.

Establishing a Financial Library

To learn more about investing and the mutual fund industry, your local library should have a reference tool called *Books In Print*, which is a useful source for finding various books and publications on investing. Financial magazines and newspapers, such as *Barron's*, *The Wall Street Journal*, *Money*, and *Kiplinger's Personal Finance Magazine*, also provide updated information on the best mutual funds for one's investment needs. Certain subscription-based financial or investment newsletters may be helpful. It is also recommended that you start your own home library of financial information and investing books, including Charles J. Givens's practical *More Wealth Without Risk*, Vanita Van Caspel's latest edition of *Money Dynamics*, George S. Clason's masterpiece *The Richest Man in Babylon*, and Napoleon Hill's classic *Think and Grow Rich*. These works provide exciting and informative insights on the topics of investing, prosperity, and wealth acquisition.

Gambling and Investing

For those who think of investing as just another form of gambling, the Writings clearly indicate that this is not the case. In the

1. *Lights of Guidance*, no. 1862, pp. 548-549.
2. Ibid., no. 1865, p. 549.
3. Ibid., no. 1869, p. 550.

Kitáb-i-Aqdas, Bahá'u'lláh states that the under age children of deceased parents should have their inheritance *"invested on their behalf in trade and business until they come of age."* [1] Also, the Universal House of Justice endorses investing as a means of preserving capital. In a letter written on its behalf, the House of Justice directed a national spiritual assembly to preserve the real value of the Bahá'í funds in its care: "The Assembly is the trustee of the funds in its care, and its primary concern in investing such funds should be to try to preserve their real value. Obtaining a good income from such investments is also desirable, but is a secondary consideration and should not be sought if this would endanger the value of the principal." [2] By following the guidelines for investing as outlined in this and similar books, spiritual assemblies can keep ahead of inflation and increase the value of the funds entrusted to their care through wise investing.

Non-U.S. Citizenship

If you are not a U.S. citizen, one of the disadvantages of investing in the U.S. market is that every mutual fund company is obligated to impose, on behalf of the U.S. Government, a yearly tax on the profits (the distribution of dividends and capital gains) realized by the fund and payable to you. Although the country where you are a citizen may allow you a tax credit on the foreign taxes paid outside of your own country, if you are a non-U.S. citizen, you should learn about the specific tax consequences of investing in the U.S. market (or any other foreign market) before doing so, especially if you can make larger after-tax gains in your own country. However, for the average American citizen, or for those wishing to keep their money in U.S. dollars, U.S. mutual funds are considered to be one of the best investment vehicles available.

Interest Rate Fluctuations

Another important aspect to keep in mind when investing in mutual funds is changes in the government's prime interest rate. The value of stock and bond funds is usually dependent on the fluctuation of government interest rates as determined by the Federal Reserve. When the long-term outlook for interest rates is on the rise, it may be necessary to switch your money from stock and bond funds to money market funds in order to preserve your capital and protect your gains, since stock and bond prices usually decline when interest rates are rising. When the long-term trend in interest rates begins to decline, it may be time to reinvest in stock and bond funds, since their value will usually increase during periods of lower interest rates. Although financial markets and specific investment vehicles are cyclical in their movements, all switching to and from stock, bond, and money mar-

---

1. *Kitáb-i-Aqdas,* K27, p. 28.
2. Lights of Guidance, no. 888, p. 264.

ket funds is made much easier through a mutual fund family which has a wide variety of these different types of funds.

Future Potential

Mutual funds should be the foundation for most investment portfolios. It is anticipated that mutual fund investing will play a significant role in the financial lives of people well into the twenty-first century. In order to capitalize on these advantages, you should begin your investment program now. The present opportunities are too great to pass up. Over the next few years, as humanity approaches the reality of world unity, the world's financial markets could explode in new growth and expansion. As the worldwide integration of nations becomes stronger, economic prosperity should assume greater proportions. Everything seems to be coming together for an unprecedented and unparalleled growth of business during the next several decades. Those who have invested in the right mutual funds could well be at the forefront of this economic expansion. The eventual planetary cessation of war and terrorism, caused by the establishment of universal peace, will result in the dawning of a worldwide renaissance of prosperity. The next and final chapter of this book explains why we should take advantage of these golden opportunities.

Chapter 15

Participating in the Current Golden Age

I am the Lord thy God which teacheth thee to profit, which leadeth thee by the way that thou shouldest go.–Isaiah 48:17

The fifth principle of prosperity requires that we participate in the richest period ever known in human history by investing in the global market place. Although the immediate future of the human race may look foreboding, Bahá'u'lláh has established the basis for a glorious and attainable future. While the fulfillment of the promise of a divine civilization may still seem to be a reality of the distant future, the initial dynamics of the New World Order are currently being experienced in its embryonic stages. All organic entities experience one or more transitional phases from a lower to a higher state of being. The same can be said of human civilization—its development is moving, in stages, toward an ever greater golden age. Bahá'u'lláh has designated man's supreme golden age as the Most Great Peace. Prior to the Most Great Peace, mankind will pass through a series of lesser golden eras, including the Lesser Peace. 'Abdu'l-Bahá has also called the twentieth century, the century just prior to the Lesser Peace, the Century of Light.

Unprecedented Opportunities

The marvels associated with the Age of Bahá'u'lláh offer unprecedented opportunities for participating in the prosperity of the next several decades. Not only are we living in the Century of Light, but we are also at the beginning of a material golden age the likes of which have never before been witnessed by the nations and peoples of the earth. As a result of the energizing power released through the Revelation of Bahá'u'lláh, a vast expanse of undreamt-of prosperity waits for mankind to embrace it full force. The world of humanity is "pregnant with the promise of a future so bright that no previous age in the annals of mankind can rival its glory."[1] Although human civilization is undergoing a period of convulsive change and spiritual reformation, it is destined to emerge revitalized and enlightened.

Since the path to the Golden Age of the Faith of Bahá'u'lláh lies directly through the material golden age of this and the next century, we are in a prime position to take advantage of the many unprecedented opportunities generated by this spiritual Springtime. This is especially evident since the natural confluence of humanity's progress and advancement is toward a global civilization, a unified planet, and a united world government. Among other things, this unity will consist of a global system of economics, a worldwide currency, and a universal standard of weights and measures.

The vast vista of financial prosperity which a federated system of nations can bring to the peoples of the world is truly formidable. Once the governments of the earth have eliminated war, fear, hunger, want, and poverty, and the resources of the planet are harnessed for the benefit of all peoples, the material well-being of the entire world will be assured and promoted. We are privileged to be living at the dawn of a new and wondrous period of prosperity for all mankind. We should avail ourselves of the extraordinary opportunities for success provided by this new era of affluence. It is our birthright.

Evidence of the Existing Golden Age

According to the teachings of the world's great religions, the peoples of the world must pass through cycles of change and turmoil before receiving the promised benefits of a divine civilization known as "the Kingdom of God." Man's present-day civilization, according to Shoghi Effendi, is undergoing two simultaneous, though diametrically opposed, transformations: "We stand on the threshold of an age whose convulsions proclaim alike the death-pangs of the old order and the birth-pangs of the new."[2] The first transformation being experienced by the world today is "fundamentally disruptive" in that it "tends to tear down, with increasing violence, the antiquated barriers that seek to block humanity's progress towards its destined goal;" while the second transformation is "essentially an integrating process," which "as it steadily evolves, unfolds a System which may well serve as a pattern for that world polity towards which a strangely-disordered

---

1. Shoghi Effendi, *The Advent of Divine Justice*, p. 43.
2. *The World Order of Bahá'u'lláh*, p. 169.

world is continually advancing."[1] Since it is nearly impossible for any transformation to work in isolation, each of these processes is effected by the other.

Although the violent and painful disintegration of the old world order is clearly evident, the peaceful and steady construction of the new world order is not as readily discernible, especially to those who have not recognized the Revelation of Bahá'u'lláh. Since the impact of society's decline seems more striking than the influence of its spiritual reshaping, it is easy to emphasize the former over the latter. Although the integrating process is not always noticeable in everyday life, we should focus on those positive trends in the world today which are contributing to the foundation of a future world society.

The nations and peoples of the world have recently witnessed the birth of an economic renaissance through the expansion of capital markets around the globe. With the effective demise of political totalitarianism in most countries of the former Soviet-bloc, and the virtual collapse of economic communism throughout the planet, the Second World (the former Communist-bloc countries) is struggling to obtain its fair share of the material prosperity readily available in the Western World. Now, with both the Second and Third worlds bent on achieving parity with their brothers and sisters in the First World, humanity is entering the initial stages of a material golden age that is destined to permeate the entire planet. It is an age which must precede and eventually culminate in a spiritual golden age that has been designated by Bahá'u'lláh as the Most Great Peace, and which Shoghi Effendi has explained is "a peace that must inevitably follow as the practical consequence of the spiritualization of the world and the fusion of all its races, creeds, classes and nations."[2]

Just as people were blind to the economic opportunities available in the aftermath of the Second World War, most of which were created by the cessation of global warfare and the establishment of an embryonic world government (known as the United Nations), many people will also miss the opportunities for growth and prosperity afforded by the establishment of the Lesser Peace and the strengthening of the world's political unity in the years ahead. Once the nations of the world cease squandering their material resources on weapons of destruction, and limit their armaments to only those necessary for safeguarding their own territories, an immense burden will have been lifted from the shoulders of the peoples and governments of the world. When the complete cessation of warfare finally occurs throughout the planet, the fortunes of mankind will be substantially increased. In other words, once the poverty caused by war is eliminated, the prosperity brought on by peace can flourish. 'Abdu'l-Bahá states that when a vast reduction in military expenditures on the weapons of war

1. *The World Order of Bahá'u'lláh*, p. 170.
2. Ibid., p. 162.

occurs, there will follow *"universal development and prosperity."* [1]
Shoghi Effendi has envisioned the potential of a peaceful world in
these terms:

> The enormous energy dissipated and wasted on war,
> whether economic or political, will be consecrated to such ends
> as will extend the range of human inventions and technical
> development, to the increase of the productivity of mankind, to
> the extermination of disease, to the extension of scientific re-
> search, to the raising of the standard of physical health, to the
> sharpening and refinement of the human brain, to the exploita-
> tion of the unused and unsuspected resources of the planet, to
> the prolongation of human life, and to the furtherance of any
> other agency that can stimulate the intellectual, the moral, and
> spiritual life of the entire human race. [2]

How each of us personally decides to participate in the economic flourishing afforded by the strengthening of the world's political
unity will not only determine the extent of our future prosperity, but
also the meaningful expansion of a unified planetary system of economics. As believers in the inevitable unification of the planet into a
single world order, Bahá'ís are uniquely positioned to take advantage
of this trend as it begins to develop and take root worldwide. It is an
opportunity that should not be missed.

Technological Advancement and Expansion

Technological development, though still in its infancy, has become the central cause of our modern lifestyle and provides us with
most of the tools for our physical comfort and efficiency. Without the
advances of modern technology, human beings could not have pro-
gressed to the point where they find themselves today. The impact of
technology on the lifestyle of man is redefining how he views society
and the purpose of existence. Technology is propelling us toward a
world that is literally on the edge of our imagination. Technological
advances are also having a positive effect on our economic systems,
since they can shorten the disparities between the nations of the
world. Furthermore, many of the world's citizens are no longer toler-
ant of being deprived or excluded from access to these advancing
technologies.

For example, it would be very difficult for totalitarianism to exist
in a society with access to modern communications, since control
over their use cannot be absolutely maintained. Furthermore, any nation desiring to compete economically in the modern world would
have to acquire and use advanced computer technology and telecommunications in order to survive. This situation would require such a

---

1. *The Secret of Divine Civilization*, p. 66.
2. *The World Order of Bahá'u'lláh*, p. 204.

government to relinquish some of its control over the use of communications and computer-based technology. The irony is that by using such technologies to enhance and maintain a country's economic viability, oppressive governments would be forced to open the doors to social and political change, which would eventually lead to their restructuring or downfall.

The survival of almost any country's economy may find itself vulnerable to adverse financial conditions without access to modern technology. The world's banking, medical, manufacturing, transportation, communication, energy, and entertainment systems, as well as a country's various governmental departments and agencies, are critically dependent on computer technology for their daily operation. Computers are becoming vital to most social, business, and education organizations throughout the world. The entire structure and functioning of human society is becoming more computer-dependent and technology-driven as the Information Age transforms the daily life of people. This dependency on computers and advanced technology is only just beginning to change the pattern of thinking in the modern world. In its broadest sense, technology includes all practical knowledge and information about any subject. Humanity's reliance on such information will probably continue for many decades, if not for many centuries.

One of the greatest challenges facing humanity, as it enters the computer age, will be in maintaining the integrity of its collective cultural and societal values, which have been gained over many centuries of precomputer civilization. The new computer age will find its greatest impact in the ultimate transformation of humanity's traditional and deep-rooted values. The computer revolution is already overwhelming our capacity to cope with change as it redefines our priorities, outdates our laws, reorganizes our economy and workplace, and alters our views of reality. Whether we like it or not, the technology revolution precludes turning back to a more primitive and ignorant lifestyle.

As the world becomes more automated, the inherent demand for technololgy-related products has accelerated. This trend has produced a desire for digital dissemination in all areas of life, especially in the fields of personal computers, client-server software, wireless communications, and networking equipment. This situation makes the investment opportunities in nearly any field, including technology itself, vast and far-reaching. Computers have only recently appeared on the world scene, yet they are now indispensable to our daily functioning and permeate all areas of our life. The automobile has gone from a relatively simple machine to a complex computer-operated vehicle with over fifty semiconductors on board. Liquid-lens technology and high-resolution film have revolutionized space satellite photography. By using lasers and computers, stores have automated inventory and accounting procedures through the use of the Universal Bar Code. Advances in laser technology have also sharply improved musical acoustics through compact disc players, while laser imaging has revolutionized the field of medicine and enhanced the quality of medical care. Personal computers now routinely use CD Rom technology to store ever more data. Cellular telephones allow people to communicate (via satellite or microwave) from nearly every location on the planet, while fax machines and computer networking systems allow people to communicate electronically with all parts of the globe. Integrated telecommunication systems are at the forefront of the upcoming information superhighway network, which will include electronic shopping malls, on-line retrieval capabilities, and long-distance computer-based learning.

The information superhighway infrastructure is being laid with optic fiber, satellite, and digital technology through which users can transfer up to 100 million pieces of information per second. The advent of high-resolution, high-definition television sets with 500-channel capability, access to multimedia information, electronic libraries, interactive entertainment, and the use of virtual reality technology are now just beginning. Beyond this is the dawning of the earth's first artificial intelligence system and neural network conduit, similar to the brain and central nervous system in the human body. Advancements in nearly every sphere of technology have made information one of the most valuable commodities in the world. The Information Age is expected to have a far greater impact on man's overall development than did the Industrial Revolution. Never before has civilization been so thoroughly transformed by advancements in technology.

Due to these technology trends, any current investment portfolio should include part of its funds in companies which have a stake in the development and success of the information superhighway. The technological foundation of the future, especially in the early decades of the twenty-first century, is being laid by this new electronic and communications network. When this network is in place and fully functional, it will shrink the earth's time-distance continuum to the size of a small neighborhood and the planet will physically become one global community. Once this occurs, and the obstacles to achieving planetary unity in the political sphere have been permanently abolished, the spiritual reality of world unity should not be far behind.

Global Economic Integration

The process of social integration and economic interdependence of the peoples and nations of the world is more than just a coincidence. It is the preparation of humankind for the advent of universal peace. In order for the unity of mankind to be universally realized in all spheres of life, human beings must first develop the capacity to understand the Message of Bahá'u'lláh:

> Throughout succeeding centuries and ages the call of civilization hath been raised, the world of humanity hath been advancing and progressing day by day, various countries have been developing by leaps and bounds, and mate-

rial improvements have increased, until the world of exis-
tence obtained universal capacity to receive the spiritual
teachings and to hearken to the Divine Call.[1]

As the transformation of national economies into one global system increases, and the conversion of separate financial markets into
one global entity speeds up, the nations and peoples of the world will
more readily accept the idea of one universal economic order. With
the prosperity of the world's nations now totally dependent on international trade, countries are becoming more economically integrated
than ever before. Not surprisingly, this type of cooperation and interdependence is starting to produce greater prosperity for nearly all
nations.

At the vanguard of this global economic integration has been the
pioneering efforts of many multinational companies. When companies
expand beyond their national borders, they no longer regard the rest
of the world as outside their natural domain. In fact, they expand
their production and marketing capacities to incorporate a global
viewpoint. Whenever possible, they spearhead efforts to lessen the
political tensions in those countries in which they have economic interests. Political and social unrest are not conducive to a productive
or profitable free enterprise environment. Tariff and trade barriers
normally hinder the growth and expansion of business, while free
trade practices spur development and cause greater efficiency in manufacturing and productivity. Many multinational companies also recognize that a hostile populace in a host country will eventually destroy
any hope of making a profit in that country. Therefore, many of
these companies train, educate, and employ local citizens to work in
all levels of the company, including managerial positions. After people
are hired and prove themselves capable, they can transfer to other
parts of the world where their company has other operations. In the
best of circumstances, employees of a multinational company can be
considered a microcosm of world citizenry.

In recent times, even small companies have expanded internationally without too much difficulty, since global networking and computer technology can provide access to foreign markets. As the
electronic information network continues to expand, so will the global
appetites of many businesses. Worldwide economic integration is the
wave of the future.

Another indicator of worldwide economic integration consists of
the buying power and taste of the individual (now global) consumer.
Every person can find products in their home that come from at least
a dozen different countries. An American has products from Asia and
Europe; a European owns products from Asia and America; and an
Asian possesses products from Europe and America. With the former
Eastern-bloc countries and China opening their markets, the expan-

---

1. 'Abdu'l-Bahá, *Selections from the Writings*, no. 225, p. 285.

sion of trade and economic integration becomes that much greater. Even the nations of Africa are realizing that it is better to develop their economies and trade internationally than to destroy one another in pointless vendettas and tribal warfare. The new international consumer is not only developing a taste for products manufactured outside of his own country, but he is also accepting it as normal.

Another example of global economic integration is that some products are made in one country, but assembled in another country. Also, various corporations which have their headquarters in one country, often open factories and branch offices in other countries, even if these countries are on different continents. Although the whole process of economic integration has deeply and permanently infiltrated the world economy, it only serves as a preamble for the birth of a future global economy, which will eventually lead to the establishment of a world commonwealth.

If the growth rate of the world's population continues to increase at its present speed, many more goods and services will be needed to meet the demands of this growing population. The population explosion is causing the leaders of the nations of the world to pursue viable economic policies which will not only increase production, but also allow the fruits of this increased productivity to be passed on to the populace. No longer will the great majority of the world's population tolerate any limitations on access to those material goods which have usually been reserved for a privileged class of people.

The availability of abundant and diverse foodstuff, pleasant living conditions, comfortable and colorful clothing, stimulating multi-level entertainment, and the material comforts and tools brought about by advanced technology has generated a justifiable desire for these goods and services throughout the world. People from the less developed nations are demanding their fair share of the material abundance made available by modern technology. The past two World Wars, which were primarily fought by the nations of the Industrial World, have produced in the Non-Industrial World a "vast army of embittered citizens impotent to procure for themselves the material goods and necessities"[1] which others have deliberately destroyed. There has been untoward emotional suffering and material loss caused by man's disunity and animosity toward his fellow world citizen. With the advent of nuclear and other fearful weapons of destruction, the risk of continuing this insanity could bring annihilation upon all humanity.

Fortunately, the future Bahá'í World Commonwealth, the foundation of which is now being laid by the Bahá'í Administrative Order, is the blueprint for tomorrow's just and spiritual society. Although the term "commonwealth" has no specific legal meaning, its original meaning signifies the coming together of different people for the common good or public welfare. Later, the term was adopted to

---

1. Shoghi Effendi, *The World Order of Bahá'u'lláh*, p. 189.

mean a loosely knit confederation of independent nation-states for the common benefit of all concerned. Although there are many examples of commonwealths in the world today, one of the distinctive features of a commonwealth is its ability to create unity among a number of diverse and separate entities for the expressed purpose of enhancing the wealth and protection of each member. Eventually, as the Bahá'í Faith spreads throughout the planet, it is "destined to attain, in the fullness of time, the status of a world-embracing Commonwealth, which would be at once the instrument and the guardian of the Most Great Peace." [1] Today's gradual global economic integration is a significant step on the path to this future world commonwealth.

The Inevitable Prosperity of Humankind

One of the reasons for recognizing that we have been created rich is to help us expand our vision of a prosperous future and assist us in taking the necessary steps for realizing this prosperity. Eliminating the degradation of extreme poverty, partially by expanding our spiritual consciousness, will help make universal prosperity a general reality. It is unthinkable that the future Golden Age promised by Bahá'u'lláh will accept, much less tolerate, a condition of material poverty among the masses of mankind. Extreme poverty is a material aberration caused by injustice and spiritual bankruptcy. Prosperity and an abundantly rich lifestyle, on the other hand, should become the common condition or status quo for all people. Never before has the future promised so much for so many.

When thinking about the future World Order of Bahá'u'lláh and the flowering of the human race, we can visualize this future period as one of universal prosperity and success, widespread affluence and abundance, and undreamed of progress and opportunities. The eventual elimination of the extreme wealth of some, as well as the unbearable poverty of others, does not mean that those with a prosperous lifestyle will become poorer; it means that the poor will learn to prosper and will be protected from destitution and injustice. Moderate prosperity will be available to all. It is evident from the writings of Bahá'u'lláh that we have been created rich and noble, and that these qualities are intended to be mirrored both in our spiritual nature and in our material environment. If we have not yet formulated a prosperity consciousness concerning this innate condition, we may wish to alter our thinking in light of the Guardian's description of humanity's future:

> The unity of the human race, as envisaged by Bahá'u'lláh, implies the establishment of a world commonwealth in which all nations, races, creeds and classes are closely and permanently united, and in which the autonomy of its state members

---

1. Shoghi Effendi, *The World Order of Bahá'u'lláh*, p. 196.

and the personal freedom and initiative of the individuals that compose them are definitely and completely safeguarded. This commonwealth must, as far as we can visualize it, consist of a world legislature, whose members will, as the trustees of the whole of mankind, ultimately control the entire resources of all the component nations, and will enact such laws as shall be required to regulate the life, satisfy the needs and adjust the relationships of all races and peoples. A world executive, backed by an international Force, will carry out the decisions arrived at, and apply the laws enacted by, this world legislature, and will safeguard the organic unity of the whole commonwealth. A world tribunal will adjudicate and deliver its compulsory and final verdict in all and any disputes that may arise between the various elements constituting this universal system. A mechanism of world inter-communication will be devised, embracing the whole planet, freed from national hindrances and restrictions, and functioning with marvelous swiftness and perfect regularity. A world metropolis will act as the nerve center of a world civilization, the focus towards which the unifying forces of life will converge and from which its energizing influences will radiate. A world language will either be invented or chosen from among the existing languages and will be taught in the schools of all the federated nations as an auxiliary to their mother tongue. A world script, a world literature, a uniform and universal system of currency, of weights and measures, will simplify and facilitate intercourse and understanding among the nations and races of mankind. In such a world society, science and religion, the two most potent forces in human life, will be reconciled, will cooperate, and will harmoniously develop. The press will, under such a system, while giving full scope to the expression of the diversified views and convictions of mankind, cease to be mischievously manipulated by vested interests, whether private or public, and will be liberated from the influence of contending governments and peoples. The economic resources of the world will be organized, its sources of raw materials will be tapped and fully utilized, its markets will be coordinated and developed, and the distribution of its products will be equitably regulated.

National rivalries, hatreds, and intrigues will cease, and racial animosity and prejudice will be replaced by racial amity, understanding and cooperation. The causes of religious strife will be permanently removed, economic barriers and restrictions will be completely abolished, and the inordinate distinction between classes will be obliterated. Destitution on the one hand, and gross accumulation of ownership on the other, will disappear....

A world federal system, ruling the whole earth and exercising unchallengeable authority over its unimaginably vast resources, blending and embodying the ideals of both the East and the West, liberated from the curse of war and its miseries, and bent on the exploitation of all the available sources of energy on the surface of the planet, a system in which Force is made the servant of Justice, whose life is sustained by its universal recognition of one God and by its allegiance to one common Revelation—such is the goal towards which humanity, impelled by the unifying forces of life, is moving.[1]

---

1. Shoghi Effendi, *The World Order of Bahá'u'lláh*, pp. 203-204.

Bibliography

'Abdu'l-Bahá. *The Promulgation of Universal Peace: Talks Delivered by 'Abdu'l-Bahá During His Visit to the United States and Canada in 1912.* Comp. Howard MacNutt. 2nd ed. Wilmette: Bahá'í Publishing Trust, 1982.

_____.*The Secret of Divine Civilization.* Trans. Marzieh Gail with Ali-Kuli Khan. 3rd ed. Wilmette: Bahá'í Publishing Trust, 1975.

_____. *Selections from the Writings of 'Abdu'l-Bahá.* Comp. Research Department of the Universal House of Justice. Haifa: Bahá'í World Centre, 1978.

_____. *Some Answered Questions.* Trans. Laura Clifford Barney. 4th ed. Wilmette: Bahá'í Publishing Trust, 1981.

The American Bahá'í. The monthly publication of the National Spiritual Assembly of the Bahá'ís of the United States.

Bahá'í Funds: Contributions and Administration. Extracts from the letters of the Guardian and the Universal House of Justice. Thornhill, Ontario: Bahá'í Canada Publications, 1974.

Bahá'í World Faith: Selected Writings of Bahá'u'lláh and 'Abdu'l-Bahá. 3rd ed. Wilmette: Bahá'í Publishing Trust, 1976.

Bahá'u'lláh. *Epistle to the Son of the Wolf.* Trans. Shoghi Effendi. 3rd ed. Wilmette: Bahá'í Publishing Trust, 1971.

_____. *Gleanings from the Writings of Bahá'u'lláh.* Trans. Shoghi Effendi. 2nd ed. Wilmette: Bahá'í Publishing Trust, 1976.

_____. *The Hidden Words.* Trans. Shoghi Effendi with the assistance of some English friends. Wilmette: Bahá'í Publishing Trust, 1932.

_____. *The Kitáb-i-Aqdas: The Most Holy Book.* Trans. Shoghi Effendi and the Universal House of Justice. Wilmette: Bahá'í Publishing Trust, 1992.

_____. *The Kitáb-i-Íqán: The Book of Certitude.* Trans. Shoghi Effendi. Wilmette: Bahá'í Publishing Trust, 1931.

_____. *Tablets of Bahá'u'lláh revealed after the Kitáb-i-Aqdas.* Comp. Research Department of the Universal House of Justice. Rev. ed. Wilmette: Bahá'í Publishing Trust, 1988.

Barron's. A weekly financial news and information magazine. A Publication of Dow Jones & Company, Inc., New York.

Business Week. A weekly international business magazine published by McGraw-Hill, New York.

Each One Teach One, A Call to the Individual Believer. Comp. National Teaching Committee and the National Education Committee of the National Spiritual Assembly of the Bahá'ís of the United States. Wilmette: Bahá'í Publishing Trust, 1975.

Esslemont, J. E. *Bahá'u'lláh and the New Era.* 5th rev. ed. Wilmette: Bahá'í Publishing Trust, 1980.

Holy Bible. King James Authorized Version. Cleveland, Ohio: The World Publishing Company, circa 1965.

Holy Bible. New International Version. Colorado Springs, Colorado: International Bible Society, 1973.

Huqúqu'lláh: A Study Guide. Issued by the Research Department of the Universal House of Justice with an address by Hand of the Cause of God, Dr. 'Alí-Muhammad Varqá, Trustee of Huqúqu'lláh. London: Bahá'í Publishing Trust, 1989.

Huqúqu'lláh: The Right of God. Extracts from the Writings of Bahá'u'lláh, 'Abdu'l-Bahá, Shoghi Effendi, and the Universal House of Justice. Comp. Research Department of the Universal House of Justice. rev. ed. London: Bahá'í Publishing Trust, 1989.

Khavari, Khalil and Sue Khavari. *Together Forever: A Handbook for Creating a Successful Marriage.* Oxford: Oneworld Publications Ltd, 1993.

Kimbro, D. and Napoleon Hill. *Think and Grow Rich: A Black Choice. A Guide To Success for Black Americans.* New York: Fawcett Crest Books, 1991.

Lifeblood of the Cause: Bahá'í Funds and Contributions. A compilation of extracts from the Bahá'í Writings. Comp. Research Department of the Universal House of Justice. rev. ed. London: Bahá'í Publishing Trust, 1989.

Lights of Guidance: A Bahá'í Reference File. Comp. Helen Hornby. 2nd rev. ed. New Delhi: Bahá'í Publishing Trust, 1988.

Rabbaní, Rúhíyyih. *The Priceless Pearl.* London: Bahá'í Publishing Trust, 1969.

Shoghi Effendi. *The Advent of Divine Justice.* Wilmette: Bahá'í Publishing Trust, 1939.

_____. *Bahá'í Administration.* rev. ed. Wilmette: Bahá'í Publishing Trust, 1968.

_____. *Citadel of Faith: Messages to America, 1947–1957.* Wilmette: Bahá'í Publishing Trust, 1965.

_____. *Dawn of a New Day: Messages to India, 1923–1957.* New Delhi: Bahá'í Publishing Trust, 1970.

_____. *Guidance for Today and Tomorrow.* A selection from the Writings of Shoghi Effendi. London: Bahá'í Publishing Trust, 1953.

_____. *The World Order of Bahá'u'lláh, Selected Letters.* Wilmette: Bahá'í Publishing Trust, 1938.

Taherzadeh, Adib. *The Revelation of Bahá'u'lláh. Volume 1: Baghdád 1853–1863; Volume 2: Adrianople 1863–1868; Volume 3: 'Akká, The Early Years 1868–1877; and Volume 4: Mazra'ih & Bahjí 1877–1892.* Oxford: George Ronald. 1974 through 1987.

Trustworthiness. Extracts from the writings of Bahá'u'lláh, the Báb, 'Abdu'l-Bahá, and Shoghi Effendi. Comp. Research Department of the Universal House of Justice. London: Bahá'í Publishing Trust, 1987.

United States Federal Trade Commission Staff Report, 1979.

United States Government Statistics, Social Security Administration, 1993.

Universal House of Justice. Letter to all National Spiritual Assemblies, October 31, 1993.

_____. Letter to all National Spiritual Assemblies, January 4, 1994.

_____. *Messages from the Universal House of Justice: 1968–1973.* Wilmette: Bahá'í Publishing Trust, 1976.

_____. *Wellspring of Guidance: Messages from the Universal House of Justice: 1963–1968.* Wilmette: Bahá'í Publishing Trust, 1970.

_____. *A Wider Horizon: Selected Messages from the Universal House of Justice: 1983–1992.* Riviera Beach, Florida: Palabra Publications, 1992.

Women in the Bahá'í Faith. Comp. Research Department of the Universal House of Justice. Oakham, England: Bahá'í Publishing Trust, 1986.